ZAGATSURVEY.

2005/06

NEW JERSEY RESTAURANTS

Local Editors: Andrea Clurfeld and Shannon Mullen

Editor: Robert Seixas

Published and distributed by
ZAGAT SURVEY, LLC
4 Columbus Circle
New York, New York 10019
Tel: 212 977 6000
E-mail: newjersey@zagat.com
Web site: www.zagat.com

Acknowledgments

We thank Beth Ambrose, Liz Fuerst, Maria Gallagher, Craig LaBan, Pat Mack, Andrew Meyer, Lily, May and Eileen Mullen, Cindy Nevitt, Sue Perkins and Steven Shukow. We are also grateful to our assistant editor, Emily Parsons, and editorial assistant, Jason Briker, as well as the following members of our staff: Reni Chin, Larry Cohn, Victoria Elmacioglu, Schuyler Frazier, Jeff Freier, Natalie Lebert, Mike Liao, Dave Makulec, Robert Poole, Thomas Sheehan, Joshua Siegel and Sharon Yates.

The reviews published in this guide are based on public opinion surveys, with numerical ratings reflecting the average scores given by all survey participants who voted on each establishment and text based on direct quotes from, or fair paraphrasings of, participants' comments. Phone numbers, addresses and other factual information were correct to the best of our knowledge when published in this guide; any subsequent changes may not be reflected.

© 2005 Zagat Survey, LLC
ISBN 1-57006-716-3
Printed in the United States of America

Contents

About This Survey	5
What's New	6
Ratings & Symbols	7
Most Popular	9

TOP RATINGS
Food: Cuisines, Features, Locations	10
Decor: Outdoors, Romance, Rooms, Views	14
Service	15
Best Buys	16

RESTAURANT DIRECTORY
Names, Addresses, Phone Numbers, Web Sites, Ratings and Reviews	17

INDEXES
Cuisines	162
Locations	174
Special Features	
Breakfast	188
Brunch	188
Buffet Served	168
Business Dining	189
BYO	189
Catering	193
Celebrity Chefs	194
Child-Friendly	194
Cigars Welcome	196
Dancing	197
Delivery/Takeout	197
Dessert	198
Entertainment	198
Family-Style	199
Fireplaces	199
Historic Places	200
Hotel Dining	201
Jacket Required	202
Late Dining	202
Local Favorites	202
Meet for a Drink	204
Microbreweries	205
Noteworthy Newcomers	205
Offbeat	206
Outdoor Dining	207
People-Watching	207
Power Scenes	208
Pre-Theater Dining	208
Private Rooms	208
Prix Fixe Menus	208
Quick Bites	209
Quiet Conversation	209

Raw Bars	209
Romantic Places	210
Senior Appeal	210
Singles Scenes	211
Sleepers	212
Special Occasions	212
Tasting Menus	213
Transporting Experiences	214
Trendy	214
Twentysomethings	215
Views	215
Visitors on Expense Account	216
Warm Welcome	216
Waterside	217
Winning Wine Lists	217
Worth a Trip	218
Wine Chart	220

About This Survey

Here are the results of our *2005/06 New Jersey Restaurant Survey,* covering 843 restaurants as tested, and tasted, by 5,469 local restaurant-goers.

This marks the 26th year that Zagat Survey has reported on the shared experiences of diners like you. What started in 1979 as a hobby involving 200 of our friends rating local NYC restaurants has come a long way. Today we have over 250,000 active surveyors and now cover entertaining, golf, hotels, resorts, spas, movies, music, nightlife, shopping, sites and attractions as well as theater. As a companion to this guide, we also publish *New Jersey Shore Restaurants* along with guides to the next door cities of New York and Philadelphia. All of these guides are based on consumer surveys. Our *Surveys* are also available on PDAs, cell phones and by subscription at zagat.com, where you can vote and shop as well.

By regularly surveying large numbers of avid customers, we hope to have achieved a uniquely current and reliable guide. This year's participants dined out an average of 2.9 times per week, meaning this *Survey* is based on roughly 834,000 meals. Of these 5,000 plus surveyors, 51% are women, 49% men; the breakdown by age is 11% in their 20s; 24%, 30s; 23%, 40s; 25%, 50s; and 17%, 60s or above. Our editors have synopsized surveyors' opinions, with their comments shown in quotation marks. We sincerely thank each of these people; this book is really "theirs."

We are especially grateful to our editors, Andrea Clurfeld, the restaurant critic and food editor for the *Asbury Park Press*, and Shannon Mullen, a features writer at the newspaper.

To help guide our readers to New Jersey's best meals and best buys, we have prepared a number of lists. See Most Popular (page 9), Top Ratings (pages 10–15) and Best Buys (page 16). In addition, we have provided 50 handy indexes.

To vote in any of our upcoming *Surveys,* just register at zagat.com. Each participant will receive a free copy of the resulting guide when it is published. Your comments and even criticisms of this guide are also solicited. There is always room for improvement with your help. Just contact us at newjersey@zagat.com.

New York, NY
May 16, 2005

Nina and Tim Zagat

vote at zagat.com

What's New

There are plenty of new NJ restaurants this year – enough in fact to give Garden State food lovers a lot to crow about.

Outward Bound: The finest chefs aren't necessarily cloistering close to cities. Paul Ingenito's success at Perryville Inn has spawned his and wife Lorraine's second spot in rural western Hunterdon County, The Grand Colonial, while Greg Manning left the comfy confines of county seat Toms River to find fans flocking to his Olde Corner Deli in teeny-tiny tucked-away Island Heights. Bradley Boyle's Bula World Cuisine is the toast of northwestern Sussex County, and Sri Chandupatla's exotic Ganges is luring more than locals to West Windsor.

One-Stop Shopping: It's all happening under one roof – music, mingling, munching, spotlight seeking. Spend an entire night at complete-package destinations such as the big-and-beautiful Pan-Latin number, Lua, in Hoboken; the chic Teak, a Pan-Asian arrival in Red Bank; and Mixx, the ultrahot Asian at the Borgata.

Small-Plate Update: A bevy of baby-age boîtes are making noshers nuts about nibbling in NJ. They include: Paramus' Chakra, a slick new address upping sexiness to the umpteenth degree; the glitzy Elements in Sea Bright; and Red Bank's cool-customer, Savanna.

Move Over, Blackjack: The Borgata's big-deal restaurants need to make some elbow room considering this year's opening of AC's Old Havana–themed Quarter at the Tropicana and its eateries. Already packing 'em in are The Palm steakhouse (the group's first foray into Jersey) and P.F. Chang's, a satellite of the Chinese fusion chain.

The Second Coming: Not since The Ryland Inn debuted in 1991 has the promise of a big-ticket restaurant caused this much stir. Set to open at press time in Bedminster is The Pluckemin Inn, where Philly vet Matthew Levin will take charge of the New American kitchen. Diners will be cosseted in one of four elegant rooms, and a 1,000-label wine list will help keep things flowing.

Butt Out: Our surveyors want to clear the Jersey air – literally. Speaking with their hearts and lungs, an overwhelming 93% of them are resolute in their conviction that smoking should be banned in restaurants across the state.

Toll Fare: No matter if the $35.03 average cost of a meal is relatively high, since denizens from all corners of the Garden State seem quite willing to lay down a fair share of green.

Neptune, NJ
May 16, 2005

Andrea Clurfeld
Shannon Mullen

Ratings & Symbols

Name, Address, Phone Number & Web Site

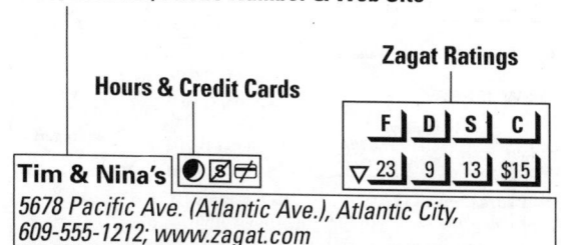

Zagat Ratings

Hours & Credit Cards

F	D	S	C
▽ 23	9	13	$15

Tim & Nina's ◐ ✗ ⌿

5678 Pacific Ave. (Atlantic Ave.), Atlantic City, 609-555-1212; www.zagat.com

"Miles from the boardwalk but still not far enough away", this "never-closing" AC "eyesore" ("Bette Davis would agree: what a dump!") "single-handedly" started the "saltwater-taffy pizza craze" that's "sweeping the casino capital" like "a run of bad luck"; don't forget to "visit the all-you-can-stomach buffet" – "it's to die for" (or from) – but don't look for ambiance because "T & N don't know from design", or service, for that matter.

Review, with surveyors' comments in quotes

Restaurants with the highest overall ratings and greatest popularity and importance are printed in CAPITAL LETTERS.

Hours: ◐ serves after 11 PM
✗ closed on Sunday

Credit Cards: ⌿ no credit cards accepted

Ratings are on a scale of **0** to **30**. Cost **(C)** reflects our surveyors' estimate of the price of dinner with one drink and tip.

F Food	D Decor	S Service	C Cost
23	9	13	$15

0–9 poor to fair
10–15 fair to good
16–19 good to very good
20–25 very good to excellent
26–30 extraordinary to perfection
▽ low response/less reliable

For places listed without ratings, such as a newcomer or survey write-in, the price range is indicated as follows:

| **I** | $25 and below | **E** | $41 to $65 |
| **M** | $26 to $40 | **VE** | $66 or more |

vote at zagat.com

Most Popular

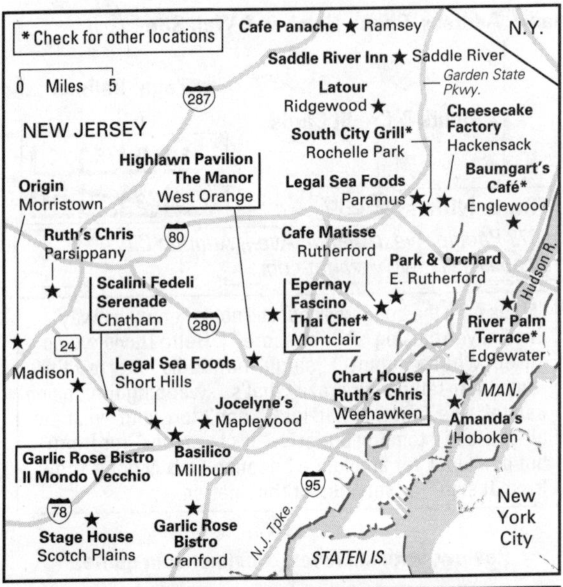

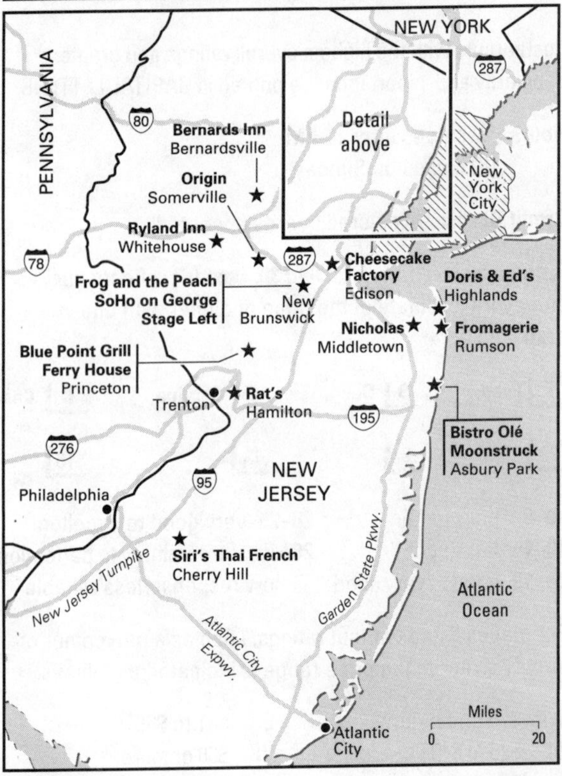

Map 1 (Northern New Jersey):

- *Check for other locations
- 0 Miles 5
- Cafe Panache ★ Ramsey
- Saddle River Inn ★ Saddle River
- Latour – Ridgewood ★
- Cheesecake Factory – Hackensack
- South City Grill* – Rochelle Park
- Legal Sea Foods – Paramus
- Baumgart's Café* – Englewood
- NEW JERSEY
- Highlawn Pavilion / The Manor – West Orange
- Origin – Morristown
- Ruth's Chris – Parsippany
- Cafe Matisse – Rutherford
- Park & Orchard – E. Rutherford
- Scalini Fedeli / Serenade – Chatham
- Epernay / Fascino / Thai Chef* – Montclair
- River Palm Terrace* – Edgewater
- Madison ★
- Legal Sea Foods – Short Hills
- Jocelyne's – Maplewood
- Chart House / Ruth's Chris – Weehawken
- Amanda's – Hoboken
- Garlic Rose Bistro / Il Mondo Vecchio – Madison
- Basilico – Millbrook
- Stage House – Scotch Plains
- Garlic Rose Bistro – Cranford
- STATEN IS.
- New York City

Map 2 (Central/Southern New Jersey):

- NEW YORK
- Detail above
- PENNSYLVANIA
- Bernards Inn – Bernardsville
- Origin – Somerville
- Ryland Inn – Whitehouse
- Frog and the Peach / SoHo on George / Stage Left – New Brunswick
- Cheesecake Factory – Edison
- Doris & Ed's – Highlands
- Nicholas ★ – Middletown
- Fromagerie – Rumson
- Blue Point Grill / Ferry House – Princeton
- Trenton •
- Rat's – Hamilton
- Bistro Olé / Moonstruck – Asbury Park
- NEW JERSEY
- Philadelphia •
- Siri's Thai French – Cherry Hill
- Atlantic Ocean
- Atlantic City •
- Miles 0 – 20

8   subscribe to zagat.com

Most Popular

1. Ryland Inn
2. Scalini Fedeli
3. Bernards Inn
4. Frog & Peach
5. Amanda's
6. River Palm
7. Nicholas
8. Serenade
9. South City Grill
10. Legal Sea Foods
11. Saddle River Inn
12. Moonstruck
13. Cheesecake Factory
14. Highlawn Pavilion
15. Origin
16. Rat's
17. Stage Left
18. Blue Point
19. Baumgart's Café
20. Jocelyne's
21. Ruth's Chris
22. Fascino
23. Cafe Panache
24. Cafe Matisse
25. Fromagerie*
26. Park & Orchard
27. Basilico
28. Ferry House*
29. Thai Chef
30. Siri's Thai French
31. Latour
32. Stage House
33. SoHo on George
34. Bistro Olé
35. Epernay
36. Garlic Rose
37. Doris & Ed's
38. Il Mondo
39. Chart House
40. Manor

It's obvious that many of the restaurants on the above list are among New Jersey's most expensive, but if popularity were calibrated to price, we suspect that a number of other restaurants would join the above ranks. Given the fact that both our surveyors and readers love to discover dining bargains, we have added a list of over 80 Best Buys on page 16. These are restaurants that give extraordinary quality at extremely modest prices.

---

* Indicates a tie with restaurant above

vote at zagat.com

Top Ratings

Excludes places with low voting,

Top 40 Food

28 Nicholas
   Ryland Inn
27 DeLorenzo's
   Cafe Panache
   Cafe Matisse
   Scalini Fedeli
   Serenade
   Saddle River Inn
   Augustino's
   Origin
   Whispers
   Jocelyne's
   Green Gables
   White House
   Washington Inn
   Dining Room
   La Isla
26 Stage House
   Bernards Inn
   Chez Catherine

Chez Dominique
Chef Vola's
Latour
Rosemary & Sage
Anthony David's
Chef's Table
Zoe's*
Lu Nello
Sagami
Fromagerie
Perryville Inn
Stage Left
Bistro Olé
Siri's Thai French
Brighton Steak
Village Green
Grimaldi's Pizza
Giumarello's
Bobby Chez
Frog & Peach

By Cuisine

American (New)
28 Nicholas
27 Saddle River Inn
   Whispers
   Dining Room
26 Bernards Inn

American (Traditional)
27 Washington Inn
26 Latour
   Doris & Ed's
25 Ram's Head Inn
24 Dock's Oyster

Asian (Misc.)
26 Tina Louise
24 Saigon R
   Ritz Seafood
   Ming
23 Mixx

Caribbean/Cuban
27 La Isla
25 410 Bank St.
23 Rebecca's
22 Azúcar
20 Martino's

Chinese
25 Far East Taste
   Suilan
   Lotus Cafe
24 Chengdu 46
23 Meemah

Continental
24 Black Forest Inn
23 Bareli's
   Don Pepe's Steak
   Stony Hill Inn
22 Ivy Inn

Eclectic
27 Cafe Panache
   Cafe Matisse
   Green Gables
26 Tomatoes
25 Savaradio

French
27 Saddle River Inn
   Jocelyne's
26 Chez Catherine
   Chez Dominique
   Latour

10   subscribe to zagat.com

Top Food

French (Bistro)
- **26** Chef's Table
- **24** Dennis Foy's
  - La Petite France
  - Le Fandy
- **23** Manon

French (New)
- **28** Ryland Inn
- **27** Serenade
  - Origin
- **26** Stage House
- **24** Rat's

Indian
- **24** Moghul
  - Passage to India
  - Bombay Gardens
- **23** Aangan
- **22** Raagini

Italian
- **27** Scalini Fedeli
  - Augustino's
- **26** Chef Vola's
  - Anthony David's
  - Lu Nello
  - Giumarello's
  - Fascino
- **25** Capriccio
  - La Tartuferia
  - Girasole (Bound Brook)
  - Mélange Cafe
  - Casa Dante

Japanese
- **26** Sagami
- **25** Sono Sushi
  - Ixora
  - Midori
  - Wasabi House

Mediterranean
- **25** Hamilton's Grill
- **24** Moonstruck
- **23** Il Villino
  - Frescos
- **22** Napa Valley

Mexican
- **23** El Meson
  - Tortilla Press
  - Los Amigos
  - Tortuga's Mexican
- **22** Casa Maya

Pizza
- **27** DeLorenzo's
- **26** Grimaldi's Pizza
- **23** Margherita's
- **22** Kinchley's Tavern
  - Brooklyn's Pizza

Sandwiches
- **27** White House
- **24** Kibitz Room
  - Hobby's Deli
- **21** Richard's
- **20** Sallee Tee's

Seafood
- **26** Bobby Chez
  - Doris & Ed's
  - Blue Point
  - Shipwreck Grill
- **25** Daniel's on B'way

South American/Latin
- **25** Cucharamama
  - Zafra
- **24** Sabor
- **23** Mixx
- **22** Brasilia

Southern/Cajun
- **25** Mélange Cafe
  - 410 Bank St.
- **20** Delta's
  - Luchento's
  - Oddfellows

Spanish/Portuguese
- **26** Bistro Olé
- **23** Casa Vasca
  - Fornos of Spain
  - Segovia
- **22** Tony Da Caneca

Steakhouses
- **26** Brighton Steak
- **25** Ruth's Chris
- **24** Morton's Steak
  - Old Homestead
  - River Palm

Thai
- **27** Origin
- **26** Siri's Thai French
- **25** Far East Taste
  - Thai Thai
- **24** Sri Thai

vote at zagat.com

Top Food

By Special Feature

Breakfast
- 25 Zafra
- 24 Hobby's Deli
- 23 Meil's
- 21 Christopher's
- 20 Java Moon

Brunch
- 26 Anthony David's
-    Amanda's
- 24 La Campagne
-    Rat's
-    Frenchtown Inn

BYO
- 27 Cafe Panache
-    Cafe Matisse
-    Saddle River Inn
-    Origin
-    Whispers

Child-Friendly
- 26 Zoe's
-    Blue Point
-    Tina Louise
- 25 Mud City
- 24 Rat's

Hotel Dining
- 27 Whispers/Hewitt
-    Green Gables
-    Dining Rm./Hilton
- 26 Ebbitt Rm./Virginia
- 25 Suilan/Borgata

Newcomers/Rated
- 26 Zoe's
-    Fascino
- 25 Cucharamama
- 22 Teak
- 21 Lawrenceville Inn

Newcomers/Unrated
-    Black Trumpet
-    Ganges
-    Grand Colonial
-    Lodos
-    Lua
-    Ocino
-    Olde Corner Deli
-    Palm
-    Porto Leggero
-    Savanna

Offbeat
- 27 La Isla
- 26 Chef Vola's
-    Siri's Thai French
-    Tina Louise
- 25 Far East Taste

People-Watching
- 26 Bernards Inn
-    Zoe's
- 25 Cucharamama
-    Ixora*
- 24 South City Grill

Power Scene
- 28 Ryland Inn
- 27 Cafe Panache
-    Serenade
-    Saddle River Inn
-    Washington Inn

Singles Scenes
- 26 Shipwreck Grill
- 25 Cucharamama
- 24 South City Grill
- 23 Cenzino
-    Clydz

Trendy
- 27 DeLorenzo's
-    Cafe Matisse
-    Scalini Fedeli
-    Origin
-    White House

Winning Wine Lists
- 28 Nicholas
-    Ryland Inn
- 27 Serenade
-    Washington Inn
- 26 Stage House

Worth a Trip
- 28 Ryland Inn
-      Whitehouse
- 27 DeLorenzo's
-      Trenton
-    Cafe Panache
-      Ramsey
-    Scalini Fedeli
-      Chatham
-    Saddle River Inn
-      Saddle River

subscribe to zagat.com

Top Food

By Location

Atlantic City
- **27** White House
- **26** Chef Vola's
  Brighton Steak
- **25** Capriccio
  Suilan

Cape May/West Cape May
- **27** Washington Inn
- **26** Ebbitt Room
- **25** Daniel's on B'way
  410 Bank St.
- **24** Peter Shields

Cherry Hill
- **26** Siri's Thai French
  Bobby Chez
- **25** Mélange Cafe
- **24** La Campagne
  Emerald Fish

Collingswood
- **26** Sagami
  Bobby Chez
- **24** Nunzio
- **23** Word of Mouth
  Tortilla Press

Hoboken
- **27** Augustino's
  La Isla
- **26** Anthony David's
  Grimaldi's Pizza
  Amanda's

Lambertville
- **25** No. 9
  Hamilton's Grill
- **24** Ota-Ya
- **23** Manon
  Tortuga's Mexican

Middletown
- **28** Nicholas
- **25** Sono Sushi
- **23** Navesink Fishery
- **21** Crown Palace
- **20** Lincroft Inn

Montclair
- **26** Fascino
- **23** Epernay
- **22** Tuptim
  Thai Chef
  Raymond's

Morristown
- **27** Origin
- **25** Tim Schafer's
  Grand Cafe
- **24** Moghul
  La Campagna

Newark
- **24** Hobby's Deli
- **23** Casa Vasca
  Fornos of Spain
- **22** Brasilia
  Tony Da Caneca

New Brunswick
- **26** Stage Left
  Frog & Peach
- **24** SoHo on George
- **23** Panico's
  Clydz

Princeton
- **26** Blue Point
- **24** Ferry House
- **23** Tortuga's Mexican
- **22** Lahiere's
- **21** Masala Grill

Red Bank
- **24** La Petite France
- **23** Sogno
  Down to Earth
  Siam Garden
- **22** Molly Pitcher

Ridgewood
- **26** Latour
  Village Green
- **25** Zarolé
- **23** Bazzini
  Sakura-Bana

Somerville
- **27** Origin
- **25** Wasabi House
- **24** da Filippo
  Chao Phaya
  Shumi

Voorhees
- **26** Bobby Chez
- **25** Little Café
- **24** Catelli
  Ritz Seafood
- **23** Laceno Italian

vote at zagat.com

Top 40 Decor

- **28** Rat's
  Highlawn Pavilion
- **27** Chakra
  Elements
  Ryland Inn
  Raven & Peach
  Cucharamama
  Nauvoo Grill
- **26** Suilan
  Dining Room
  Peter Shields
  Serenade
  Chart House
  Sergeantsville Inn
  Cafe Matisse
  Bernards Inn
  Ombra
- **25** Capriccio
  Molly Pitcher
  Amanda's

  Stony Hill Inn
  Old Homestead
  Inn at Millrace
  Manor*
  Saddle River Inn*
  Fromagerie
  Moonstruck
  Colligan's
  Harvest Bistro
  Grand Cafe
  Shadowbrook
  Washington Inn
  Tomatoes
  Scalini Fedeli
- **24** Daniel's on B'way
  Nicholas
  Ebbitt Room
  Mansion on Main
  Elysian Cafe
  Il Capriccio

Outdoors

Avon Pavilion
Axelsson's
Daniel's on B'way
Diamond's
Frenchtown Inn
Hamilton's Grill

Jonathan's
Lilly's on Canal
Misto
Moonstruck
Shipwreck Grill
Windansea

Romance

Beau Rivage
Cafe Matisse
Colligan's
Creole Cafe
Daniel's on B'way
Ebbitt Room

Perryville Inn
Rat's
Raven & Peach
Ryland Inn
Sergeantsville Inn
Washington Inn

Rooms

Bernards Inn
Bistro Olé
Chakra
Dining Room
Elements
Food for Thought

Nauvoo Grill
Peter Shields
Porto Leggero
Savanna
Serenade
Suilan

Views

Arthur's Landing
Café Gallery
Chart House
Clark's Landing
Highlawn Pavilion
Liberty House

Lua
Matisse
McLoone's
Molly Pitcher
Rooney's
Zoe's

subscribe to zagat.com

Top 40 Service

- *28* Nicholas
- *26* Ryland Inn
  - Dining Room
  - Serenade
  - Cafe Matisse
  - Washington Inn
- *25* Whispers
  - Fromagerie
  - Bernards Inn
  - Zoe's
  - Saddle River Inn
  - Capriccio
  - Green Gables
  - Stage Left
  - Nanni Ristorante
  - Grand Cafe
  - Cafe Panache
- *24* Ebbitt Room
  - Il Villino
  - Jocelyne's
- Scalini Fedeli
- Peter Shields
- Lu Nello
- Panico's
- Chez Catherine
- Amanda's
- Chez Dominique
- Stage House*
- Daniel's on B'way
- Siri's Thai French
- Perryville Inn
- Brighton Steak
- Manor
- Suilan
- Frog & Peach
- La Fontana
- Latour
- Beau Rivage
- Fascino
- Il Capriccio

vote at zagat.com

Best Buys

Top 40 Bangs for the Buck

1. White House
2. Benny Tudino's
3. DeLorenzo's
4. Kibitz Room
5. Grimaldi's Pizza
6. Tacconelli's
7. Irish Pub
8. La Isla
9. Hobby's Deli
10. Lotus Cafe
11. Far East Taste
12. Raymond's
13. Country Pancake
14. Mie Thai
15. Thai Kitchen
16. Richard's
17. Hunan Chinese
18. El Azteca
19. Down to Earth
20. Fedora Cafe
21. Norma's
22. Meemah
23. Brooklyn's Pizza
24. Simply Radishing
25. Tortuga's Mexican
26. Kinchley's Tavern
27. Bobby Chez
28. Sri Thai
29. Thai Thai
30. Pad Thai
31. Tick Tock
32. Wolfgang Puck
33. Chao Phaya
34. Ali Baba
35. Jack Cooper's
36. El Meson
37. Juanito's
38. Tortilla Press
39. Hunan Taste
40. Mastoris

Other Good Values

Aamantran
Aby's Mexican
Athens Café
Baker's Treat
Bell's
Beyti Kebab
Bien Hoa
Blue Danube
Broadway B&G
Casa Maya
Cloves
Cubby's BBQ
Cuzco
Diaz
El Familiar
El Salvadoreno
Ganges
Hot Dog Johnny's
Hurricane House
Indigo Smoke
Je's
King of India
Lada Cafe
Lodos
Los Amigos
Marco & Pepe
Mazi
Mexico Lindo
M-R Chefs Café
Navesink Fishery
Ocino
Olde Corner Deli
Passage to India
Penang
Quiet Man
Siam
Squan Tavern
Surf Taco
Tina Louise
West Lake
Wonder Seafood
Zafra

Restaurant Directory

vote at zagat.com

| F | D | S | C |

Aamantran ▽ 22 | 18 | 20 | $22
Victoria Plaza, 1594 Rte. 9 S. (Churchill Rd.), Dover Township, 732-341-5424
This BYO Indian "hidden" in a Dover Township strip mall has developed a loyal, far-flung following for its "wonderful" food that includes "flavorful" tandoori specialties outputted from the pair of ovens in the dining room; "good" service and "extremely reasonable" lunch buffets add to its attraction.

Aangan 23 | 18 | 17 | $26
A & M Plaza, 3475 Rte. 9 N. (Three Brooks Rd.), Freehold Township, 732-761-2900
"Flavorful" fare complements servers "willing to explain" the "wide selection" of dishes at this Freehold Township BYO; admirers aver that those out for Indian can expect a "distinctly better experience" here than from others in its genre; N.B. the restaurant now shares space with another eatery, Ginger Thai.

Abbey, The 16 | 21 | 17 | $37
Ramsey Golf & Country Club, 105 Lakeside Dr. (Franklin Tpke.), Ramsey, 201-818-9298; www.ramseycountryclub.com
The "clubby feel" and "lovely setting" of this "castlelike" Traditional American golf course eatery in Ramsey make it a "dependable" choice for those seeking a "romantic", "quiet dinner for two" or an "unhurried" meal with the kids; still, some aren't terribly taken with a menu that "needs a makeover" and service that's "inconsistent."

Aby's Mexican Restaurant ▽ 22 | 12 | 19 | $18
141 Main St. (Brown St.), Matawan, 732-583-9119
For "real" Mexican food, respondents recommend heading to this "*mexcellent*" Matawan storefront that's "a cut above the chains"; an "enthusiastic" staff and cute, homey touches (e.g. "paper napkins") turn it into a "treat."

Acacia 25 | 21 | 22 | $45
2637 Main St. (bet. Craven Ln. & Phillips Ave.), Lawrenceville, 609-895-9885; www.acaciacuisine.com
Chef-owner Bryan Brodowski's "tantalizing", "top-drawer" New American BYO opposite the Lawrenceville High School is a "real winner", with "consistently delicious, innovative" fare served in a "tight space" that's "packed" on weekends; while some respondents reel from "noise that can be a bit much", the "professional staff" and "romantic ambiance" make this "a nice place for a celebration."

Acqua ☒ 21 | 20 | 20 | $40
777 Rte. 202 N. (bet. 1st Ave. & Ortho Dr.), Raritan, 908-707-1777; www.acquaristorante.com
There's a "festive" vibe at this "large", "upscale" Italian in Raritan with an "innovative" menu and "professional" service; though "a bit pricey" to some, it's still "nice for a

special dinner or a drink"; N.B. look out for a hoppin' weekend bar scene and live jazz on most nights.

Acquaviva delle fonti   23 | 21 | 21 | $43
115 Elm St. (Broad St.), Westfield, 908-301-0700; www.acquaviva-dellefonti.com
An "elegant" dining room and "fabulous", "attractively presented" Northern Italian cuisine draw "a serious crowd" to this Westfield "standout"; prices may be "on the high side", but most don't mind, since you can bank on a pretty big bonus – an "attentive" staff.

Adega Grill   20 | 24 | 21 | $34
130-132 Ferry St. (bet. Madison & Monroe Sts.), Newark, 973-589-8830; www.adegagrill.com
For a "wonderful night out", make a trip to this "romantic" Newark Iberian for its "beautiful" decor and "good food" served in "huge portions" by a "gracious" staff that's "eager to please"; there's also "excellent" sangria, which helps explain why it's "crowded with young party-goers" on the weekends.

Ajihei   – | – | – | E
11 Chambers St. (Nassau St.), Princeton, 609-252-1158
Downtown Princeton is home to this small storefront Japanese where the chef transforms raw fare into sushi that "rivals the best" around; "ask for the BMW Roll and they'll know you're a regular" at the BYO whose "friendly staff is a big plus."

Akbar   19 | 17 | 18 | $26
21 Cortland St. (Patrick Ave.), Edison, 732-632-8822
While the expansion of this Indian "party-hall fave" in Edison may have made it more "lively" than ever, a few sullen sorts lament a new "focus given to catered parties"; despite this, surveyors still swear by a lunch buffet that offers "a nice variety" of "authentic" dishes.

Aladin's Ⓢ   ▽ 18 | 14 | 19 | $24
45 W. Main St. (Division St.), Somerville, 908-722-9001; www.aladinsrestaurant.com
Fans of this "authentic" Middle Eastern BYO in Downtown Somerville appreciate its "tasty" Lebanese fare and "helpful" service; though you'll find "nothing spectacular", it keeps locals and the courthouse crowd coming for an "interesting" "change of pace" at "reasonable" prices.

Alan@594 ⓈA   19 | 19 | 15 | $36
594 Valley Rd. (Bellevue Ave.), Upper Montclair, 973-744-4120
Diners arrive with "high expectations" at this new BYO that's generated quite a "buzz" in Upper Montclair, where admirers cite "simple" yet "creative" Northern Italian fare, "friendly" service and "cozy" digs; others who can't comprehend "what all the fuss is about" are outvoted.

| F | D | S | C |

Alchemist & Barrister | 17 | 16 | 18 | $34 |
28 Witherspoon St. (Nassau St.), Princeton, 609-924-5555;
www.alchemistandbarrister.com
An "old standby" of an American pub, this Princeton "institution" that's a "favorite of the gray-haired and preppy set" is a "decent" spot for "grabbing a pint and a casual meal"; regulars regard the "nice", heated year-round patio and "comfortable, dark" tavern as "better" options than the more formal dining room up front.

Al Dente Ristorante | 23 | 18 | 20 | $41 |
1665 Stelton Rd. (Ethel Rd.), Piscataway, 732-985-8220
Known for "sumptuous" Northern Italian and "courteous" service, this Piscataway BYO is an "old-world" "delight"; while some feel "it's pricier than it should be", most are "surprised" to find such a "gem" "in a strip mall" – just try "to get a handle on" the "over-the-top-decor."

Aldo & Gianni ☒ | 20 | 14 | 20 | $34 |
A&P Shopping Ctr., 108 Chestnut Ridge Rd. (Grand Ave.),
Montvale, 201-391-6866
268 Huyler St. (bet. Essex & Green Sts.), South Hackensack,
201-487-4220
www.aldoandgianni.com
Expect a "noisy, festive" atmosphere at these "storefront" Italians that offer "generous" portions of "yummy" fare, "generally friendly" service and a "casual" atmosphere, though critics contend the decor "could use a little updating"; N.B. the South Hackensack location is BYO.

Alexander's | ▽ 22 | 23 | 21 | $47 |
Alexander's Inn, 653 Washington St. (bet. Franklin & Ocean Sts.),
Cape May, 609-884-2555; www.alexandersinn.com
The "lovely" "Victorian ambiance" at this "very pretty" Cape May BYO is complemented by "wonderful, creative" French cuisine and "outstanding" service; it may be a "tad stuffy", but most maintain it's an "exquisite setting" for a "delightful" meal; N.B. there's a five-course Sunday brunch for $18.95.

Ali Baba | 19 | 12 | 17 | $19 |
912 Washington St. (bet. 9th & 10th Sts.), Hoboken,
201-653-5319; www.alibabahoboken.com
"Fly away happy" from this Hoboken Middle Easterner with "satisfying" "comfort food", a "friendly" staff and "extremely reasonable" prices; while critics are less entranced by the "dreary" decor, it's still a "reliable" "neighborhood favorite" for take out or dining in.

Alisa Cafe | ▽ 21 | 19 | 20 | $35 |
Barclay Farms Shopping Ctr., 112 Rte. 70 E. (Kings Hwy.),
Cherry Hill, 856-354-8807
While a bit "out of place" in its new "strip mall" home, chef-owner Tony Kanjanakorn's "lovely" Cherry Hill BYO

| F | D | S | C |

features the same "high-end" Thai-accented French fare and "attentive" service found in its former West Philly digs; note to Philadelphians: now *you* need to "cross the bridge."

Allendale Bar & Grill ❶ | 16 | 11 | 16 | $23 |
67 W. Allendale Ave. (Rte. 17), Allendale, 201-327-3197
This Allendale beer-and-brew joint keeps on chugging after 70 years with "decent" American fare (such as "delicious sweet potato fries") and a "cheerful atmosphere"; "kids love the free baskets of popcorn", and "people of all types, from yuppies to landscapers", laud the tabs.

AMANDA'S | 26 | 25 | 24 | $43 |
908 Washington St. (bet. 9th & 10th Sts.), Hoboken, 201-798-0101; www.amandasrestaurant.com
Still "elegant and wonderful", this "romantic" Hoboken "jewel" in a "beautiful" restored brownstone is renowned for its "fabulous", "creative" New American cuisine, a "thoughtfully" selected wine list, "impeccable" service and "lovely" decor – "and how can you beat their early-bird special?": a "stupendous bargain" at $12.50 per person.

Amarone | 20 | 16 | 23 | $38 |
63 Cedar Ln. (Teaneck Rd.), Teaneck, 201-833-1897
"The service will keep you coming back" and the Northern Italian food is "absolutely delicious" at this "charming", "casual" "neighborhood place" in Teaneck that's "always packed with regulars"; depending on your outlook, the decor is either "lackluster" or lends a "nice" "homey touch."

American Fare | 21 | 15 | 21 | $39 |
175 Maplewood Ave. (bet. Baker St. & Highland Pl.), Maplewood, 973-763-4005
Patrons fare well at this "elegant", "cramped" Maplewood BYO, a "tiny" "pearl" of a place where the kitchen creates "hearty", "eclectic" New American "comfort food" and the "earnest" staff does what it can to "accommodate" you; P.S. a recent paint job has "brightened" things up a bit.

Amici Milano | 22 | 18 | 22 | $34 |
600 Chestnut Ave. (Roebling Ave.), Trenton, 609-396-6300; www.amicimilano.com
Primo Italiano!: this "old-school" Italian "favorite" in the heart of Trenton's Chambersburg section turns out "wonderful" food, and the "pleasant" staff and "reasonable" prices make it "worth the wait if it gets a little crowded"; N.B. use one of the restaurant's free parking lots if you can't find a street spot.

An American Grill | – | – | – | E |
246 Rte. 10 W. (I-287), Randolph, 973-442-9311; www.anamericangrill.com
"A real find" in Randolph is this "relaxed and pleasant" American where the "short rib ravioli are to die for" and the

vote at zagat.com 21

| **F** | **D** | **S** | **C** |

rest of the fare on the menu, though "not high gourmet", is "well executed"; it's "worth a regular visit", say those who kick back in the dining room or "prefer to eat at the bar"; P.S. the wine list is "terrific."

Andaman ▽ 23 | 14 | 15 | $29
147 Morris St. (bet. Elm & King Sts.), Morristown, 973-538-5624
Fans of Thai-French cuisine are "very excited" about "perfectionist" chef-owner Santhaya Meunsuk's "inventive" menu at her brand-new Morristown BYO; it still has some things to work out (the "decor needs a face-lift", the "staff needs to get it together"), but "give it time" – "it's a sleeper" with "potential."

Andiamo 18 | 14 | 16 | $32
23 Hardenburgh Ave. (bet. Knickerbocker & Schraalenburgh Rds.), Haworth, 201-384-1551
"There's always a crowd" at this "friendly" "neighborhood" Italian in Haworth whose "large" "something-for-everyone" menu includes "specials that are actually special"; a coterie of critics grumble about "ordinary" food and "slow-motion" service, but "locals" laud its "cozy", "casual" ambiance, "nice wine list" and "warm, welcoming" staff.

André's ☒ 25 | 19 | 21 | $50
188 Spring St. (bet. Adams & Jefferson Sts.), Newton, 973-300-4192; www.andresrestaurant.com
André de Waal's "wonderfully creative" New American is a "must go" if you're in the Newton area, and "worth the drive" if you're not; while this "remote haven" can get a "bit cramped", the "inventive" fare, "gracious" service and "simple yet stylish" decor are sure to please; N.B. there's an on-site wine bar/boutique open Wednesdays–Saturdays.

Angelo's Fairmount Tavern 21 | 15 | 19 | $30
2300 Fairmount Ave. (Mississippi Ave.), Atlantic City, 609-344-2439; www.angelosfairmounttavern.com
After 70 years, this "old-fashioned" Atlantic City Italian is "still a classic"; it's "loud" and the "'50s decor" may feel "dated", but no matter, most say, since the "terrific" "no-nonsense" menu and "house Chianti" keep locals and tourists alike coming back.

Anjelica's 24 | 17 | 20 | $43
1070 Ocean Ave. (bet. Peninsula Ave. & River St.), Sea Bright, 732-842-2800; www.anjelicas.com
This "remarkable" BYO opposite the beach in Sea Bright has a "vast" Southern Italian menu, but "insiders" say "don't decide on your entree" until you've heard the "extensive list" of "mouthwatering" specials; though "a madhouse in the summer", if you can deal with the "din" and prices that may be "higher than you'd expect", you're in for a "nice evening."

| F | D | S | C |

Anna's Italian Kitchen ▽ 20 | 17 | 17 | $35
Fountain Ridge Shopping Ctr., 1686 Rte. 35 S. (Old Country Rd.), Middletown, 732-275-9142
Chef-owner Anna Perri's "Mulberry Street" menu at her Tuscan BYO in Middletown is "fantastic" ("the gnocchi is lighter than air"), but a vocal crew of critics say it's "pricey", the "staff needs some training" and the "cold", "unattractive strip-mall" milieu distracts diners from the "deliciously prepared" food.

ANTHONY DAVID'S 26 | 20 | 21 | $37
953 Bloomfield St. (10th St.), Hoboken, 201-222-8399; www.anthonydavids.com
Admirers "love, love, love" chef-owner Anthony Pino's "tiny", "first-class" Hoboken BYO, where the "superb", "evolving" Eclectic–Northern Italian fare is complemented by an "excellent cheese selection"; fans are also quite fond of the "wonderful" weekend brunch and "jazzy, casual" ambiance; here's a tip: "book a reservation in advance."

Anton's at the Swan 22 | 24 | 20 | $47
Swan Hotel, 43 S. Main St. (Swan St.), Lambertville, 609-397-1960; www.antons-at-the-swan.com
You can "sit by the fire" or "dine alfresco under the stars" at this "beauty" in a "historic" Lambertville hotel, where chef-owner Chris Connors "puts imagination" into his New American menu; lovebirds will appreciate that "quiet" ambiance + "warm and inviting service" = "romance."

Aozora ▽ 29 | 22 | 22 | $38
407 Bloomfield Ave. (Church St.), Montclair, 973-233-9400
The "amazing selection" of "fresh", "imaginative" and "beautifully" presented sushi and other "spectacular" Japanese-French items has sparked more than minor interest in this "incredible" two-year-old BYO in Montclair; partisans who "could eat every night" in its "Zen"-like setting declare it a "true winner."

Aquila Cucina 22 | 18 | 20 | $38
30 South St. (Springfield Ave.), New Providence, 908-464-8383; www.aquilarestaurant.com
Surveyors swoon over this New Providence "local favorite", a "pleasant" Italian BYO that's a showcase for "creative", "well-prepared" cooking and "attentive" service, and sports a new "bistro look" that "adds to the ambiance" (thanks to a fairly recent redo); "bring your earplugs", however, 'cause it's "bedlam on weekends."

Aria Ristorante 20 | 21 | 19 | $38
4 Little Falls Rd. (Passaic Ave.), Fairfield, 973-227-6066; www.ariaristorante.com
Though it looks "like a typical North Jersey catering hall" on the outside, this Fairfield Northern Italian dishes "yummy"

vote at zagat.com

| F | D | S | C |

eats in a "lively", "fun" setting; it's got a "nice" staff, admirers affirm, while a company of contrarians chime it's "not a showstopper"; P.S. "the weekend piano player adds a nice touch."

Arthur's Landing | 20 | 24 | 20 | $49 |
1 Pershing Rd. (Bergenline Ave.), Weehawken, 201-867-0777; www.arthurslanding.com
The food plays second fiddle to the "astonishing" view of Manhattan's West Side at this Weehawken waterfront New American; there's another view here too: though "good", the menu items "simply don't" "warrant" prices way above "sea level"; still, "it's hard to beat the pre-theater package" – $50 per person for valet parking, a three-course meal and round-trip NYC ferry transport.

Arthur's Tavern | 18 | 11 | 15 | $25 |
214 Kinderkamack Rd. (Lincoln Blvd.), Emerson, 201-265-5180
237 Washington St. (3rd St.), Hoboken, 201-656-5009
700 Speedwell Ave. (Littleton Rd.), Morris Plains, 973-455-9705
644 Georges Rd. (Milltown Rd.), North Brunswick, 732-828-1117
www.arthurstavern.com
Cost-conscious carnivores think they're in "hog heaven" when they visit these "no-frills" chophouses that are "cheaper" than the "fancy schmancy" joints in Manhattan; the decor is "not great" and service "can be rushed", but it's "just plain fun", those steaks are "huuuge", the beers are "cold" and "the game" is always on – if you can see it through the "smoke"; P.S. the "cash only" policy at Morris Plains is "kind of a pain."

Arturo's | 21 | 18 | 19 | $43 |
41 Central Ave. (bet. Godwin & Greenwood Aves.), Midland Park, 201-444-2466; www.arturos-restaurant.com
They offer a "good selection" of "classical" Southern Italian dishes at this "upscale" "family place" in Midland Park known for its "yummy" pizza; though former fans feel it was "better as a BYO" and think it's become too "pricey", partisans praise the "fantastic", "homestyle" fare and "sweet" service.

Assembly Steak House | 18 | 18 | 17 | $48 |
495 Sylvan Ave. (Palisades Ave.), Englewood Cliffs, 201-568-2616
Nostalgic sorts still think something was lost in translation at this "undeservedly popular" Englewood Cliffs steakhouse that's "a shadow" of its late-'90s self across the river; though put-the-past-behind types proclaim it's a "great hangout" with "good chops" and "attentive" service, and add it "sure is a lot prettier" than the NYC original.

| F | D | S | C |

Athenian Garden ▽ 24 | 12 | 20 | $25
619 S. New York Rd. (bet. Holly Brook Dr. & W. Brook Ln.), Galloway Township, 609-748-1818
Plausible theories as to why this "cozy", rustic Greek BYO in Galloway Township is growing in popularity include its "great fish" and other "delicious" fare from the exposed kitchen and "value prices"; in short, the convinced conclude it's "worth it."

Athens Café 20 | 11 | 20 | $22
Sawmill Vlg., 404 Rte. 70 E. (Brookmead Dr.), Cherry Hill, 856-429-1061
Get past the "passable" decor and head on over to the strip mall where this "informal" Cherry Hill BYO outputs "delicious" Greek cooking and is "the only place around to get a good gyro"; you'll be grateful for a "good value" meal and a "cheerful" staff that "makes you feel like family."

Atrio Cafe 22 | 19 | 21 | $37
515 Bridge St. (bet. NJ Rte. 29 & PA Rte. 32), Stockton, 609-397-0042
Groupies gush about this "terrific" New American BYO "by the Delaware River" in Stockton, where the "exciting" South American–influenced food gets a "standing-O"; it's "casual" and "cozy", but "forget about having a conversation", since it tends to get "noisy"; N.B. you can pick up some vino next door at Philips Fine Wines.

AUGUSTINO'S ⇗ 27 | 19 | 24 | $37
1104 Washington St. (bet. 11th & 12th Sts.), Hoboken, 201-420-0104
Expect a "treat" if you're "lucky enough" to score a reservation at this "intimate" Hoboken Southern Italian, where the prize is "glorious" "homespun" cooking, a "tiny", "cozy" brick-walled dining room and "mouthy" but "ultrafriendly" waitresses who "act like you're a regular"; be sure to call ahead – "unless you know someone."

Avon Pavilion 19 | 16 | 17 | $29
600 Ocean Ave. (bet. Norwood & Woodland Aves.), Avon-by-the-Sea, 732-775-1043; www.avonpavilion.com
This "seasonal favorite" right on the boardwalk in Avon purveys breakfast, lunch and dinner menus that feature "good" American standards served by an "attentive" staff; though it seems "pricey" to some ("especially for a BYO"), the ocean breezes, views that "can't be topped" and a "laid-back" vibe keep loyalists lining up.

Axelsson's Blue Claw 23 | 21 | 20 | $45
991 Ocean Dr. (Rte. 109), Cape May, 609-884-5878; www.blueclawrestaurant.com
You can "dine by the fireplace and enjoy the piano" at this year-round Cape May "secret" turning out "terrific" bounty from the sea including "great" crab cakes all brought to

| F | D | S | C |

table by a "super" staff; though a little on the "high end" side and "a bit off the beaten track", it's a "beautiful place" to watch the sunset.

Azúcar | 22 | 18 | 19 | $38 |
10 Dempsey Ave. (River Rd.), Edgewater, 201-886-0747; www.azucarcubancuisine.com
If you appreciate "imaginative" "homestyle" Cuban cooking and a "lively", "welcoming" atmosphere, you may feel quite at home in this "small" and "stylish" Edgewater BYO on the site of a former speakeasy; while the "smoke" from the upstairs cigar lounge is a "turn off" to some, fans try not to let it obscure the experience.

Babalu Grill ☒ | ▽ 18 | 23 | 21 | $36 |
2020 Atlantic Ave. (Arkansas Ave.), Atlantic City, 609-572-9898; www.serioussteaks.com
A "civilized" island in a sea of casinos, this "sophisticated" Cuban is a "refreshing" addition to the Atlantic City dining scene; "it hasn't hit it big yet", but those who enjoy its "good" food, "excellent mojitos" and flashy decor think such a "cool place" "should be busier than it is."

Bacari Grill | 20 | 22 | 20 | $41 |
800 Ridgewood Rd. (Pascack Rd.), Washington Township, 201-358-6330; www.bacarigrill.com
This "romantic" "jewel" set in the heart of Washington Township offers a "relaxing", "rustic" setting, a "creative" New American menu and a "cool" bar; though the "too-noisy", "NYC" ambiance irks some, regulars like it that way; P.S. the restaurant's two private rooms with fireplaces are "great for family events."

Bahama Breeze | 18 | 22 | 18 | $26 |
Cherry Hill Mall, 2000 Rte. 38 (Haddonfield Rd.), Cherry Hill, 856-317-8317; www.bahamabreeze.com
Cheerleaders of this "fun", "friendly" tropical-themed Cherry Hill Caribbean go bananas for its "terrific piña coladas" and "tasty" island fare that's "better than you'd expect from a chain"; "live music" adds to the getaway ambiance, though some are less sunny about "long lines" on weekends.

Bahrs Landing | 15 | 15 | 16 | $34 |
2 Bay Ave. (bet. Hillside Ave. & South St.), Highlands, 732-872-1245; www.bahrs.com
A Highlands "tourist favorite", this "old-fashioned" fish house that's "been around forever" (since 1917, to be exact) "remains true to its deep-sea roots" with an "unpretentious" American menu ("soups are its strong point") and "salty" atmosphere; though some wish the "mediocre" grub "was more interesting", others say just put your eyes on the "wondrous" seaside views and "stick to the basics."

| F | D | S | C |

Baja 20 | 16 | 18 | $25

104 14th St. (Washington St.), Hoboken, 201-653-0610
117 Montgomery St. (bet. Grove & Warren Sts.), Jersey City, 201-915-0062
www.bajamexicancuisine.com

Groups are giddy about this "lively" Mexican duo in Hoboken and Jersey City catering to a "young crowd" that appreciates "tons" of "authentic", "dependable" fare, an "extraordinary collection of tequilas" and "terrific margaritas"; don't mind the "tight squeeze" since "everyone is having a blast" – even those who think "everything's better after a few drinks."

Baker's Treat – | – | – | I

14 Turntable Junction (bet. Central Ave. & Church St.), Flemington, 908-782-3458 ⓢ
9B Church St. (bet. Main & Union Sts.), Lambertville, 609-397-2272
www.bakerstreat.com

Good food for a good cause is the motto of these Hunterdon County bakery/cafes with a noble aim (100% of their profits go to programs for women recovering from alcohol and drug addiction); N.B. not only do they cater, but they'll bake up and ship treats to any U.S. destination.

Bamboo Grille 17 | 17 | 19 | $33

Basking Ridge Country Club, 185 Madisonville Rd. (N. Maple Ave.), Basking Ridge, 908-766-8200;
www.growthrestaurants.com

Though situated on the property of a private country club, this "comfortable", "tropical"-themed Basking Ridge oasis that "overlooks the golf course" is open to the public and "very friendly"; proponents praise the "tasty" American-Eclectic fare and the "efficient" staff, while a few conclude that things here are not always "up to par."

Bamboo Leaf ▽ 25 | 22 | 19 | $27

724 Main St. (bet. Lareine & McCabe Aves.), Bradley Beach, 732-774-1661

An "extensive" menu of "amazing" Thai-Vietnamese goodies is helping fuel a "fast-growing reputation" and creating "long lines" at this new Bradley Beach "storefront" BYO; while it may get "a little cramped" now and then, it's still a "great addition" to the Monmouth County dining scene.

Bangkok Garden 23 | 13 | 20 | $25

261 Main St. (E. Salem St.), Hackensack, 201-487-2620;
www.bangkokgarden-nj.com

"Oh-soooo-flavorful" treats are in store for those who wander into this Thai in an "in-the-middle-of-nowhere" part of Hackensack; "out-of-this-world" pad Thai and the "gracious" staff that "won't hurry you out the door" help make the "banal" ambiance more palatable.

vote at zagat.com

| F | D | S | C |

Bareli's ☒   23 | 19 | 23 | $51
219 Rte. 3 E. (Plaza Center Dr.), Secaucus, 201-865-0473
The "wonderful" staff and "fabulous" fare draw a crowd to this "lovely" Secaucus Italian near the Meadowlands; while some find comfort in its "great" bar, "wide variety" of specials and game-oriented, "machismo" atmosphere, others "don't understand the attraction", and say "save-it-for-the-expense-account" prices means "you better not leave home without it."

Barnacle Ben's   19 | 18 | 18 | $27
Acme Shopping Ctr., 300 Young Ave. (bet. Marne Hwy. & Marter Ave.), Moorestown, 856-235-5808;
www.barnaclebens.com
If you "want a good piece of fish" at a "reasonable price", this BYO "hidden" in the Acme parking lot in Moorestown may be the place, where an "inventive" seafood menu features some "unusual combinations"; though a few "want to put it out to sea", most want to keep it on the mainland.

Barnacle Bill's ☾   20 | 15 | 17 | $25
1 First St. (River Rd.), Rumson, 732-747-8396
"Post-collegiate prepsters" and their "baby boomer parents" rave about the "irresistible", "belly busting" burgers and "convivial" atmosphere of this "rustic" Rumson American, where you can throw "peanut shells on the floor" and enjoy a "good, cold" pint of grog while taking in the "magnificent view" of the Navesink River; it's "noisy" and "smoky" and there's "always a wait", but "who cares?" – it's "fun."

Barone's   21 | 17 | 18 | $27
Barclay Farms Shopping Ctr., 210 Rte. 70 E. (Kings Hwy.), Cherry Hill, 856-354-1888
280 Young Ave. (Main St.), Moorestown, 856-234-7900
www.baronerestaurants.com

Villa Barone
753 Haddon Ave. (bet. Frazer & Washington Aves.), Collingswood, 856-858-2999; www.baronerestaurants.com
This family-owned trio is known for its "generous portions" of "delicious", "garlicky" Italian fare and its "nice" outdoor seating; though some have issues with staff "attitude", "lots of people" like the three, right down to their "fake Italian courtyard" decor "that somewhat works."

Barrel's   20 | 12 | 17 | $25
199 New Rd. (Central Ave.), Linwood, 609-926-9900 ☒
9 S. Granville Ave. (Ventnor Ave.), Margate, 609-823-4400
206 E. 11th St. (bet. Haven & West Aves.), Ocean City, 609-399-1700
"Local" loyalists laud these "informal" "red-gravy" BYOs along the shore for their "authentic" "South Philly"–style Italian food, "bargain" prices and "service with a smile";

| F | D | S | C |

it's also "good for takeout", though a crew of critics wishes the place would take away the "so-so" decor.

BASILICO 23 | 21 | 20 | $41
324 Millburn Ave. (Main St.), Millburn, 973-379-7020; www.basilicomillburn.com
Before milling about the Paper Mill Playhouse, theatergoers head to this "chic" Millburn BYO known for its "marvelously prepared" Northern Italian fare, "dependable" service and "phenomenal" desserts; it can get "noisy", but "for a night out with friends" or a "romantic dinner" "you can't go wrong here" – just don't forget to "make reservations", since it's "always crowded."

Basil T's ● 17 | 17 | 17 | $31
183 Riverside Ave. (Bridge Ave.), Red Bank, 732-842-5990; www.basilt.com
The "homemade" hops are the "main attraction" at this Red Bank microbrewery/American-Italian eatery that also packs in a lunch crowd seeking "big burgers", "good pastas and pizzas" and an antipasta bar that folks "love"; despite critics who complain of "slow" service and "generic" fare, an "active" bar scene and live music make for a "lively" time.

BAUMGART'S CAFÉ 20 | 14 | 18 | $25
59 The Promenade (River Rd.), Edgewater, 201-313-3889
45 E. Palisade Ave. (bet. Dean & Engle Sts.), Englewood, 201-569-6267
158 Franklin Ave. (N. Walnut St.), Ridgewood, 201-612-5688
www.baumgartscafe.com
Sure, it's a "strange combo" – American diner by day, Chinese-Thai BYO by night – "but somehow it works": the food, from stir-fried chicken to chicken pot pie, is "delicious", the "homemade" ice cream is "heavenly" and the service is "fast and friendly"; though the Ridgewood location is "prettier" than the others, hearts are set on the Englewood original; N.B. they recently added sushi.

Bayou Cafe ∇ 22 | 13 | 18 | $25
209 First Ave. (bet. Brielle Rd. & Main St.), Manasquan, 732-223-6678; www.bayoucafe.net
New Orleans native and chef-owner Tim Paris "knows his gumbo" and "isn't afraid to spice things up" at his "wonderful" storefront "hideaway" near the beach in Manasquan, where delighted diners dig into "very good", "down-home" Cajun cooking; Bayou backers'll also love that it's "funky" and "friendly", to boot.

BayPoint Prime ∇ 20 | 13 | 16 | $53
1805 Ocean Ave. (Rte. 35), Point Pleasant Beach, 732-295-5400
Dennis Foy and chef Kevin Pomplun (ex Ryland Inn) have transformed a Point Pleasant Beach Italian eatery into a "high-class" steakhouse purveying "high-end" steaks and

vote at zagat.com

F D S C

burgers "to die for"; not everyone, however, is primed for a return visit, since it seems "pricey", and the quality of the food is "undone" by a space "in need of a redo" and "so-so" service.

Bazzarelli ▽ 20 | 14 | 17 | $25
117 Moonachie Rd. (Joseph St.), Moonachie, 201-641-4010
A pizza toss away from the Meadowlands, this "small" "mom-and-pop" Moonachie Italian serves "good", "old-school" food brought to table by a staff that makes you "feel like family"; while the quarters are "bland", and it gets "loud" ("bring cotton for your ears") and "smoky", it remains a "nice" choice for the area.

Bazzini at 28 Oak Street ⌧ 23 | 16 | 20 | $44
(fka 28 Oak Street)
28 Oak St. (bet. Franklin & Ridgewood Aves.), Ridgewood, 201-689-7313
Chef-owner Paul Bazzini's "beautifully prepared", "upscale" New American "comfort food" brings fans "again and again" to his Ridgewood BYO, where the service is "considerate without being overbearing"; while the "dated" decor and "high prices" can be "a let down", most feel it's time and money well spent for a "wonderful" experience.

Beau Rivage 23 | 24 | 24 | $51
128 Taunton Blvd. (Tuckerton Rd.), Medford, 856-983-1999
"First class" all the way, this "romantic", "special-occasion" Medford French offers a "beautiful" château setting complemented by *belle cuisine* and "formal" service; a few modern-minded who find it all a little "stuffy" can opt for the basement wine cellar bistro, a "great alternative" to the fancier, Louis XVI–style dining room upstairs, where jackets are required.

Beechwood Cafe & Market _ | _ | _ | I
290 Grove St. (Mercer St.), Jersey City, 201-985-2811; www.beechwoodcafe.com
Popping up opposite City Hall is this brand-new BYO in Jersey City offering a slate of Traditional American eats all day in cheery, comfy digs; if you haven't had your fill supping on sandwiches, pastries and the like, consider purchasing items for home in the adjacent retail shop.

Beignet's Pub ▽ 18 | 19 | 16 | $38
618 Boulevard (Blaine Ave.), Seaside Heights, 732-830-1255
Fans of this New American/Cajun-Creole combo with a "very hip bar" (featuring live jazz on weekends) wonder how a "slick" spot like this "wound up in Seaside"; though faultfinders think it isn't worth dealing with the "smog" from cigarettes, it's still an "unexpected change" in the "land of the sausage and pepper sandwich"; N.B. open Fridays and Saturdays in winter, and Wednesday–Sunday in the summer.

subscribe to zagat.com

F	D	S	C

Bella Sogno — — — E
600 Main St. (Brinley Ave.), Bradley Beach, 732-869-0700
Subtle nuances in Med-Italian standards elevates the fare at this clubby, wood-paneled BYO tucked away on a side street just off the main drag in the coastal community of Bradley Beach; fans who have been keeping the little-known spot to themselves recommend the hearty rustic pastas and salads as the best route to a night filled with – as the name suggests – beautiful dreams.

Bellissimo's 23 20 21 $46
1 Rte. 23 S. (Rte. 46), Little Falls, 973-785-4225
The "long recitation" of "amazing" specials will "make your head spin", but with such a "huge variety" of offerings, everyone "can find something" "delicious" at this "elegant", "upscale" Italian in Little Falls; hats off to the "superb" waiters who memorize all those dishes, but "beware" the "high prices" that accompany them.

Bell's ⌀ 19 10 17 $25
183 N. Union St. (bet. Buttonwood & Elm Sts.), Lambertville, 609-397-2226; www.bellstavern.com
Locals make a point of "getting in early" to this Lambertville landmark that "fills up quickly" because of its "yummy" Italian-American eats and "well-stocked bar"; though "shabby" on the inside, and "loud" and "smoky" once things gets humming, it's "an institution" for a reason: you'll have a "good" time "on the cheap."

Bell's Mansion — — — E
11 Main St. (Rte. 183 S.), Stanhope, 973-426-9977; www.bellsmansion.com
Set in a grand brick homestead (circa 1840) in Stanhope, this elegant special-occasion destination offers traditional tavern fare in its Tap Room (featuring a late-19th-century oak bar) and more sophisticated New American comestibles in the other dining rooms; there's talk that some of the house's departed inhabitants linger in spirit – in light of the mansion's considerable charms, it's easy to see why.

Belmont Tavern ⌀ 22 6 12 $27
12 Bloomfield Ave. (15 St.), Bloomfield, 973-759-9609
"It's all about" the signature dish at this Bloomfield "dive" that's "still going strong", cooking up an "amazing" chicken Savoy on an all-around "outstanding" menu that has kept "generations" of "locals" "coming back"; the Italian fare, though, had better be good to compensate for waitresses who "treat you like a nobody."

Belvedere 20 17 19 $36
247 Piaget Ave. (Main Ave.), Clifton, 973-772-5060
They "do everything right", "year after year", affirm acolytes who praise this "old-time" "favorite" in Clifton for its

vote at zagat.com

| F | D | S | C |

"delicious" Italian food and "quality" service; critics warn you may end up "feeling like an ashtray" in the dining room, and "parking can be an issue", but a crowd of "regulars" thinks it's still a "gem."

Benito's ▽ 20 | 19 | 20 | $37
(fka Toscana Trattoria)
44 Main St. (Rte. 24), Chester, 908-879-1887
"Consistently good" Northern Italian fare and "decadent" desserts delivered by a staff that's "friendly" "without being overbearing" are hallmarks of this "romantic" Chester BYO; while you may not find a lot of "imagination" in the "traditional" menu, it's champions don't care, and consider the place a "hidden treasure."

Benny Tudino's ●⊄ 21 | 7 | 14 | $11
622 Washington St. (bet. 6th & 7th Sts.), Hoboken, 201-792-4132
Size matters at this Hoboken pizza "landmark", a "Friday night favorite" with a "loyal following" thanks to its "gigantic", "$2 slices on steroids" that are "meals in themselves" – no surprise then that BT remains one of the best Bangs for the Buck in our *Survey*; so if you stumble in before, during or after a night out at the bars, ignore the decor and stuff yourself "silly."

Berkeley Restaurant & 18 | 11 | 17 | $27
Fish Market
Central & 24th Aves. (J St.), South Seaside Park, 732-793-0400
South Seaside Park's 60-year-old seafooder is better known for its "beautiful views" of Barnegat Bay and Island Beach State Park than for its culinary creativity; though doubters dub it a destination for "day-trippers" rather than serious fish fans, the kind opine that considering its past, the "food has really improved."

BERNARDS INN, THE 26 | 26 | 25 | VE
27 Mine Brook Rd. (Quimby Ln.), Bernardsville, 908-766-0002; www.bernardsinn.com
The verdict's in: despite much talk about Ed Stone's departure last year, chef Corey Heyer's tenure at the "grande dame" of "special-occasion" dining in Bernardsville has been "exceptional", and the "magic" of this "classic" in the land of "blue bloods" remains on all fronts, from the "blue-ribbon" New American cuisine, to "superb" service to an "incredible wine list" backed by a "knowledgeable" sommelier; though the prices may seem "exorbitant", the "experience" here is likely to be "memorable."

Berta's Chateau ▽ 21 | 17 | 21 | $46
7 Grove St. (Prospect St.), Wanaque, 973-835-0992; www.bertaschateau.com
Bring a compass to zero in on this "hard-to-find" "charmer" in Wanaque known for "wonderful" Northern Italian fare that "captures the simple homemade pleasures" of The

| F | D | S | C |

Boot backed by a "welcoming" ambiance and "extensive", Barolo-heavy wine list; it may "look tired around the edges", but most feel it's "stood the test of time."

Beyti Kebab ▽ 25 | 10 | 19 | $25
4105 Park Ave. (bet. 41st & 42nd Sts.), Union City, 201-865-6281; www.beytikebab.com
This "terrific" Turkish treasure in Union City is "the real thing", with "superb" fare that's the "best of its kind this side of the Bosporus", "smoky", "no-frills" atmosphere and belly dancing (weekends only); when "no one around you is speaking English", "you know it's good"; N.B. there's a halal butcher shop attached to the restaurant.

Bien Hoa ▽ 21 | 9 | 18 | $15
2090 Rte. 27 (Talmadge Rd.), Edison, 732-287-9500
Though *not* a sight for sore eyes, this "small" Vietnamese BYO in an Edison strip mall is the "only place to go" "when you crave pho"; pho-ponents and others in search of "something a little different" are also content with "cheap" prices that make the "tasty" offerings even more enticing.

Big Ed's BBQ 17 | 10 | 16 | $22
259 Rte. 130 (bet. Jerome St. & Lincoln Ave.), Burlington, 609-387-3611
305 Rte. 34 N. (Low Rd.), Old Bridge, 732-583-2626
535 Rte. 9 S. (Birdsall St.), Waretown, 609-693-7222
www.bigedsbbq.com
Oink oink! "bring the kids" and a "big appetite" and have a sloppy "good" time at this trio of BBQ "pig-out" palaces serving "succulent, fall-off-the-bone" ribs; they're "loud" and "messy" and easier on your wallet than on your eyes, but most brave "long lines" 'cause these places are "fun to chow down in"; P.S. "avoid indigestion" by "steering clear of karaoke night" at the Burlington location.

Big Fish Seafood 18 | 19 | 16 | $32
3535 Rte. 1 (Meadow Rd.), Princeton, 609-919-1179; www.muer.com
"Funky" decor and a "stylish" bar set the tone for this "hip", "happening" Princeton seafood "chain" spot whose "reliable" fare and "bustling weeekend" scene attract a "young crowd" that doesn't mind the "cacophony"; it's also clear that "spotty" service can't keep 'em away, since most say it's a "cool" place for those who "aren't ready to head home" anytime soon.

Bistro at Red Bank, The 21 | 18 | 17 | $36
14 Broad St. (bet. Front & Mechanic Sts.), Red Bank, 732-530-5553; www.thebistroatredbank.com
There's "always a scene" at this BYO Eclectic in Downtown Red Bank, whose "global", "far-out" menu "has something for everyone", "from sushi to pizza" to "inventive" seafood dishes (the crackling calamari salad is "killer"); fans feel it's

vote at zagat.com

| F | D | S | C |

"very chic", but critics suggest the "disinterested" staff "lose the attitude."

BISTRO OLÉ 26 | 19 | 23 | $36
230 Main St. (bet. Cookman & Mattison Aves.), Asbury Park, 732-897-0048; www.bistroole.com
Adding a second dining room has given more folks a chance to check out chef Wil Vivas' "lively", "exceptional" cooking, a "celeb"-worthy greeting from host-owner Rico Rivera and "enthusiastic" service at this "swanky" Spanish-Portuguese "pearl" in Asbury Park; "the waits to get in" can be "insane", but be patient and you'll have an "amazing" time.

Black Duck on Sunset ▽ 26 | 21 | 22 | $43
1 Sunset Blvd. (Broadway), West Cape May, 609-898-0100
Chef-owner Christopher Hubert (Union Park) is showing an "innovative" touch at this Eclectic BYO that's "off the beaten track" in West Cape May; "exquisite" food such as honey roast duck and "romantic" ambiance means it's "worth hunting down."

Black Forest – | – | – | M
42 S. Main St. (south of Rte. 195), Allentown, 609-259-3197
Celebrate Oktoberfest year-round at this genial German BYO in one of the oldest buildings in Allentown; now shepherded by chef Kevin Warner, the veteran's classics draw in droves of hearty eaters lusting after gravy-soaked pork shanks and sauerbraten, while the cheery staff ensures the welcome's as warm as the steaming potato pancakes.

Black Forest Inn 24 | 22 | 21 | $41
249 Rte. 206 N. (I-80, exit 25), Stanhope, 973-347-3344; www.blackforestinn.com
"If sauerbraten excites you", this "enchanting" Teutonic "old-timer" is "worth the drive" to Stanhope's "backwoods" for "first-rate" German-Continental fare, "expert" service and unabashedly "traditional" decor; though the place is "huge", it's "divided into small spaces" for more "intimacy."

Black Horse Tavern & Pub 19 | 19 | 18 | $34
1 W. Main St. (Rte. 124), Mendham, 973-543-7300; www.blackhorsenj.com
Whether you opt for the "casual" pub or the slightly "more conservative" tavern at this Mendham American, the "ol' mare'll" provide "reliable" fare and "great Cosmos"; there's a "stable" crowd of "soccer moms" and "younger yuppies" here, and day-trippers don't mind "popping in for a beer and burger" after a trip through the heart of horse country.

Black Swan, The 24 | 20 | 21 | $32
Super G Shopping Ctr., 127 Ark Rd. (Rte. 38), Mount Laurel, 856-866-0019
Admirers swoop down on this "strip-mall surprise" in Mount Laurel that turns out "excellent" Eclectic–New

American food with service to match; indeed, the BYO's "hidden" location belies a "quality" place that's "great to celebrate or impress someone"; N.B. their 'heart check' menu items feature ingredients low in cholestorol.

Black Trumpet | – | – | – | E |

The Sandpiper Inn, 7 Atlantic Ave. (Ocean Ave.), Spring Lake, 732-449-4700; www.theblacktrumpet.com

The new sensation in genteel Spring Lake is this warmly welcomed arrival from chefs Mark Mikolajczyk and Dave McCleery (both ex Whispers), a New American in a gracious space a seashell's skip from the Atlantic; start off with lamb brushed with pomegranate molasses and move on to scallops with a splay of the namesake mushrooms at this immediately fashionable BYO.

Bloomfield Steak & Seafood | 17 | 13 | 17 | $35 |

409 Franklin St. (Broad St.), Bloomfield, 973-680-4500; www.bloomfieldsteakandseafood.com

Once a hiding place for George Washington from the Redcoats, this Bloomfield eatery in a 17th-century building now has a more mundane mission – to feed folks "pretty good" surf 'n' turf in a "friendly" atmosphere; some, though, want to reach for a candle, saying the "dark" digs could use an "update."

Blue | 24 | 21 | 22 | $43 |

1016 Long Beach Blvd. (11th St.), Surf City, 609-494-7556; www.bluerestaurantlbi.com

Vacationers from "more urban environs" who "don't want to leave the pleasures of big-city dining behind" consider this "funky" seasonal California-Eclectic BYO a "standout" amid Long Beach Island's "countless" "fish and pasta factories"; it's a "sophisticated treat" for those who appreciate "daring" cuisine (smoked salmon cannoli, anyone?) served up by a "well-versed" staff in a "sleek" and "spare" space.

Blue Danube | ∇ 19 | 15 | 18 | $27 |

538 Adeline St. (Elm St.), Trenton, 609-393-6133

"When you're in the mood for something different", the "good", "hearty" Continental–Eastern European comfort fare (Czech, German, Russian, you name it) and "charming" ambiance at this "tiny" Trentoner provides a "nice break" from the city's "Italian" food scene; though service "can be slow", at least it's "always courteous", and prices are "reasonable" given the "large" portions.

Blue Eyes | – | – | – | E |

139 Egg Harbor Rd. (Blackwood Barnsboro Rd.), Sewell, 856-227-5656; www.blueeyesrestaurant.com

The Rat Pack's back – or at least it feels that way at this Washington Township American that pays tribute to Frank, Dean, Sammy and the gang nightly with a hoppin' bar and

| F | D | S | C |

lounge, lots of steaks, seafood and chops, and continuous clips from the crooners' '50s–'60s flicks shown on easy-viewing flat screens; if it all sounds very Vegas, well, it is – South Jersey style.

Blue Moon Mexican Cafe 16 | 14 | 15 | $23
21 E. Palisade Ave. (bet. Dean St. & Grand Ave.), Englewood, 201-541-0600
Bi-State Shopping Plaza, 216 Old Tappan Rd. (Central Ave.), Old Tappan, 201-263-0244
42 Kinderkamack Rd. (Prospect St.), Woodcliff Lake, 201-782-9500
Boulder Run Shopping Area, 327 Franklin Ave. (bet. Goodwin Ave. & Main St.), Wyckoff, 201-891-1331
www.bluemoonmexicancafe.com
"You can depend on" this "family-friendly" Mexican chain for its "*grande*" servings of "good" grub at "fair" prices; though traditionalists deem it "McMexican", kids "love the clown" (weekends) and few complain about leaving with a "full belly" and overall "happy buzz"; P.S. the Wyckoff location is BYO, but the others have a "lively" bar scene.

BLUE POINT GRILL 26 | 15 | 21 | $34
258 Nassau St. (Pine St.), Princeton, 609-921-1211; www.bluepointgrill.com
Scoring points for its "amazing" "variety" of "flawless", "super-fresh" seafood preparations "kept simple" is this "casual" Princeton BYO that's usually "packed to the gills"; the "great" raw bar and "efficient" staff keep "hooking" 'em despite "long" lines and "noise."

Bobby Chez 26 | 10 | 17 | $20
Village Walk Shopping Ctr., 1990 Rte. 70 E. (bet. Old Orchard & Springdale Rds.), Cherry Hill, 856-751-7373 ⌧
33 W. Collings Ave. (bet. Cove Rd. & Norwood Ave.), Collingswood, 856-869-8000 ⌧
8007 Ventnor Ave. (S. Gladstone Ave.), Margate, 609-487-1922
Southgate Plaza, 1225 Haddonfield-Berlin Rd. (Lippard Ave.), Voorhees, 856-768-6660 ⌧
www.bobbychezcrabcakes.com
"Crab cakes!" sums up the appeal of this South Jersey seafood chain that's primarily a "take-out" spot; loaded with "lump meat", the signature "hockey pucks" are the "best around", according to those who can stand the "brutal" waits in the summer; the lobster mashed potatoes and "underrated" shrimp cakes collect kudos too.

Bombay Gardens 24 | 13 | 20 | $24
Center 18 Mall, 1020 Rte. 18 N. (bet. Gunia St. & Hillsdale Rd.), East Brunswick, 732-613-9500; www.bombaygardens.com
Beloved backers of this "small" BYO in East Brunswick say be sure to "try the tandoori" and the "great selection of breads" on the "mouthwatering" menu of Indian eats

subscribe to zagat.com

| F | D | S | C |

brought to you by "accommodating" servers; don't let the "kitschy" decor and "strip mall" locale throw you, since the place "continues to amaze."

Boulevard Grille 19 | 15 | 17 | $32
1033 MacArthur Blvd. (bet. Corporate Dr. & Ridge Rd.), Mahwah, 201-760-9400; www.boulevardgrille.com
Finding "creative" "well-prepared" New American fare in a mini-mall is "unexpected", so this Mahwah BYO earns plaudits for its "great bread basket" and "large" dessert list; though pundits profess the place "seems to be slipping", citing "weak" service and a "sterile" setting, they're overruled by a majority that thinks it still has "potential."

Braddock's Tavern 20 | 23 | 20 | $39
39 S. Main St. (Coates St.), Medford, 609-654-1604; www.braddocks.com
There may be nothing revolutionary on the menu, but the Traditional American chow is "solid" nonetheless at this Medford "charmer" whose staff adds to the "historical" ambiance by donning Colonial-era garb; though it feels "like it's been around forever", and some swear it's high time for a "makeover", it ranks as a "popular" destination for "special occasions."

Brandl. 23 | 16 | 20 | $44
703 Belmar Plaza (bet. Main St. & 9th Ave.), Belmar, 732-280-7501; www.brandlrestaurant.com
"Tucked away" on a pedestrian plaza in Downtown Belmar, this "busy" "cosmopolitan" New American BYO is a "nice surprise" for the Shore; you may have to shout above the "noise" to "have a conversation" (maybe it's "the tin ceiling"?), but the service is "first rate", and the "lavishly prepared" cuisine is "exceptionally good" – period.

Brasilia 22 | 12 | 21 | $28
132 Ferry St. (bet. Madison & Monroe Sts.), Newark, 973-465-1227
"International fans" of Brazilian BBQ who want to "talk soccer" and score "endless skewers" of "delicious" "all-you-can-eat" grilled meats at "modest prices" head to this "gem in the heart of Newark"; "it's not anything to look at", but with a "club downstairs on weekends" it's a "rocking place for carnivores" looking for a "carnival"-like time.

Brass Rail, The 20 | 20 | 19 | $39
135 Washington St. (2nd St.), Hoboken, 201-659-7074; www.thebrassrailrestaurant.com
An "upscale" "standby", this Washington Street New American is a "classy" escape from Hoboken's well-documented "frat" scene; supporters swear you'll find gold in an "eclectic" menu matched by "excellent" wine selections that'll "delight" enthusiasts; P.S. the "romantic" upstairs dining room is a more formal counterpart to the casual area downstairs.

vote at zagat.com

| F | D | S | C |

BRIGHTON STEAKHOUSE   26 | 24 | 24 | $55
Sands Hotel & Casino, 136 S. Kentucky Ave. (Pacific Ave.), Atlantic City, 609-441-4300; www.acsands.com
The odds are stacked in your favor at this slabhouse in the Sands serving some of the "best steaks in AC"; fans take comfort in the "excellent" service and "fabulous" decor, but they also pray that someone else picks up the bill, 'cause the beef isn't the only thing that's "premium" here.

Brioso   24 | 18 | 19 | $38
Willow Pointe Shopping Ctr., 184 Hwy. 9 (Union Hill Rd.), Marlboro, 732-617-1700; www.briosoristorante.com
Despite the fact that "you can't be assured of a quiet meal", devotees declare "there are few finer" spots in the area than this "friendly", "bistro-like" Italian BYO in a Marlboro strip mall with a "wonderful selection" ("what other Italian restaurant serves sweetbreads?") of "delicious" fare; in spite of a vocal minority that mutters about "inconsistent" service, most bet "you'll come back."

Brix 67   19 | 20 | 15 | $39
67 Union Pl. (Summit Ave.), Summit, 908-273-4448
Evoking some of SoHo's "hipness", this Asian-Eclectic in suburban Summit is "typically packed" with "lots of pretty ones" who like the vibe and the "broad" menu – with everything from brick-oven pizza to sushi, there's "something for everyone"; the scene is a little "too cool" for some, however, particularly those not into "inattentive" service.

Broadway Bar & Grill ●   ▽ 14 | 12 | 15 | $19
106 Randall Ave. (Broadway), Point Pleasant Beach, 732-899-3272
Though the "food isn't anything special", this "cheap", "laid-back" Point Pleasant Beach American is a "favorite" of "fishermen from the docks across the street" and landlubbers who like it because this "neighborhood" "hang" makes "everyone feel like a regular"; P.S. there's "good live music" every night.

Brooklyn's Coal-Burning   22 | 10 | 14 | $17
Brick-Oven Pizzeria
Edgewater Commons Shopping Ctr., 443 River Rd. (Hudson River Rd.), Edgewater, 201-945-9096
161 Hackensack Ave. (Emerald St.), Hackensack, 201-342-2727
15 Oak St. (Ridgewood Ave.), Ridgewood, 201-493-7600
"Ex–New Yorkers" say "you'll feel like you're back in Brooklyn" when you visit these "busy" Bergen County pizza joints pumping out "crispy", "thin-crust" treats from their brick ovens; though they're "nothing fancy" on the inside, and neither "lax" service nor the no-slice policy win over fans, many remain focused on pies "comparable to some of NYC's best."

| F | D | S | C |

Brothers Moon 22 | 16 | 21 | $36
7 W. Broad St. (Greenwood Ave.), Hopewell, 609-333-1330;
www.brothersmoon.com
"Funky" and "quaint", this "storefront" BYO in Hopewell attracts a "loyal clientele" who appreciate chef-owner Will Mooney's "inventive" New French menu that makes "artful" use of "fresh", local organic produce and meats; the "prompt" service from an "oh-so-friendly" staff may put you over the moon.

Brunello Ristorante 21 | 17 | 20 | $37
120 Terhune Dr. (Hamburg Tpke.), Wayne, 973-616-0999;
www.brunelloristorante.com
A "nice place to host a party", this Wayne Italian draws praise for its "delicious" food and "great" service; though a snobbish set snort that it's "romantic" in a "tacky" way, and the "attempt at elegance" "falls short", most sense "it's a cut above the rest."

Bruschetta ☒ 22 | 20 | 20 | $44
292 Passaic Ave. (bet. Bloomfield Ave. & Rte. 46), Fairfield, 973 227-6164; www.bruschettarestaurant.com
This "special place" in Fairfield, "a charming find on an otherwise industrial stretch" of Passaic Avenue, purveys "solid" Northern Italian food in an "intimate" space; though "pricey" to some and "not too different than the other places" in the area to others, most agree it's a "dependable" choice for a "great meal."

Buca di Beppo 16 | 19 | 20 | $25
2301 Rte. 38 (Haddonfield Rd.), Cherry Hill, 856-779-3288;
www.bucadibeppo.com
If "softball-size meatballs" are your thing, come to this "entertaining", "family-oriented" Cherry Hill chain spot featuring "trough loads" of "decent" Italian amid decor "corny" enough to inspire many "conversations"; it can be "entertaining", especially if you "go with a big group."

Bula World Cuisine ☒ – | – | – | M
134 Spring St. (Rte. 206), Newton, 973-579-7338;
www.bularestaurant.com
Chef Bradley Boyle's exotic Eclectic menu covers the gastronomic globe from Europe to Korea to the Caribbean at his 90-seat Newton storefront that's routinely jammed with the area's newly relocated professionals who dig the rock shrimp cakes with mango salsa as much as they do the chicken paprikash or beef bulgoki; fyi, it's BYO.

Busch's Seafood ∇ 19 | 16 | 18 | $38
8700 Landis Ave. (87th St.), Sea Isle City, 609-263-8626;
www.buschsseafood.com
Born in 1882 and still standing, this "classic" Sea Isle City seafooder's fame largely rests on its "standout" she-crab

vote at zagat.com

soup on a shellfish-strong menu that "hasn't changed in years"; "it's update time", some insist, but the "lines" of "locals" and "tourists" suggest many folks like it just the way it is.

Cabin, The | 17 | 16 | 16 | $24
984 Rte. 33 E. (Fairfield Rd.), Howell, 732-462-3090; www.thecabinrestaurant.net
"Unpretentious" to say the least, this "lively" Howell roadhouse, where "jeans" and a "pickup truck" outside are de rigueur, serves up "simple" American fare (burgers, steaks, etc.) in "rustic" quarters; "families" luck out with the "huge portions", while sports nuts find it a "fun place" to "catch a football game."

Cafe Abbraci | 22 | 15 | 22 | $36
140 Durham Ave. (Central Ave.), Metuchen, 732-548-6077
Talk about a role reversal: this "quaint", "little" Metuchen BYO used to be a "biker bar" but is now an "intimate date place" with "high-quality" Italian fare and "top-notch" service; though the decor may call for a "redo", it's still a "cozy" place where "everyone feels welcome."

Cafe Arugula | 22 | 17 | 19 | $36
59 S. Orange Ave. (bet. Scotland Rd. & Vose Ave.), South Orange, 973-378-9099; www.cafearugula.com
It's hard to "save room for the gelato" considering there's "generous portions" of "delicious", "imaginative" Italian food at this "delightful" BYO in South Orange known for its "extensive list of specials"; the staff has an "easygoing" style, and supporters see that their wallets won't wilt, given "down-to-earth" pricing.

Cafe at Rosemont, The | 21 | 16 | 20 | $29
88 Kingwood-Stockton Rd. (Rte. 519), Rosemont, 609-397-4097; www.cafeatrosemont.com
Whether for breakfast, brunch or dinner, this "adorable" BYO in a 200-year-old "general store" in rural Rosemont is "always a winner"; the "innovative" New American "comfort" comestibles ("don't miss the butterscotch pudding"), "eclectic" decor "with local art for sale" and "friendly" staff "that calls everyone 'hon'" tend to draw a "diverse crowd" of folks who consider it a place to go for a "true respite."

Cafe Coloré | 21 | 17 | 20 | $32
Chadwick Sq., 3333 Rte. 9 N. (Adelphia Rd.), Freehold Township, 732-462-2233; www.greatrestaurantsnj.com
"Dress up or down" at this Freehold Township BYO in a strip mall that offers a variety of "tasty" Italian dishes "at affordable prices", and whose digs are "simple" yet "pleasant"; P.S. bonus for parents and kids: the "reliable" servers will provide crayons for the young ones.

| **F** | **D** | **S** | **C** |

Cafe Cucina 🚭 | 21 | 20 | 20 | $39 |
3366 Rte. 22 W. (bet. County Line & Readington Rds.), Branchburg, 908-526-4907; www.cafecucina.com
The "new decor looks great" at this "cute but noisy" Branchburg BYO whose "wonderful" Italian cooking is matched by an "excellent" martini list; it's "a bit expensive" and "not always consistent", some say, but most maintain the "enjoyable ambiance" makes it a "pleasant surprise."

Cafe Emilia | 23 | 21 | 22 | $42 |
705 Rte. 202 N. (Milltown Rd.), Bridgewater, 908-429-1410; www.cafeemilia.com
"Warm" and "friendly" and "anxious to please", this Bridgewater Italian "in the shadow" of the Wegmans store is a "wonderful find" on "busy" Route 202 that gets high marks for its "terrific" "homemade pasta", "excellent sauces" and "lovely" space; admirers affirm that it can swing two ways – as a "good bet" for "a business lunch", or a "romantic" dinner.

Café Everest | 18 | 14 | 19 | $30 |
45 Broad St. (White St.), Red Bank, 732-933-9848
It may be "less exciting" than climbing a mountain, but this Russian-Armenian BYO in Red Bank is still an "interesting" "change of pace" for reviewers recommending its "simple" fare that includes "delicious pierogi" and "killer chicken Kiev"; though the staff is "gracious", the decor may be "less than thrilling."

Café Gallery | 21 | 24 | 21 | $33 |
219 High St. (Pearl St.), Burlington, 609-386-6150; www.cafegalleryburlington.com
This "beautiful" Burlington "favorite" with an art-gallery alter ego boasts a "gorgeous view" of the "Delaware River" and a "superb" "Sunday brunch" to boot; admirers attest to the "solid" French-Continental fare and "reasonable" prices, while detractors dish that service, though "friendly", can be "slow."

Cafe Graziella | 21 | 15 | 18 | $31 |
Cost Cutters Shopping Ctr., 390 Rte. 206 (Hillcrest Rd.), Hillsborough, 908-281-0700
A strip-mall locale hides this Hillsborough BYO and its "terrific, earthy" Italian cuisine, a staff that provides the goods "in seconds" and a "relaxing" atmosphere; some feel the interior "could use an upgrade", but overall, it's an "excellent value."

Cafe Italiano | 18 | 13 | 17 | $35 |
14 Sylvan Ave. (Irving Ave.), Englewood Cliffs, 201-461-5041
Satisfied surveyors say the "delicious" pastas and "homey" ambiance at this Englewood Cliffs Italian in "cute" quarters make it a "nice" option; regulars "love the outdoor dining"

vote at zagat.com

| F | D | S | C |

and "great early-bird specials", though dismayed diners dock the place for its "off nights"; P.S. there's a "reasonable" corkage fee for those who tote their own.

Cafe Loren ▽ 26 | 20 | 24 | $44
2288 Dune Dr. (23rd St.), Avalon, 609-967-8228;
www.cafeloren.com
We "wish it were open 365 days a year" proclaim fans of this "charming" seasonal BYO in Avalon whose "fabulous" New American food and "wonderful" service translate into return visits for those undeterred by the "tight" seating setup; N.B. open May–September.

CAFE MATISSE 27 | 26 | 26 | $60
167 Park Ave. (bet. E. Park Pl. & Highland Cross),
Rutherford, 201-935-2995; www.cafematisse.com
A "go-to place" for a "special-occasion" "splurge", this "romantic" Rutherford BYO in a "charmingly decorated" renovated firehouse wows with a "consistently amazing" Eclectic menu, a "pastry chef who works wonders" and a "knowledgeable" staff that "pays attention to details"; the "velvet chairs" and "jeweled chandeliers" add to "beautiful" decor even the maestro would have approved; P.S. there's a wine shop up front – "how perfect is that?"

Cafe Metro 21 | 16 | 18 | $24
60 Diamond Spring Rd. (bet. 1st Ave. & Orchard St.),
Denville, 973-625-1055; www.thecafemetro.com
"If healthy eating is your passion", you're in for a treat at this "Victorian" BYO in Denville whose red-meat-be-gone, veggie-centric Eclectic lineup includes "interesting" chicken, pasta and seafood dishes prepared with "fresh", organic ingredients; it's "bright" and "airy" – literally – since it's "smoke free."

CAFE PANACHE ⓈⒷ 27 | 21 | 25 | $52
130 E. Main St. (Rte. 17), Ramsey, 201-934-0030
It's no surprise that reservations are "hard to come by" at "one of Bergen's best", a Ramsey BYO via "magician" chef-owner Kevin Kohler that "delights" both "palate" and soul with an "ever-changing" menu of "terrific" Eclectic fare incorporating "fresh" ingredients "sourced from local farmers"; "impeccable" service and a recent "upgrade" of the decor adds to a "wonderful" experience.

Cafe Zbra Ⓢ ▽ 23 | 14 | 19 | $44
9 E. Somerset St. (Thompson St.), Raritan, 908-722-0445;
www.cafezebra.com
Get an "enthusiastic" greeting from the "entertaining" owner of this "cute" Raritan New American sporting a "funky" "zebra-themed" interior; though not everyone's "crazy about" the "no-printed menu" thing (you have to hear dishes recited "over and over as each table is seated"), most go nuts over the "imaginative" and "tasty" cuisine.

| F | D | S | C |

Caffe Aldo Lamberti 22 | 21 | 20 | $38
2011 Rte. 70 W. (Haddonfield Rd.), Cherry Hill, 856-663-1747; www.lambertis.com
Devotees have "nothing but good things to say" about this Cherry Hill Italian that's "worth a trip" for its "wonderful specials", "superb" service and "surprisingly good list" of vinos featuring some "amazing bargains"; the few who feel it tends to "run hot or cold" are outvoted; N.B. the restaurant offers private dining in their two wine cellars for parties of 16 or more.

California Grill 20 | 14 | 18 | $24
Dansk Plaza, 1 Rte. 31 (US Hwy. 202), Flemington, 908-806-7141
The only thing that's changed is the ownership at this "casual" "strip-mall" Eclectic in Flemington, a "favorite" "lunch stop" for bargain-hunters looking to "recharge" after a "hectic" hustle at the nearby shopping outlets; the "interesting", "vegetarian-friendly" menu includes "wonderful" salads, "creative soups" and "very good gourmet pizzas", while a "pleasant" atmosphere may inspire return visits.

Capriccio 25 | 25 | 25 | $64
Resorts Atlantic City Casino & Hotel, 1133 Boardwalk (North Carolina Ave.), Atlantic City, 609-340-6789
Consider playing the slots to pay for a meal at this "pretty" Italian in the Resorts, where fans say you've "hit the jackpot" since the food is "superb", the staff is "excellent" and the big bonus is the "ocean view" (though "not visible at night"); "even if you're not comped", it's "worth every poker chip" in your pocket.

Captain Jack's 20 | 17 | 18 | $31
68 Main Ave. (bet. New York Ave. & Pilgrim Pathway), Ocean Grove, 732-869-0770; www.captainjacksog.com
All hands are on deck applauding the "well-prepared" New American fare and "arty" ambiance of this "reliable" BYO on Ocean Grove's "main drag", where the "diverse" menu spans offerings from fried calamari to filet mignon; it's "fun", even for "bored kids" who'll appreciate gazing at the fish in the "huge" tank.

Capt'n Ed's Place 18 | 13 | 18 | $31
1001 Arnold Ave. (Pine Bluff Ave.), Point Pleasant, 732-892-4121; www.captainedsplace.com
Though the practice of "cooking your own" on a "hot stone" may seem a tad Neolithic, it also may ensure your food is "exactly to your liking" and help explain why this "typical" Jersey Shore surf 'n' turf joint in Point Pleasant gets "jammed"; those who complain of "ridiculously long waits" and "slow" service, however, advise you can always opt to "stay home and cook."

vote at zagat.com

	F	D	S	C

Cara Mia Café ☒   _ | _ | _ | E
218 Main St. (Church St.), Hackettstown, 908-684-3801
It's not just locals who are fond of this 48-seat Italian BYO in Hackettstown, whose homey appeal extends throughout Warren County; chef Tommaso Wohlrob makes the trip worthwhile with crowd-pleasers such as filet mignon and Brazilian lobster tail in a garlic-arugula cream sauce; N.B. closed Sundays and Mondays for private parties.

Carpaccio   17 | 16 | 18 | $31
651 Bound Brook Rd. (2nd St.), Middlesex, 732-968-3242
This "fairly typical" Italian in Middlesex features a "great pasta fagiole" on a menu "without surprises" and "good" service; supporters say it's "worth a try" considering the "nice prices", though critics carp about the "dated" "'60s wedding banquet" decor and the "ordinary" fare.

Caruso's Tuscan Grill   17 | 18 | 16 | $38
65 Rte. 4 W. (N. Farview Ave.), Paramus, 201-556-9111
Scene trumps cuisine at this Paramus Northern Italian, whose "trendy bar" helps hook in a "hip", "young" crowd; depending on your luck, service is "fast" or "slow", and as for the fare, it's "nothing memorable", though a committed crew sees it as "better than average."

Casa Dante   25 | 19 | 22 | $43
737 Newark Ave. (bet. Kennedy Blvd. & Summit Ave.), Jersey City, 201-795-2750
A red-sauce specialist for over 30 years, this Jersey City Southern Italian cooks up "out of this world" cuisine served by a staff that knows how to "take care" of an audience made up of "power brokers" and "loyal" customers; sure, the decor may be "unremarkable", but it doesn't matter – this place is "a classic."

Casa Giuseppe   ∇ 24 | 19 | 25 | $39
487 Rte. 27 (Oaktree Rd.), Iselin, 732-283-9111; www.casagiuseppe.com
Though "hidden" among "all the offices" in the Metropark area, this Iselin Southern Italian is a "great surprise", where the "flavorful" food, "exceptional" service and "upscale" ambiance mean "you can't go wrong"; it's "expensive" to a few, but "worth every penny" to most.

Casa Maya   22 | 17 | 18 | $25
615 Meyersville Rd. (Hickory Tavern Rd.), Meyersville, 908-580-0799; www.casamayamexican.com
Way out there, somewhere "in the middle of nowhere", is this "funky" Meyersville Mexican cantina that comes in a size "small", but where folks take a ticket and endure "long waits" to corral a table; fans say it's the "only game around" – albeit a "good" one; P.S. strictly a BYO operation, so "don't forget" to bring a side order of "Coronas."

44   subscribe to zagat.com

| F | D | S | C |

Casa Vasca
23 | 14 | 22 | $31

141 Elm St. (Prospect St.), Newark, 973-465-1350
The "tasty" Spanish, Basque and Portuguese specialties at "fantastic values" keep this "terrific" Ironbound Iberian "packed" with patrons "ready for a show" at NJPAC; if the "noise" frays your nerves, the "relaxed" service should put you at ease; P.S. the nearby "parking lot is a plus."

Catelli
24 | 24 | 23 | $46

Plaza 1000 Main St. (bet. Evesham & Kresson Rds.), Voorhees, 856-751-6069; www.catellirestaurant.com
"Beautiful" decor and a "capable" staff complement the "creative" fare at this "upscale" Voorhees Italian whose "great bar area" attracts a well-heeled group of "older singles"; "act like a king" if you can, since "premium" pricing means you'll need pockets as deep as one.

Cathay 22
23 | 17 | 20 | $31

124 Rte. 22 W. (Hillside Ave.), Springfield, 973-467-8688; www.cathay22.com
You'll know by "consistently imaginative", "spicy" Szechuan treats and "charming" service that this unassuming Springfield "staple" is "no-run-of-the-mill" joint; some surmise that even "Chinese diplomats" would go here.

Cenzino ☒
23 | 21 | 22 | $46

589 Ramapo Valley Rd. (Franklin Ave.), Oakland, 201-337-6693; www.cenzinos.com
A "tuxedoed" staff and "congenial" owner provide "first-class" service at this "clubby" and "comfortable" Oakland "oasis", an Italian "bistro" where the food "shines" and where you know it's "loud inside" once you see that the "parking lot is full of high-end European cars"; in sum, it's a "wonderful experience" "time after time."

CHAKRA
20 | 27 | 18 | $53

144 Rte. 4 E. (Arcadian Way), Paramus, 201-556-1530; www.chakrarestaurant.com
"Sexy singles" and "suburban housewives" "love" this "exotic" Paramus newcomer whose "jaw-dropping" decor features a "tranquil" water wall and "cozy" seating with "lots of pillows" that will "transport" you to "Marrakesh" – or at least someplace "far away"; the "tantalizing" New American menu and "hopping" bar are equally "trendy"; P.S. bring "infrared goggles" – it's "quite dark."

Champps Americana
16 | 16 | 15 | $22

Menlo Park Mall, 418 Menlo Park Dr. (Rte. 1), Edison, 732-906-1333
Marlton Crossing Shopping Ctr., 25 Rte. 73 S. (Rte. 70), Marlton, 856-985-9333
www.champps.com
If you're looking for a "quintessential" sports bar, these "popular" American spots in Edison and Marlton cover the

F | D | S | C

bases – "giant burgers", "frosty beers", "balloons for the kids" and, of course, "a ton of TVs"; they're "noisy" and "crowded" and the service ebbs and flows like the "game" you're watching, but the atmosphere is "fun" and "lively", and the prices are "reasonable."

Chand Palace   21 | 12 | 18 | $22
257 Littleton Rd. (Parsippany Rd.), Parsippany, 973-334-5444; www.chandpalace.com
"You won't miss meat" once you sample the fare at this vegetarian strip-mall Indian in Parsippany with a "great buffet" that has a "variety" of "interesting" dishes at a "really good value"; a "standard" experience to some, few deride this BYO's "friendly" staff and "no-smoking" policy.

Chao Phaya   24 | 16 | 21 | $24
9 Davenport St. (W. Main St.), Somerville, 908-231-0655
Considering the "wonderful flavors" in "every dish", "you can't go wrong" at this Somerville Thai, where fans are fired up about the BYO's "exceedingly fresh" fare that "has some zip" to it ("spicy" stuff), "warm" service and "pleasant" digs that put it in a league with "NJ's best."

Charley's Ocean Grill   20 | 13 | 18 | $33
29 Avenel Blvd. (Ocean Ave.), Long Branch, 732-222-4499
Locals tramp to this "reliable" Long Branch surf 'n' turfer near the ocean for its "good burgers", "hearty seafood chowder" and "homey", "pub" atmosphere; it's "smoky" and "always crowded", but most agree it's a "comfy" "hang."

Chart House   21 | 26 | 21 | $46
Lincoln Harbor, Pier D-T (Harbor Blvd.), Weehawken, 201-348-6628; www.chart-house.com
Respondents revel in an "unbelievable" view of the Big Apple from the vantage point of this Weehawken American "celebration place" whose food, though not as "dazzling" as the vista, is "delicious" enough to leave many incredulous that it's part of a chain; so, "get a window seat", "impress a date" and "enjoy."

CHEESECAKE FACTORY, THE   19 | 19 | 16 | $27
Menlo Park Mall, 455 Menlo Park Dr. (Rte. 1), Edison, 732-494-7000
Riverside Square Mall, 197 Riverside Sq. (Hackensack Ave.), Hackensack, 201-488-0330 ◐
www.thecheesecakefactory.com
"Getting to dessert" is "difficult" at these Edison and Hackensack branches of a national chain: first, there's the "ridiculously long wait"; then, the main course: "surprisingly good" Traditional American fare doled out in portions so "enormous" it's a challenge to "save enough" real estate in your stomach for the "divine", namesake confection; one thing's for sure – they're "popular."

46   subscribe to zagat.com

| F | D | S | C |

CHEF'S TABLE, THE 26 | 17 | 23 | $45
Franklin Square Shopping Ctr., 754 Franklin Ave. (Pulis Ave.), Franklin Lakes, 201-891-6644
Nonbelievers need to know that "great" things can show up in "unlikely places", and the strip-mall location of this "tiny" BYO French bistro in Franklin Lakes proves just that, with chef-owner Claude Baills' "marvelous" creations of country "classics" and "delightful" service from a staff that "does all it can" to ensure a "pleasurable" experience; N.B. reservations required.

CHEF VOLA'S ⌿ 26 | 10 | 22 | $44
111 S. Albion Pl. (Pacific Ave.), Atlantic City, 609-345-2022
You may have to "know the right people" who can get you in to this reservations-only "find" in an AC "basement", "one of the more original places around" that delivers with "sensational" Italian fare, "incredible hospitality" and a "quirky" "non-decor" that's "part of the charm"; P.S. "bring cash", and don't forget a bottle, since it's BYO.

Chengdu 46 24 | 18 | 20 | $39
1105 Rte. 46 E. (bet. Valley Rd. & Van Houten Ave.), Clifton, 973-777-8855; www.chengdu46.com
This "high-end" Chinese BYO in Clifton "continues to amaze" respondents who report that it "rivals anything across the Hudson", citing the "tantalizing" Szechuan goodies, an "impressive" wine selection and "attentive" staff; it's "pricey" and a few who aren't inclined to "spend a pretty penny" think it's "living on its reputation", but do note that its "20+ years following" can only mean that it has "staying power."

CHEZ CATHERINE ⌧ 26 | 21 | 24 | $57
431 North Ave. (E. Broad St.), Westfield, 908-654-4011; www.chezcatherine.com
Edith and Didier Jouvenet are "doing a marvelous" job carrying on the tradition set by their predecessor; their "pink" and "cozy" French "landmark" in Westfield treats its audience to "beautiful" preparations of sometimes "otherworldy" cuisine and "first-class" service, making it a "superb" choice for a "special day or date"; N.B. closed Sundays and Mondays.

CHEZ DOMINIQUE ⌧ 26 | 17 | 24 | $45
4 Bedford Ave. (Washington Ave.), Bergenfield, 201-384-7637; www.chezdominique.com
"Exquisite" Classic French food helps turn this "tiny" "charmer" in Bergenfield into "a must" when a "trip to Paris" is out of the question and you need a culinary reminder of the city's classic dishes; chef-owner Dominique Payraudeau is a "true artist" "who cares"; "excellent" service adds to the "warm" atmosphere.

vote at zagat.com

| F | D | S | C |

Chez Elena Wu 22 | 19 | 21 | $31
Ritz Shopping Ctr., 910 Haddonfield-Berlin Rd. (White Horse Rd.), Voorhees, 856-566-3222
The name may tell you something about this "upscale" strip maller in Voorhees, namely that it's the address of chef-owner Elena Wu and her "high-quality" Asian-French fare; add "fine" service and a new sushi bar, and it's no surprise this spot's been a "winner since day one."

Chez Z 19 | 18 | 18 | $28
Village Shopping Ctr., 1260 Springfield Ave. (South St.), New Providence, 908-665-4000
This "unassuming" neighborhood cafe in a New Providence strip mall has an "interesting variety" of "reasonably priced" New American dishes, and an even more interesting decor that's "cute as a button" or "tacky", or at least "fit for Liberace"; P.S. the BYO policy is "an added plus", and the "early-bird menu" is a "great value."

Chilangos ∇ 21 | 15 | 20 | $23
272 Bay Ave. (Sea Drift Ave.), Highlands, 732-708-0505; www.chilangosnj.com
Considering the "well-stocked bar" featuring upwards of 80 types of tequila, and fare that showcases "authentic" ingredients (including cactus), it's clear that this Highlands Mexican is "anything but cookie-cutter"; with chef-owner Leo Cervantes "always around for recommendations", it's "worthy of a visit."

Christie's 23 | 18 | 21 | $35
Howell Center Mall, 2420 Rte. 9 S. (W. Farms Rd.), Howell, 732-780-8310; www.christiesrestaurant.us
Though the "strip-mall setting can be a turnoff", admirers of this Howell BYO have their eyes and mouths set on this Italian that "brings a touch of class" to "fast-food" Howell; "it's your fault if you go away hungry", since its "wonderful" food comes in "bountiful portions", but you may not be able to do much about the "noise."

Christopher's Cafe 21 | 13 | 18 | $25
41 Rte. 34 (Rte. 537), Colts Neck, 732-308-3668
"Hidden" in a shopping center, this "little" "neighborhood" BYO in Colts Neck cooks up "creative" American comfort food "prepared with care" for breakfast, lunch or dinner; the "homey" ambiance "leaves a lot to be desired" to some, but regulars say the working "fireplace" lends some "coziness."

Cinque Figlie ⌧ 23 | 19 | 21 | $43
302 Whippany Rd. (Park Ave.), Whippany, 973-560-0545; www.fivedaughters.com
The owners' "five daughters should be proud" of this eatery named after them, since this Whippany Italian located in a "pretty" "restored house" whips up "very good"

| F | D | S | C |

food brought to you by a "gracious" staff; it's been years now, but some continue to "miss" the "smaller" digs and lower prices of the original BYO in Morristown, but most have moved on to appreciate the extra "elbow room."

City Bistro
19 | 20 | 17 | $33

56-58 14th St. (bet. Hudson & Washington Sts.), Hoboken, 201-963-8200

"Bustling" and undeniably "trendy", this all-the-way-Uptown New American in Hoboken boasts a "fantastic view" of NYC from its rooftop bar that's a cool bet on warm days; its "terrific ambiance" is further abetted by a "scene" of "pretty people" sipping some "excellent martinis" and tucking into "sophisticated" fare; N.B. the first-floor lounge offers a more casual bar menu to the more extensive options on the second floor.

Clark's Landing
19 | 21 | 18 | $34

847 Arnold Ave. (Bay Ave.), Point Pleasant, 732-899-1111; www.clarksbarandgrill.com

A "spectacular view" of the Manasquan River and a "lively" "bar scene" for "singles" "over 40" are the main attributes of this American docked on a Point Pleasant marina that offers a "good variety" of fare; the staff may be "friendly", but the service tips toward "unprofessional", and others claim the setting is offset by a place that's "inconsistent."

Claude's
– | – | – | E

Anglesea Vlg., 100 Olde New Jersey Ave. (1st Ave.), North Wildwood, 609-522-0400

Chef Claude Pottier and his wife, Mary, recently relocated their BYO from Stone Harbor to North Wildwood, bringing along French standards (sole meunière) and their patented signature, shrimp Thailandaise; loyalists report this one's an elegant change from the area's other offerings.

Clouseau's
∇ 20 | 17 | 15 | $35

12 New St. (Main St.), Metuchen, 732-205-0058

This "sleeper" of a BYO is a "great addition" to Metuchen's dining scene, where the French-Eclectic cooking "abounds in brilliant flavors" and the "dim, romantic" ambiance "makes you forget the world outside"; but a small crew of divided diners detect something "amateurish" here, particularly in the "disorganized" service, that makes "comparisons" to Peter's Seller's "Inspector irresistible."

Cloves
∇ 21 | 19 | 23 | $25

61 International Dr. (Main St.), Budd Lake, 973-347-9290; www.clovesindiancuisine.com

Locals in-the-know say this "lone outpost" in Budd Lake serves "good" Indian food in an "odd location" in Northwest New Jersey; its "great specials" and "excellent" service help counteract "cafeteria-style" decor that may need a little spicing up; N.B. lunch is buffet only.

vote at zagat.com

| F | D | S | C |

Clydz ⬤ | 23 | 17 | 20 | $43 |
55 Paterson St. (Spring St.), New Brunswick, 732-846-6521;
www.clydz.com
A "huge selection" of martinis and an "eccentric" lineup of "excellent" New American fare turn this "basement" bar/eatery into "*the* place to be" if and when in New Brunswick; post-collegians plop down a "pretty penny" and "jostle for space" to become part of the "cool", "cramped" and "noisy" " scenery" that plays host to folks "from all walks of life", who receive a bonus in the form of "down-to-earth" service.

Coconut Bay Asian Cuisine | – | – | – | M |
Echelon Village Plaza, 1120 White Horse Rd. (Berlin Rd.), Voorhees, 856-783-8878;
www.coconutbayasiancuisine.com
This new Southeast Asian specialist in Voorhees is tantalizing taste buds with Korean barbecued beef and Malaysian pineapple shrimp in a high-tech setting softened by Buddhas and glowing paper lanterns; BYO keeps the costs cool.

Colligan's Stockton Inn | 20 | 25 | 19 | $43 |
Colligan's Stockton Inn, 1 Main St. (Bridge St.), Stockton, 609-397-1250
Now under a new chef and owners, this "quaint" Colonial country-inn restaurant in Stockton has "improved" its French–New American fare that's now "expertly prepared"; though the service hasn't "pulled together yet", the decor is "as beautiful as ever", and most maintain it's "romantic" and "overflowing with character."

Columbia Inn | 21 | 13 | 16 | $31 |
29 Main Rd./Rte. 202 (Morris Ave.), Montville, 973-263-1300;
www.thecolumbiainn.com
Loyalists who praise the "paper-thin crust" pizzas, "great salads" and "fresh fish" at this "casual" "local hangout" in Montville insist the Italian fare is "good enough to compensate" for any "drawbacks" in the decor area; the "only place in town worth talking about", however, also has some snickering about "noise."

Copper Canyon | 25 | 18 | 18 | $37 |
Blue Bay Inn, 51 First Ave. (bet. Bay & Center Aves.), Atlantic Highlands, 732-291-8444; www.bluebayinn.com
Forced to relocate to new and larger digs across the street after a 2004 fire, this Atlantic Highlands Tex-Mex "hasn't missed a beat": the "Southwestern" cuisine remains "inventive" and "delicious" and there are still tons of "tequilas" to choose from; despite the expansion, diners still "have to cram themselves in" and service "can be "disappointing", but that "hip" "young" crowd is "glad" to have their hangout "back."

| F | D | S | C |

Country Pancake House ⊘   19 | 9 | 15 | $15
140 E. Ridgewood Ave. (Walnut St.), Ridgewood, 201-444-8395
Why "count carbs" when you can load up on "fantastic" flapjacks the "size of manhole covers" and other portions of AM faves?, ask patrons of this "frill-less" American in Ridgewood; though the "unending" menu includes "hearty" lunch and dinner dishes, those in-the-know "don't order anything but breakfast food" – if they first make it through the "eternal waits" for a table.

Court Street   22 | 18 | 20 | $31
61 Sixth St. (bet. Hudson & Washington Sts.), Hoboken, 201-795-4515; www.courtstreet.com
In the court of public opinion, this "casual" Continental "hidden" on a side street is one of Hoboken's "best-kept secrets" purveying "wonderful" food to "parents" and couples "on a date" who can look forward to "friendly" service and "great" wines; P.S. regulars "adore" the Sunday brunch and "bargain" early-bird Mondays–Thursdays.

Crab's Claw   16 | 13 | 17 | $31
601 Grand Central Ave. (President Ave.), Lavallette, 732-793-4447; www.thecrabsclaw.com
"Fresh" seafood, a "really nice" bar and "superior" beer and wine lists are the hallmarks of this Lavallette "standby" that attracts "long lines" of "vacationers"; while those expecting "gourmet" goods might leave in a "crabby" mood, it remains "a guaranteed Shore destination."

Crab Trap   20 | 16 | 18 | $33
2 Broadway (Somers Point Circle), Somers Point, 609-927-7377; www.thecrabtrap.com
This "old-fashioned" seafood shack in Somers Point is "busy" "even in the off season" on account of its "excellent crab cakes" and other "fresh", "nothing-spectacular" fare; few argue that the "joint" is touristy, but it's a matter of debate whether the "hassle" of "long waits" is worth it.

Cranbury Inn   15 | 17 | 16 | $33
21 S. Main St. (Rte. 130), Cranbury, 609-655-5595; www.thecranburyinn.com
With a "history" that's "almost as rich as the desserts", this pre-Revolutionary era landmark in Cranbury serving American "home cooking" is a "favorite" with "older" "locals" who consider it a "pleasant place for Sunday lunch"; subjects, though, cite "uneven" performance in the kitchen and a dining room that could use a "refurb."

Creole Cafe   ▽ 27 | 19 | 21 | $31
1333 Black Horse Pike (Corkery Ln.), Williamstown, 856-262-2334; www.creole-cafe.com
"You'll swear you're in New Orleans!" exclaim fans of this "quaint" Williamstown Cajun-Creole BYO that most "wish

vote at zagat.com

| F | D | S | C |

were closer" but is "worth the drive" to South Jersey for its "terrific" standards; the "great specials" and "cute little rooms" are further incentives to head down there.

Crown Palace   21 | 20 | 18 | $27
8 N. Main St. (Rte. 79), Marlboro, 732-780-8882
1283 Hwy. 35 (Kings Hwy.), Middletown, 732-615-9888
Followers are fully behind this "perennially" "popular" duo, claiming their "fabulous" Chinese cuisine that's "served with style" separates them from pretenders to the throne of "best in Monmouth County"; "purists" praise the "excellent dim sum" (available for lunch on weekends), and are thankful for a "warm" ambiance.

Cubby's BBQ Restaurant   17 | 7 | 12 | $16
249 S. River St. (bet. E. Kennedy & Water Sts.), Hackensack, 201-488-9389
For a "fast and cheap" fix, fans ignore the inside of this Hackensack rib joint and go for the "awesome" barbecue goodies and sides such as their "superb onion rings"; even if it may be a "cafeteria masquerading as a restaurant", others see a "fun family place" and a staff "dedicated to the hearty consumption of 'cue."

CUCHARAMAMA   25 | 27 | 22 | $41
233 Clinton St. (bet. 2nd & 3rd Sts.), Hoboken, 201-420-1700
Maricel Presilla's "amazing" Hoboken newcomer a block away from her sister restaurant, Zafra, "will delight your senses" with "powerful flavors" and an "ingenious use of ingredients" revealed in the "phenomenal" South American fare that's backed by "sexy", "swanky" sub-equatorial decor; "small" and sometimes "tough to get into", those who don't mind "waiting" are glad they did.

Cucina Rosa   19 | 16 | 19 | $34
Washington Street Mall, 301 Washington St.
(bet. Jackson & Perry Sts.), Cape May, 609-898-9800;
www.cucinarosa.com
"Good, basic" Italian food and a "welcoming" ambiance make folks "return" to this "reliable" BYO in a Cape May mall; while "nothing special in a town of great restaurants", it's important to remember that "reasonable prices" mean something in these parts.

Cuzco   – | – | – | M
56 Main St. (Obert St.), South River, 732-238-8882;
www.cuzcorestaurant.com
Those who appreciate Peruvian cuisine have found a home at this laid-back South River BYO whose specialties include certifiably tasty seviche and a jazzy, super fresh *jalea* (fried fish, shrimp and calamari topped with marinated onions and tomatoes); N.B. Latin entertainment on weekends gets the joint jumpin'.

| F | D | S | C |

da Filippo Autentica Cucina Italiana 24 | 17 | 23 | $38

132 E. Main St. (Meadow St.), Somerville, 908-218-0110; www.dafilippos.com

Chef-owner Filippo Russo "really enjoys his customers" – and the feeling is mutual: loyalists "love" the "personalized" service and "music from the kitchen" in the form of "superior pastas and seafood" at his Italian BYO "in the heart" of Somerville; "even if you go sporadically", chances are they'll "treat you like family."

Dai-Kichi 22 | 14 | 21 | $29

608 Valley Rd. (Bellevue Ave.), Upper Montclair, 973-744-2954

"Hope you like your neighbors", because the seating is "tight" at this "bustling" BYO that draws in many an Upper Montclairian with its "consistently good" sushi and other Japanese offerings; good to know that the "quick, efficient" service may be an antidote to somewhat "bare" atmosphere.

Daniel's on Broadway 25 | 24 | 24 | $51

416 S. Broadway (4th Ave.), West Cape May, 609-898-8770; www.danielscapemay.com

The "elegance" of the country inn setting is a "perfect" complement to the "sophisticated" New American menu featuring "unbelievable seafood" and an "unbeatable" Sunday brunch at this "pearl" in West Cape May; admirers sit back and watch a "staff that makes every effort to please" and delight in a "romantic" experience that some remark is "better each time."

Dan's on Main 22 | 17 | 21 | $38

426 Main St. (bet. Highland & Hillside Aves.), Metuchen, 732-549-6464; www.dansonmain.com

Dan Slobodien shows a "deft hand" with New American selections at his "storefront" BYO in Metuchen with an "inventive" menu including pierogi that people profess are "the best this side of Warsaw"; while a few have issues with the "dated" decor, a majority concludes that with "fantastic" service, a trip here is "always a pleasure."

Dante's Ristorante 22 | 17 | 21 | $34

100 E. Main St. (Cold Hill Rd.), Mendham, 973-543-5401

A recent expansion of the take-out area is testimony to the popularity of this "reliable" Italian BYO in Mendham that adherents assert has "the best pizza around"; those who choose to "eat in" find an often "overwhelmed", yet "friendly" staff serving "innovative" dishes to pleased patrons huddled in "close" quarters.

Da Vinci 18 | 16 | 18 | $35

411 Washington St. (bet. 4th & 5th Sts.), Hoboken, 201-659-2141

Hoboken regulars of this Northern Italian on Washington Street keep "going back" for its "very fine" cooking and

vote at zagat.com

| F | D | S | C |

"good value"; the staff "aims to please", and it's hard not to dig the "old-school" decor; P.S. "sit outside" when the weather permits.

De Anna's ⌫⊘   22 | 14 | 19 | $28
18 S. Main St. (Lilly St.), Lambertville, 609-397-8957
This Lambertville BYO serves "homespun" Italian food that if it "was any fresher, you'd have to slap"; indeed, the stuff on the plate includes a Sicilian meatloaf and ricotta cheesecake that consumers "love" as much as the prices, and though the space inside is "tight", go ahead and make use of the "nice" patio when the clime is right.

Déjà Vu   21 | 14 | 14 | $34
399 Bloomfield Ave. (bet. Glen Ridge & Willow Aves.), Montclair, 973-233-1126
A "symphony" of French and Thai flavors makes for an "exciting dining adventure" that's "easy on the wallet" at this Montclair BYO; though there is little dispute over the food, surveyors think they've seen the "no-one-in-charge" service act before at this place, and advise the best thing to do is to "bring a book and pillow" since you may wait awhile (or "pass out from hunger") before someone gets to your table.

DELORENZO'S TOMATO PIES ⊘   27 | 8 | 15 | $15
530 Hudson St. (bet. Mott & Swann Sts.), Trenton, 609-695-9534
If all the "universe" were filled with competitors, this Trenton "institution" with "zero" decor and no bathroom might still "surpass" all others for its "thin-crust", "perfectly crisp" pies; "join the line" "around the corner" to gain admission to the No. 1 pizza spot in our *Survey* – again – that offers up its "brilliant" creations to legions of fawning followers.

Delta's   20 | 21 | 19 | $37
19 Dennis St. (bet. Hiram Sq. & Richmond St.), New Brunswick, 732-249-1551; www.deltasrestaurant.com
Surveyors step on over to this New Brunswick Southerner for food that "sticks to your ribs" and is "good for your soul"; the "gorgeous open setting" is an "elegant" counterpoint to fare that's mostly "down home" (fried crawfish) and, on occasion, "dressed up" (duck confit spring rolls); P.S. there's "great" live jazz and R&B on Saturdays.

Dennis Foy's   24 | 13 | 20 | $47
816 Arnold Ave. (Bay Ave.), Point Pleasant Beach, 732-295-0466
A BYO in a Point Pleasant Beach "strip mall" seems an "unlikely" venue for a "master" chef, but Dennis Foy puts doubts to rest by treating Shore residents to "sophisticated" New American–French food that compares to what you can "get in Manhattan"; despite a low Decor score, diners deem the "understated" look "calming."

| F | D | S | C |

Diamond's Oceanside   22 | 19 | 21 | $43
1900 Ocean Ave. (8th Ave.), Ortley Beach, 732-793-5555; www.diamondsrestaurant.com

Diamond's Riverside
1140 River Rd. (bet. Duffield & Holder Drs.), West Trenton, 609-882-0303; www.diamondsrestaurant.com

It's a "nice surprise" to find a "unique menu" that includes calf's liver and bacon, and specials such as Kobe beef alongside "great pastas" at this Italian couple; though "pricey" for a few, "professional" service at both locations and a beachfront view that "can't be beat" (at the seasonal Ortley Beach outpost) mean most will "definitely go back."

Diaz   ∇ 24 | 10 | 27 | $21
306 Main St. (Lincoln Ave.), Avon-by-the-Sea, 732-774-0554; www.diazrestaurant.com

"If your taste buds need a strong infusion of flavor", this spartan, 40-seat "family-run" storefront BYO in Avon "is the place" to go for "fabulous" Cuban-Dominican-Puerto Rican; the namesake chef-owner, who's not shy about making "recommendations", employs a staff that shares his "passion for food and service"; N.B. closed Tuesdays, but they'll turn a bottle of wine into sangria any other day.

DINING ROOM, THE ⓈS   27 | 26 | 26 | $69
Hilton at Short Hills, 41 JFK Pkwy. (Rte. 24), Short Hills, 973-379-0100; www.hiltonshorthills.com

Reserve this "elegant" and "formal" Hilton New American near the Mall at Short Hills for those "momentous life events", or if you're just in the mood to indulge in the "epitome of fine dining in NJ"; it's "tops" in every way, from the "exquisitely prepared" food, to the "romantic" ambiance to the "superb" service – but remember to bring a "Brinks truck" to pay for it; N.B. jacket suggested.

Dish ⓈS   21 | 19 | 20 | $43
40 Brighton Ave. (Van Houten Ave.), Passaic, 973-773-9335; www.dish-nj.com

It's a "cool place to dine", crows a "young lounge crowd" that frequents this Passaic New American and cites the "inventive" cuisine, "solid" service and "trendy", Manhattan "club"-like decor; it's in a "dark warehouse area" of Passaic, but that can't stop a bar scene that's "a hoot."

Dish ⓈS   – | – | – | E
13 White St. (Broad St.), Red Bank, 732-345-7070

The straightforward style of this New American shepherded by chef Anthony Ferrando and partner Judy Matthew has ignited the passions of Red Bank's culinary cognoscenti; the modest-looking BYO brings a lineup of hearty fare to a town trembling with trends and desperately in need of a lovable, low-key delight where seconds on homemade focaccia are de rigueur.

vote at zagat.com

F	D	S	C

Dock's Oyster House   24 | 19 | 22 | $47
2405 Atlantic Ave. (Georgia Ave.), Atlantic City, 609-345-0092; www.docksoysterhouse.com
Those who like to "escape the casinos" for a while and feast on "delicious" seafood recommend this "tried and true" Atlantic City "institution" (100 years and counting) known for its "fabulous assortment of pristine oysters" and "outstanding" service; though you may have to "wait" for a table, it's still "hard to beat", especially with "free parking."

Don Pepe   20 | 15 | 18 | $35
844 McCarter Hwy. (Raymond Blvd.), Newark, 973-623-4662
18 Old Bloomfield Ave. (Changebridge Rd.), Pine Brook, 973-882-6757
www.donpeperestaurant.com
"Eat like a king" (or, *don*) at either of these "classic" Iberians famous for their "mammoth" portions of "flavorful" food and sangria that'll "knock your socks off"; the original Ironbound spot may be "better" than the Pine Brook branch, but regulars register their approval of both, saying either one makes for "great get togethers with friends."

Don Pepe's Steakhouse   23 | 16 | 19 | $42
58 Rte. 46 W. (Bloomfield Ave.), Pine Brook, 973-808-5533; www.donpepesteakhouse.com
Meat eaters who could do without the "hassle and expense" of "heading into NYC" say this Continental stronghold of surf 'n' turf in Pine Brook (a relative of the Newark original) is an "excellent" choice; though some see the site as "facelift"-ready, most are happy to report that you get "a lot of food for the money."

Doris & Ed's   26 | 20 | 23 | $53
348 Shore Dr. (Waterwitch Ave.), Highlands, 732-872-1565; www.dorisandeds.com
"Never missing an opportunity to please its patrons", this "well-honed" Highlands landmark's "excellence" lies in an "innovative" concept of 'Yesterday/Today' American menus featuring seafood "so fresh", "so superb" even a "fish would want to be cooked here", and service that "thoroughly satisfies"; fans doff their hats, moreover, to a "fantastic wine list."

Down to Earth   23 | 15 | 20 | $22
7 Broad St. (W. Front St.), Red Bank, 732-747-4542
Vegans and vegetarians "rejoice" over this meat-free BYO in Red Bank where "those with an open mind" come for fare "without mystery ingredients" that "could win over any carnivore"; the "creative" menu offers a "little something for everyone", and the name of this basement "oasis" could also describe a staff that's "eager to please"; N.B. there's a juice bar on-site.

	F	D	S	C

Dry Dock Ice Cream Bar & Grille ⊟
▽ 19 | 9 | 17 | $15

1440 Texas Ave. (Pittsburgh Ave.), Cape May, 609-884-3434; www.capemaydrydock.com

Reconnect with your "childhood" at a "great price" when you stop by this Cape May American serving "smooth" "homemade" ice cream, "incredible" burgers and some of the "best fries around"; its 40-year history attests to its staying power.

Due Amici
17 | 12 | 19 | $33

450 Main St. (Harrison Ave.), West Orange, 973-669-0027

"Nothing fancy", but this "neighborhood" BYO in West Orange still delivers "well-prepared" Italian food to fans who may indeed make friends with one another given the "tight" seating setup; the few in the ex-admirer camp who label it "standard" and think it's "lost its magic" are outvoted.

E & V ⊟
23 | 12 | 20 | $28

320 Chamberlain Ave. (bet. Preakness & Redwood Aves.), Paterson, 973-942-8080; www.evrestaurant.com

Piling on the food is this Paterson "family fave" dishing "tremendous proportions" of "delicious" Italian goods to "hungry" folk who brace themselves for "no decor" and "waits" "on weekends"; an "accommodating staff" and "great prices", however, help turn it into a "standby."

East
21 | 16 | 15 | $27

1405 Teaneck Rd. (Rte. 4), Teaneck, 201-837-1260

Expect an "amusing evening" at this "snag-what-you-want" sushi house in Teaneck where you need to "make up your mind fast enough" to figure out which piece of the "fresh", "gorgeous" and "reasonably priced" items you wish to sample; "kids have fun" watching the rotating "conveyor belt", and parents flip for the other "interesting" Japanese specialties on the regular menu.

East Coast Vegan ⊠
– | – | – | I

313 W. Water St. (Main St.), Toms River, 732-473-9555

This new and "much-needed" addition to Ocean County comes courtesy of chef-owner Michael Pollack, who's set up shop in a Downtown Toms River storefront and is "converting" the carnivorous ("it *doesn't* taste like plastic") and pleasing the herbivorous with his "excellent" vegan fare; those who duck in like the fact that you can "get in and out quickly."

East Tokyo
20 | 12 | 18 | $29

119 Rte. 10 E. (Ridgedale Ave.), East Hanover, 973-515-9898

"Delicious sushi" and a "friendly" staff that "makes you feel at home" are what draws repeat customers to this East Hanover Japanese; some are "put off" by "the fact that it shares an entrance with the [next door] bowling

	F	D	S	C

alley", and, if the decor "needs work", "takeout" is "just as good."

Ebbitt Room, The   26 | 24 | 24 | $54

Virginia Hotel, 25 Jackson St. (bet. Beach Dr. & Carpenter Ln.), Cape May, 609-884-5700; www.virginiahotel.com

"Excellence is the mantra" at the "class act of Cape May" whose "beautiful" dining room in a "charming" boutique hotel is "one of the more romantic settings" in town for "superb" New American fare that's "interesting" yet "unfussy", and "professional" service from a "caring" staff; the nightly "piano music" completes that "special getaway feeling"; P.S. if the mood hits, book a room and "have breakfast on the porch in the morning."

Eccola Italian Bistro   21 | 18 | 19 | $38

1082 Rte. 46 W. (N. Beverwyck Rd.), Parsippany, 973-334-8211

They've sold the Bernardsville location to new owners, but not the "energy", "noise" or "delicious" food that "satisfies the soul" at this "trendy" Italian "bistro" in Parsippany; so, if you can "stand the crowds" and you're taking someone to this neck of the woods, fans say "make it your ace in the hole."

Echo ⊘   ▽ 18 | 21 | 19 | $28

79 Monmouth St. (Maple Ave.), Red Bank, 732-747-8050; www.echo-redbank.com

Lounge with the "hip" at this Red Bank hipster that's "great" for "hanging out with friends" keen to "be seen" sipping martinis or checking out the Eclectic selection of "tapas-style" apps; most don't seem to mind dishing out a "pretty penny", since they seem to dig the "funky" NYC vibe.

Edo Sushi   22 | 12 | 18 | $23

Pennington Shopping Ctr., 25 Rte. 31 S. (bet. Delaware & Franklin Aves.), Pennington, 609-737-1190

Though a recent remodeling has "warmed up" the decor a bit at this Pennington Japanese-Chinese BYO in a strip mall, it's the "excellent sushi" that explains why "90-year-olds and their great grands leave smiling"; the staff aims to please, and regulars report there are some "very good" Thai additions to the menu.

El Azteca   19 | 11 | 17 | $17

Ramblewood Shopping Ctr., 1155 Rte. 73 N. (Church Rd.), Mount Laurel, 856-914-9302

The Mexican cooking at this "strip-mall" Mount Laurel BYO with "little atmosphere" "beats the stuff from the chains – hands down", aver its enthusiasts, who suggest wearing "loose pants" since the "amount of food" is "amazing for the price"; some say nay, though, and decry "run-of-the-mill" fare that means "Taco Bell has nothing to worry about."

| F | D | S | C |

El Cid   21 | 14 | 17 | $38
205 Paramus Rd. (bet. Century Rd. & Rte. 4 W.), Paramus, 201-843-0123
"Atkins" adherents appreciate the "super-sized" servings of "tasty" surf 'n' turf at this Spanish tavern in Paramus; determined diners withstand "long" waits to get a table at this "no-reserve" "meat-eater's Eden", but once seated, they may want to have a word with the decorator, since it "looks like there's a yard sale going on."

ELEMENTS ☽   18 | 27 | 19 | $41
1072 Ocean Ave. (River St.), Sea Bright, 732-842-1100; www.elementslounge.com
"NY glitz" "meets the Shore" at this bi-level "fish out of water" in Sea Bright co-owned by Matthew Bongiovi (Jon Bon Jovi's brother), where once you "get past the doormen" out front you'll discover "beautiful", "serene" decor that visually incorporates the five elements; expect "good" Eclectic "tapas-style" fare – and "lots of posturing at the bar"; P.S. become a "member" and receive "VIP" treatment.

Elements Café 🗹   ▽ 20 | 15 | 17 | $31
517 Station Ave. (White Horse Pike), Haddon Heights, 856-546-8840; www.elementscafe.com
Advocates for this New American on "reemerging Station Avenue" in Haddon Heights' "like the small-plates concept" that "allows you to try many dishes" (all priced under $10); "it's a little cramped in there", but the "presentations" are "pretty" and being a "BYO" is a "plus."

El Familiar   – | – | – | I
Stella Towne Ctr., 1246 Rte. 166 (Hilltop Rd.), Dover Township, 732-240-6613
Sincere Colombian-Mexican cooking is the heart and soul of this plain BYO storefront in a Dover Township shopping center; what's on tap might not always be familiar, but it is adored – chunky oxtail soup, arepas of several stripes and pork tinga quesadillas as addictive as Carolina BBQ.

El Meson Cafe   23 | 14 | 20 | $23
40 W. Main St. (Court St.), Freehold, 732-308-9494
This "vibrant" "storefront" BYO in Downtown Freehold is "always crowded – and for good reason": the "authentic", "fresh" Mexican fare, served up in "generous" portions by an "energetic" staff, is "the best for miles around", and the menu includes "some really original dishes"; attached to a "quaint bodega", it's "pretty small", so expect a "wait out the door" on weekends.

El Salvadoreno   ▽ 14 | 10 | 15 | $21
38 W. Front St. (Riverside Ave.), Red Bank, 732-530-1611
The few who know about this "mom-and-pop"-style BYO in Red Bank "love" the "delicious", "home-cooked Salvadoran

vote at zagat.com

food" ("try the shrimp" and "roast pork") as well as the "low prices"; though the staff could use "more help", and it "ain't very pretty" inside, the stuff they send out is "very tasty."

El Tanampa ∇ 21 | 14 | 18 | $20
Kennedy Mall, 2770 Hooper Ave. (Brick Blvd.), Brick, 732-920-0290
It may be tucked away in the far reaches of a shopping plaza, but those who've found and frequent this BYO in a "simple storefront" serving "simple" Mexican food "hope it succeeds"; you may need to "brush up your Spanish" to converse with the staff, but you'll likely be saying *muy bien* by meal's end.

Elysian Cafe ◐ 19 | 24 | 21 | $32
1001 Washington St. (10th St.), Hoboken, 201-798-5898
"Amanda's owners" have done a "wonderful job" scrubbing up a "historic" "old-man dive" that once epitomized Hoboken's rough and tumble past, transforming it into a "beautiful" new French bistro "unlike anything in town"; though a few find the food "needs some work", most are willing to give them time to "work it out" since this operation "has great potential."

Emerald Fish 24 | 15 | 22 | $30
Barclay Farms Shopping Ctr., 65 Rte. 70 E. (Kings Hwy.), Cherry Hill, 856-616-9192
Serious seafooders sold on "super-fresh" fish go to this "delightful" BYO when in Cherry Hill; though the decor "leaves something to be desired" to some, others are baited by the "fabulous" piscine-oriented paintings posted on the walls and "excellent" service that makes this strip maller a "surprisingly good" catch.

EPERNAY ☒ 23 | 17 | 19 | $40
6 Park St. (Bloomfield Ave.), Montclair, 973-783-0447; www.epernaynj.com
Francophiliacs frequenting this "cute" bi-level BYO like having a "little Balthazar" in their "backyard", especially one that serves up "out-of-this-world decadence" in the form of bistro classics that "please" *tout* Montclair; an "attentive", "courteous" staff works in "tight quarters", but do note it gets "busy" in there, so it may not be a surprise if you feel "rushed."

Eppes Essen 16 | 9 | 11 | $20
105 E. Mt. Pleasant Ave. (S. Livingston Ave.), Livingston, 973-994-1120
"Taken a turn for the better" ever since Josh Kanter took over, this newly "refurbed" ("thank goodness") Livingston "institution" that "hasn't gone out of style since it was never in style" still serves "classic" "non-kosher" Jewish-style items to a crew of deli mavens; *deli*ghted diners declare "even the food seems fresher" now.

	F	D	S	C

Espo's
23 | 12 | 19 | $23

10 Second St. (bet. Anderson & Thompson Sts.), Raritan, 908-685-9552

For more than 30 years, "locals" longing for "homestyle" "comfort food" have "crowded" into this "cheap, dark and smoky" Raritan red saucer to sample the "hearty" Southern Italian specialties scrawled on its "blackboard menu"; "what it lacks in decor, it makes up for in food" – lots of it.

Esty Street
24 | 19 | 21 | $48

86 Spring Valley Rd. (Fremont Ave.), Park Ridge, 201-307-1515; www.estystreet.com

Whether you're "entertaining clients" for lunch or out for a "romantic" night, this Park Ridge "gem in a barren land" is "always a pleasure", offering "exciting" New American fare and a "sophisticated" ambiance "without city attitude"; if some sum it up as a good fit for "expense-acounters", its many admirers think it's "first class all the way."

Eurasian Eatery
19 | 10 | 17 | $21

110 Monmouth St. (bet. Maple Ave. & Pearl St.), Red Bank, 732-741-7071

"Eclectic" best describes the veggie-centric menu at this Red Bank BYO whose food "fuses just about everything" and where you can "cure your mainstream" blues by tucking into everything from curried lasagna to Florentine dumplings (how's *that* for a twist); its "elbow to elbow" in there, but the goods are "tasty" and the prices "can't be beat."

Europa South
20 | 16 | 19 | $37

521 Arnold Ave. (Rte. 35 S.), Point Pleasant Beach, 732-295-1500; www.europasouth.com

Advocates of this "old standby" see "no need to go to Newark" for Spanish-Portuguese fare considering the "good" standards and "great" sangria at this Downtown Point Pleasant Beach Iberian; still, detractors deduct points for the "tired" decor and prices that are "no bargain."

Famished Frog, The
14 | 15 | 15 | $24

18 Washington St. (N. Park Pl.), Morristown, 973-540-9601; www.growthrestaurants.com

"Kids love" the "frog and fauna" motif at this "whimsically" adorned Morristown American that also appeals to many as a "good place" to "watch a game" over drinks and to nosh on American fare that's a "step up from what you get at a chain"; the food "ain't shabby", but wags warn "don't come looking for gourmet."

Fantasea Reef Buffet
18 | 20 | 17 | $27

Harrah's, 777 Harrah's Blvd. (Brigantine Blvd.), Atlantic City, 609-441-5052; www.harrahs.com

If gambling has left you a bit, shall we say, empty, fill up on an "endless supply" of Eclectic eats at Harrah's all-day

| F | D | S | C |

eatery that features an "excellent" selection of seafood options; it's "one of the better buffets" in AC to its champions, who add the "undersea" decor is "worth at least one trip."

Far East Taste 25 | 7 | 22 | $19
19 Main St./Rte. 35 (Broad St.), Eatontown, 732-389-9866
Chef-owner Richard Wang, a "favorite culinary personality" at the Shore, is a "true pro" who cooks to "your taste" and improvises "like a jazz musician" at this Thai-Chinese BYO in Eatontown; it's a "hole-in-the-wall", but loyalists say the "sublime", "affordable" food and "A+" service compensate.

Farnsworth House, The 20 | 18 | 20 | $35
135 Farnsworth Ave. (Railroad Ave.), Bordentown, 609-291-9232; www.thefarnsworthhouse.com
Bordentowners make this Continental comfort fooder a "first choice" for its "reliably" "delicious" fare and "intimate" ambiance; "dine downstairs" where there's a "long, narrow barroom", or opt for the "prettier room" upstairs.

FASCINO ⑤ 26 | 20 | 24 | $47
331 Bloomfield Ave. (bet. Grove & Willow Sts.), Montclair, 973-233-0350; www.fascinorestaurant.com
A "top-notch" two-year-old, this "bustling" Montclair BYO run by the "warm and talented" DePersio family has become "so hot" that "reservations" are almost "impossible" to get since there have been "nothing but raves" about its "outstanding" "nouveau" Italian cuisine (save space for some "dreamy desserts"), "superb" service and "cool", "sleek" decor; in simple words, it's "fantastic."

Fat Kat, The ⑤ ∇ 24 | 17 | 22 | $36
201 Main St. (Liberty St.), Little Ferry, 201-814-0234
Antonio Goodman's "tiny winner" of a BYO is lifting Little Ferryite spirits with its "delightful", "unique" New American menu of weekly changing comestibles; admirers appreciate having "superb" stuff in an area lacking upscale dining options, and add "cheerful" service makes it even more of a "pleasant surprise."

Federici's ⌀ 20 | 11 | 17 | $21
14 E. Main St. (South St.), Freehold, 732-462-1312; www.federicis.com
Freehold folks have been able to "count on" this "family-friendly" pizza "landmark" (in business for over 80 years) for "outstanding", "ultra-thin crust" "showstoppers"; while the other Italian items are "pretty good", "stick to" the pies and "you can't go wrong" – unless you forget to "bring cash."

Fedora Cafe 19 | 18 | 14 | $19
2633 Main St. (bet. Craven Ln. & Phillips Ave.), Lawrenceville, 609-895-0844
"Comfy couches", "funky" decor, live music – it's no wonder people find this all-day BYO "way cool", a Lawrenceville

| F | D | S | C |

Eclectic that's a "hang" for the "prep school set" and known for "imaginative" dishes and "wonderful" "bust-a-gut" desserts; it's "great for a quick bite", but, alas, service is "not so quick."

Felicity's ▽ 22 | 22 | 20 | $35

801 Bay Ave. (E. New Jersey Ave.), Somers Point, 609-927-0068

"Call ahead" so you can "match your vino" to the "creatively prepared" "specials" and other "excellent" New American fare at this "gem" in Somers Point that's relatively new to the Shore; set in a century-old Victorian house, the BYO offers "attentive" service, a "pleasant" atmosphere and views of Great Egg Bay; N.B. also serving brunch and lunch May through August.

Ferrari's Ristorante 22 | 18 | 19 | $38

A & M Plaza, 3475 Rte. 9 N. (Three Brooks Rd.), Freehold Township, 732-294-7400

Surveyor sentiment seems favorable toward the new owners of this Italian Freehold Township BYO, saying they've "restored it to its high quality"; look for an expanded seafood selection joining a "solid" menu that features "lustily seasoned old-world standards."

Ferraro's 19 | 15 | 17 | $31

8 Elm St. (North Ave.), Westfield, 908-232-1105

With separate areas for casual and formal dining, this Italian "family tradition" in Westfield is a "fine choice" for kids craving pizzas and for big people seeking something a bit more "upscale"; while critics complain about "slow" service and "plain-Jane" decor, it's such a "staple" that it's "always busy."

FERRY HOUSE, THE 24 | 19 | 22 | $47

32 Witherspoon St. (Spring St.), Princeton, 609-924-2488; www.theferryhouse.com

"Helping Princeton shake its Buffy-let's-get-a-burger" image is this "elegant, NY-ish" BYO offering "delightful" New American–French fare and a "civilized intimacy in spite of the number" they serve; "dark", "romantic" decor and a "fine" staff help foster that "warm" ambiance – and perhaps "Ivy League prices."

Fiddleheads 21 | 13 | 20 | $34

27 E. Railroad Ave. (bet. Church St. & Rte. 612), Jamesburg, 732-521-0878

This former "luncheonette" in Jamesburg has recently changed hands and reinvented itself as a "quaint bistro" thanks to new owners who have done a "perk-up" of the New American menu as well as a "spruce-up" of the decor; though it's "still a work in progress", those who continue to be fond of its "friendly" service and "innovative" fare think it's a "star."

| F | D | S | C |

Filomena 21 | 20 | 19 | $35
13 Milford Cross Keys Rd. (White Horse Pike), Berlin, 856-753-3540
Commerce Plaza, 1245 Blackwood-Clementon Rd. (Laurel Rd.), Clementon, 856-784-6166
1738 Cooper St. (N. Almonesson Rd.), Deptford, 856-228-4235
www.filomenalakeview.com
South Jerseyites have a "great time" at these "big-city quality" Southern Italians courtesy of the DiVentura brothers delivering "plenty of good" red-sauce favorites that complement a "chichi" menu and "intriguing specials"; though most find "you can't beat the atmosphere" (featuring live music most nights), others waver on service that has its "slow" or "good" "moments."

Fiorino ⓈⒷ 21 | 21 | 22 | $44
38 Maple St. (Springfield Ave.), Summit, 908-277-1900;
www.fiorinoristorante.com
A "special-occasion place", this "classy" Northern Italian in Summit summons surveyors to soak up some "fantastic" service, eat up its "excellent" food, and take in the "lovely" decor and a "bustling bar scene" that's a "hangout" for "singles"; a few sum things up in their minds saying "summit", though, "may be a good description of where the prices are"; N.B. the private wine room seats 55.

Fish Outta Water – | – | – | M
8611 Long Beach Blvd. (bet. 86th & 87th Sts.), Long Beach Township, 609-492-8340
Swimming pretty in the sprawling space long home to Charles' Seafood Garden, this seafarin' newcomer on LBI spouts laid-back style on its fish-dominated New American menu; the BYO's setting is casual, the service bright-eyed and eager, and the straightforward staples supplemented by summery specials that suit the seasonal spot's always-on-holiday mood; N.B. prepare to buck well-tanned, well-toned crowds on weekends.

Fleming's Prime Steakhouse 21 | 23 | 20 | $54
City Pl., 90 The Promenade (River Rd.), Edgewater, 201-313-9463; www.flemingssteakhouse.com
Outback Steakhouse's "upscale" family member purveys "perfectly done" steaks to a meat-eating committee of contented critics; though its Edgewater location (right next to the Hudson) is "great", some wonder why they didn't "lower the windows", because "you lose the view of NYC once you sit down."

Food for Thought 25 | 24 | 22 | $40
Marlton Crossing Shopping Ctr., 129 Rte. 73 S. (Rte. 70), Marlton, 856-797-1126; www.njfoodforthought.com
Think again if you think you can't get "first-rate" food in a strip mall after dining at this "terrific", "upscale" Marlton

| F | D | S | C |

spot, a "quaint" and "lovely" New American with "even lovelier" fare and "outstanding" service; yes, it's hard to believe the BYO lives here, and perhaps it's "too expensive" for some, but most are happy to find this "delightful" "oasis in the midst of a loud, busy world."

Formia 25 | 16 | 22 | $34
418 Broad St. (bet. Baldwin St. & Bay Ave.), Bloomfield, 973-748-8080

"Small" in stature but "big on hospitality" is this "storefront" in Bloomfield that doesn't shrink from serving "excellent" Northern Italian fare and isn't shy about its "nicely priced" wine list; if some consider the "modestly decorated" interior "upgrade"-worthy, there's little doubt that it's been a "consistent" "pleaser" "year after year."

Fornos of Spain 23 | 18 | 21 | $37
47 Ferry St. (Union St.), Newark, 973-589-4767; www.fornosrestaurant.com

There's a "party" atmosphere at this "big" and "busy" Ironbound Spaniard whose "hustling" staff serves Essex County power brokers and other longtime loyalists some "massive" helpings of "superb" Iberian food; so, with "lines out the door" sometimes, "prepare to wait", eat up and "go home happy."

410 Bank Street 25 | 21 | 22 | $48
410 Bank St. (bet. Broad St. & Lafayette Ave.), Cape May, 609-884-2127

"It's worth battling the Parkway traffic" on the way to this "foodie mecca" in a Cape May "strip mall" that's "still at the top of its game"; chef Henry Sing Cheng's "innovative" Creole-Caribbean cooking, a "friendly, knowledgeable" staff and "quaint" ambiance ("you feel like you're on someone's elegantly appointed back patio") explain why this place remains a "classic."

Francesca's ▽ 17 | 17 | 14 | $29
191 Woodport Rd. (Pine Cone Ln.), Sparta, 973-726-7771

This "rustic" Sparta Italian draws a "big happy-hour crowd" as well as "many families", which makes for a "noisy" night out; though most agree the food is "good for the area" with "limited" choices, critics say the service is "hit-or-miss", so consider going "during the week or on off hours."

Frankie & Johnnie's 23 | 20 | 20 | $46
163 14th St. (Garden St.), Hoboken, 201-659-6202; www.frankieandjohnnies.com

Square-mile city-ites have come to think of this Hoboken chophouse as a landmark that serves steaks "outstanding" enough to rival those of the "big boys across the river"; an "attentive" staff, "soothing" piano bar that's a "perfect retreat for an after dinner drink" and valet parking are all "big pluses", but just expect citified prices for the package.

vote at zagat.com

| F | D | S | C |

Frankie Fed's 20 | 10 | 19 | $21
831 Rte. 33 E. (Weaverville Rd.), Freehold Township, 732-294-1333
Freehold Township folk "look forward to going back" to this "casual" Italian BYO renowned for its "yummy" thin crusters; it also earns extra credit for "good entrees" including "creative specials", and most are ready to overlook the "nondescript" setting.

Frenchtown Inn, The 24 | 23 | 22 | $47
7 Bridge St. (Rte. 29), Frenchtown, 908-996-3300; www.frenchtowninn.com
A French-Eclectic Frenchtown "favorite" "for many years", this "lovely" "country inn" eatery on the Delaware River is a "wonderful" place to "celebrate an important moment" or relax after "a pleasant drive" through rustic Hunterdon County; expect "attentive" service and "exceptional" fare in both the "formal" dining room and "more casual" grill room; P.S. they offer a "great Sunday brunch" for $22.95.

Frescos 23 | 21 | 21 | $43
412 Bank St. (bet. Broad St. & Lafayette Ave.), Cape May, 609-884-0366
Attached to its higher profile relative, 410 Bank Street, this "BYO-friendly" Cape May spot that fans "love" turns out "excellent" tummy-pleasing takes on Med-Italian fare for the "crowds"; though some snipe at the "hype" it's received, the majority finds it "wonderful"; P.S. "sit upstairs where it's less cramped."

Fresco Steak & Seafood Grill ▽ 27 | 20 | 24 | $36
Heritage Shopping Plaza, 210 Ryders Ln. (Blueberry Dr.), Milltown, 732-246-7616; www.restaurantfresco.com
Admirers of LouCás in Edison have "yet to be disappointed" with her younger Milltown "strip-mall" sis, a BYO proffering an "excellent variety" of "consistently good" Italian specialties and surf 'n' turf standards; a "comfortable" setting turns it into a "welcome addition to the area."

FROG AND THE PEACH, THE 26 | 23 | 24 | $57
29 Dennis St. (Hiram Sq.), New Brunswick, 732-846-3216; www.frogandpeach.com
An example of "excellence on all fronts" is New Brunswick's "favorite" son, a New American that "continues to amaze" repeat visitors with "innovative", "brilliantly executed" food, "top-notch" service and a "superb" "wine list"; it's "still one of the finest" and "most beautiful" restaurants in the state, but "oy! the prices" are not for the faint of heart.

FROMAGERIE 26 | 25 | 25 | $63
26 Ridge Rd. (Ave. of Two Rivers), Rumson, 732-842-8088; www.fromagerierestaurant.com
Much to the delight of those who believe it sets the standard for "special-occasion" dining, this "romantic", "pop-the-

| F | D | S | C |

question" Classic French establishment in Rumson that "hasn't changed much" over the years is still wowing its clientele with "fabulous" fare and "fantastic" service; as "beautiful" and "civilized" and "exceptional" as it is, just "bring the deed to your house" to pay for it.

Fuji ▽ 22 | 13 | 18 | $32
404 Rte. 130 N. (New Albany Rd.), Cinnaminson, 856-829-5211; www.fujirestaurant.com
To its partisans, the "freshest sushi in the area" (is there a "tunnel to the ocean" here?) and other "creative" Japanese fare can be had at Matt Ito's Cinnaminson BYO, where the food for "adventurous" palates "outshines the setting"; don't let "the shady motel" nearby "scare you away", they say, and make sure to reserve on weekends, as it's required.

Full Moon ⌿ 18 | 13 | 15 | $21
23 Bridge St. (Union St.), Lambertville, 609-397-1096
Stop by this "comfy" and "cute" cafe in Lambertville feeding American breakfast and brunch treats (try the "best omelets anywhere") to regulars that include those on "antiquing" assignments at one of the nearby shops; though open for dinner only when there's a full moon, some wish it would stay open more than "once in a . . . ."

Fulton Crab House 16 | 10 | 14 | $30
697 Anderson Ave. (bet. Grand Ave. & Lafayette St.), Cliffside Park, 201-945-2347; www.fultoncrabhouse.com
For "fish as fresh at it comes", fans float to this Cliffside Parker that lists "the catch of the day" on a blackboard menu showcasing a "tremendous variety" of seafood; the "modest", "maritime" setting is no place for some, however, who deem this boat "too smoky."

Gaebel's 19 | 21 | 20 | $39
85 Church St. (George St.), New Brunswick, 732-247-3131; www.gaebels.com
The New American fare may be "eclectic" and "beautifully presented", but it's the "trendy bar scene" that's "the real attraction" at this "hip", yet "friendly" New Brunswick eatery-cum-nightclub; it's got that "modern", "metropolitan" touch to it, which may set just the right mood for the "huge" number of "singles" who show up, especially "when the DJ starts to spin" on weekends.

Gaetano's 22 | 17 | 19 | $33
10 Wallace St. (Broad St.), Red Bank, 732-741-1321; www.gaetanosredbank.com
A recent expansion "should help" ease the "waits" at this Italian in Red Bank, whose open kitchen creates classics (including brick-oven pizzas) that "taste good", if not "great"; the decor à la "Pottery Barn" sets a "casual" tone; N.B. it's BYO, but they do sell Garden State wines.

vote at zagat.com

| F | D | S | C |

Ganges — | — | — | M
33 Princeton-Hightstown Rd./Rte. 571 (Cranbury Rd.), West Windsor, 609-750-1550; www.gangesonline.com
Traditional dishes and little-known regional delicacies form the core of the engaging menu at chef-owner Sri Chandupatla's nouveau Indian in West Windsor; the 80-seat BYO has caught the eye of Princeton professionals, who find the burgundy-accented decor soothing and the hands-on proprietor charming.

Garlic Rose Bistro 21 | 16 | 19 | $33
28 North Ave. W. (N. Union Ave.), Cranford, 908-276-5749
41 Main St. (bet. Green Village Rd. & Waverly Pl.), Madison, 973-822-1178
www.garlicrose.com
A "vampire's" nightmare, these "novel" Eclectic BYOs in Cranford and Madison pull in patrons who pay to pay homage to the stinking rose; *everything* in the duo's "good" and garlicky repertoire is infused with the namesake herb, "even the ice cream"; so go and let a "cordial" staff greet you, along with an unmistakable "smell"; P.S. "not advisable for those on a first date."

Gaslight 19 | 15 | 18 | $28
400 Adams St. (4th St.), Hoboken, 201-217-1400; www.gaslightnj.com
Sporting a "pretty-good", "something-for-everyone" Italian-American menu is this Hoboken bar/eatery that caters to "fans" on "game day" and to those with something more "upscale" in mind; it's "fun" and "loud" and gallant enough to offer "ladies" who dine together "free entrees" on Tuesday nights as long as they buy $10 worth of drinks, desserts or apps.

Ginger Thai — | — | — | M
A & M Plaza, 3475 Rte. 9 N. (Three Brooks Rd.), Freehold Township, 732-761-2900
New Age Thai trades off with Bangkok street food classics at this Freehold Township newcomer that shares space with the Indian restaurant Aangan; though there are kinks to be worked out in the kitchen, the BYO still answers a need in a part of the state where real-deal ethnics are in short supply.

Ginza Hibachi Steakhouse & Sushi Bar ∇ 24 | 17 | 22 | $28
6708 Black Horse Pike (Tilton Rd.), Egg Harbor Township, 609-383-2588
The few who know about this "unassuming" Japanese BYO in Egg Harbor Township praise the "consistently good" food and service and say the "hibachi chefs put on a great show"; moderate prices and "creative" sushi keep those in-the-know making "multiple visits."

subscribe to zagat.com

| F | D | S | C |

Girasole | 23 | 19 | 18 | $45 |
Ocean Club Condos, 3108 Pacific Ave. (bet. Chelsea & Montpelier Aves.), Atlantic City, 609-345-5554; www.girasoleac.com
"Leave the casinos and come up for air" at this "new world" Southern Italian near the Tropicana in Atlantic City that cooks "beautiful" food for a crowd of "beautiful people" that considers it a "welcome escape" from the "buffets"; though not everyone who dines here, mind you, feels like they're "a member of the club", it's still a "real surprise" for AC; N.B. jackets are suggested.

Girasole | 25 | 20 | 22 | $37 |
502 W. Union Ave. (Thompson Ave.), Bound Brook, 732-469-1080; www.girasoleboundbrook.com
It "takes weeks" to snare a "weekend" "reservation" at this "dark" and "trendy" Bound Brook BYO, and "you'll know why" when you experience the "delectable" Italian cuisine ("even the complimentary bruschetta is fantastic") and "superb" service; "reasonable pricing" at this "rose in a thorny neighborhood" has proponents proclaiming "go, if you can."

Giumarello's | 26 | 23 | 22 | $45 |
329 Haddon Ave. (bet. Cuthbert Blvd. & Kings Hwy.), Westmont, 856-858-9400; www.giumarellos.com
To its champions, "there's no mistaking it": this "high-class", "romantic" Westmont Northern Italian is "one of, if not the best" of its breed in South Jersey; the sense of "sensuality" in the "fantastic" fare helps lure diners to its "upscale" quarters, and the "great martini list" is a further draw for those who settle in here for a few hours amid the "glitz and glam."

Grain House, The | 16 | 18 | 17 | $34 |
Olde Mill Inn, 225 Rte. 202 (I-287, exit 30B), Basking Ridge, 908-221-1150; www.oldemillinn.com
"Rustic charm" is the main attribute of this "cozy", "homey" Basking Ridge American set in a Colonial inn, whose "fireplaces beckon" "the horse crowd" "in the fall and winter"; while some feel "let down" by the "pretty average" food, loyalists laud a kitchen brigade that "does the basics pretty well"; P.S. opt to dine on the "nice outdoor patio" in the warmer months.

Grand Cafe, The | 25 | 25 | 25 | $59 |
42 Washington St. (Rte. 24 W.), Morristown, 973-540-9444; www.thegrandcafe.com
"Folks with fat wallets" love to feast on the "fabulous" fare at the "doyenne of Morris County", a "fancy French" "favorite" in Morristown where "everything" is "first class", from the "fantastic", "steady classics" to the "gorgeous" decor to a "staff that attends to your every need"; it's just

vote at zagat.com 69

| F | D | S | C |

a "grand" place "for a memorable dinner"; N.B. jackets are suggested, though it's more casual on weeknights.

Grand Colonial, The — | — | — | VE
86 Hwy. 173 W. (Rte. 78, exit 12), Union Township, 908-735-7889; www.grandcolonialnj.com

Thoroughly modern style comes to the former Coach & Paddock (circa 1685) in the form of this ambitious Eclectic in Union Township spearheaded by Paul and Lorraine Ingenito (Perryville Inn, a few football fields away); with a selection of small plates, a grill room fed by an open kitchen, cheese cave and raw bar, it's clear the team behind this $5 million baby is merging the best of old and new worlds.

Grappa ∇ 20 | 21 | 21 | $46
Somerset Hills Hotel, 200 Liberty Corner Rd. (Mt. Airy Rd.), Warren, 908-647-6700; www.grappanj.com

Guests "don't have to leave" the Somerset Hills Hotel to enjoy a "good" meal, say supporters of this "elegant" Warren Italian who go on to praise its "fantastic brunch" and "superb" service; most find it "special" for a "special occasion", especially on "Friday and Saturday" nights when the "pianist" contributes to the "perfect" ambiance.

GREEN GABLES 27 | 22 | 25 | VE
Green Gables Inn, 212 Center St. (bet. Bay & Beach Aves.), Beach Haven, 609-492-3553

Though it may be hard to find a menu here, acolytes who deem this "Victorian" Beach Haven BYO "wonderful" don't seem to mind, since the Eclectic food on the $75 five-course prix fixe menu is "phenomenal"; it's true, "you never know what you're going to get", but you can bet the farm there'll be "accommodating" service and a "romantic" setting during your "enchanted evening"; N.B. a $50 three-course prix fixe is also available.

Green Grill 17 | 13 | 16 | $31
Home Depot Shopping Ctr., 450 Hackensack Ave. (Rte. 4), Hackensack, 201-488-2885

"Come hungry", then "stuff yourself" on the stuff at the "lavish buffet" of this "all-the-meat-you-can-eat" Brazilian BBQ in a Hackensack mall near Home Depot that offers an "unbelievable" and "endless" "variety of meats" and, perhaps more unbelievably, sushi and sashimi; detractors decry a "quantity over quality" mindset, but advocates green light it, notwithstanding its "cafeteria"-like atmosphere.

Grenville, The 22 | 24 | 20 | $40
Grenville Hotel, 345 Main Ave. (bet. Harris & Karge Sts.), Bay Head, 732-892-3100; www.thegrenville.com

"Cute and frilly" and "one of the few places in the area with charm", this "memorable" Bay Head New American (with new owners that have been in charge over a year) in the Grenville Hotel is also "one of the better choices on the

| F | D | S | C |

Shore" for "romantic" dining amid "Victorian" "elegance", and where most are "especially fond of the weekend brunch"; in sum, it's "a class act."

Grill 73   22 | 14 | 20 | $35

73 Mine Brook Rd. (Woodland Rd.), Bernardsville, 908-630-0700; www.grill73.com

Fans of the "well-done", "innovative" New American fare and "hip, unpretentious" staff at this "bustling" BYO "bistro" opposite Bernardsville's "quaint old train station" say it's been a "great addition to Downtown" since the "trendy" two-year-old opened; while not everyone digs the "retro diner" look, the prices are "reasonable" and most are happy to have "a casual place" in the area "that's not a pizzeria."

Grimaldi's Pizza   26 | 12 | 18 | $18

133 Clinton St. (2nd St.), Hoboken, 201-792-0800; www.grimaldis.com

Though the Brooklyn original may upstage it, this Hoboken spin-off has resolute reviewers convinced its pies should serves as "*the* reference to which all other pies are judged"; the reward for admission in to the No. 1 pizza palace in town is (you guessed it) "awesome" "thin-crust" brick-oven specialties "worth" their weight in dough and that are, to its many backers, the "best around."

Grissini Restaurant   20 | 20 | 18 | $52

484 Sylvan Ave. (Palisade Ave.), Englewood Cliffs, 201-568-3535; www.grissinirestaurant.com

In a town not exactly known for trendy eateries, this Englewood Cliffs Italian proves the exception, an "upscale" kind of place serving up "fabulous" food and a "see-and-be-seen" scene; it's famous for its "parking lot" that some mistake for a "Mercedes dealership", and for those "willing and able" to afford the "high-priced" luxury items inside.

Groff's   ▽ 21 | 12 | 20 | $22

423 E. Magnolia Ave. (Ocean Ave.), Wildwood, 609-522-5474

For "home-cooked" favorites, Wildwood locals and vacationers know they better "line up early" to get a seat at this "dependable" American BYO, an "old standby" serving generations of "families" for 80 years; while the decor is "dated", it's "in immaculate condition", and you can always count on the "credo" of "friendly" service and "good, basic food" at "reasonable" prices.

Hamilton's Grill Room   25 | 20 | 21 | $44

8 Coryell St. (N. Union St.), Lambertville, 609-397-4343; www.hamiltonsgrillroom.com

"Excellent" meats and "sublime" seafood "grilled in front of your eyes" are yours courtesy of chef Mark Miller at this "wonderful" "rustic" Mediterranean BYO in Lambertville; "tucked away in an alley" near the Delaware River Canal, it's "hard to find", but folks "like it that way" since it's "crowded"

vote at zagat.com

| F | D | S | C |

enough as is on account of the "adventurous" menu and "convivial" atmosphere; update: they've recently added a glass-enclosed garden room that seats 25.

Harbor View Restaurant ▽ 19 | 16 | 16 | $33
954 Ocean Dr. (2 mi. east of Garden State Pkwy.), Cape May, 609-884-5444
This relatively new all-day casual dining spot in Cape May with "unbelievable" harbor views has become a popular "hangout for local boat people" and where the seafood is "well prepared"; overall, it's off to a "good" start.

Hard Grove Cafe ◐ 16 | 13 | 15 | $20
319 Grove St. (Christopher Columbus Dr.), Jersey City, 201-451-1853; www.hardgrovecafe.com
Jersey City citizens seeking a "super-cheap" fix fix their sights and stomachs on this Cuban diner that's "full of fun" and a "place to meet" for a "good breakfast"; take a seat and find fans digging into "authentic" fare and "smoking cigars" amid a "tacky" setting, but do watch out for vocal voters who find the eats "unmemorable."

Hardshell Cafe ▽ 19 | 11 | 17 | $26
150 Rte. 73 N. (Rte. 70), Marlton, 856-983-3180
"You're gonna get dirty" feasting on the "amazing" garlic crabs, the "specialty" of this "very informal" Marlton BYO that's also known for its "all-you-can-eat nights"; some wish they'd "update" the "'80s" decor, and others sense "nothing special" here besides those commendable crustaceans.

Harry's Lobster House 19 | 11 | 14 | $49
1124 Ocean Ave. (New St.), Sea Bright, 732-842-0205
Devotees of this "old-fashioned" Sea Brighter say it has the "best lobsters in town", among a seafood-focused American menu that includes "filet mignon"; "hang on to your wallet", however, since it's "unbelievably expensive", and you may want to lend an ear to detractors who decry a "frumpy", "stodgy" decor that's "in need of an interior designer."

Harvest Bistro 21 | 25 | 19 | $49
252 Schraalenburgh Rd. (Bergenline Ave.), Closter, 201-750-9966; www.harvestbistro.com
"Charming" Bergen County residents since it planted itself in Closter a little over a year ago, this "chic" and "stylish" French bistro reaps a "high-energy" crowd happy to have an "NYC-type" spot in their 'hood; it's "popular", so expect "lotsa noise" in the "gorgeous setting" that's the stage for "delicious" fare and a "very hip" and "happening bar."

Harvest Moon Inn 24 | 21 | 21 | $49
1039 Old York Rd. (Rte. 202), Ringoes, 908-806-6020; www.harvestmooninn.com
Set in an "old stone house", this "classy" New American in "low profile" Ringoes proffers "innovative", "gourmet" food

| F | D | S | C |

in its more "special-occasion"-worthy dining room, while offering more casual treats in the walk-in tavern area; the "wonderful homey atmosphere" in both venues "hides the sophisticated tastes of the chef", and an "outstanding wine list" is further reason for "making the drive" out to the "middle of nowhere."

Harvey Cedars Shellfish Co. ⌿ | 22 | 10 | 17 | $27 |
506 Centre St. (Pennsylvania Ave.), Beach Haven, 609-492-2459
7904 Long Beach Blvd. (bet. 79th & 80th Sts.), Harvey Cedars, 609-494-7112
"Plain" and "homey" as they may be, this cash-only duo on Long Beach Island lures folks from far and wide who endure "long lines" in their "flips" and "bathing suits" for a chance to sit at one of the "picnic tables" and sample "fresh", "fabulous" and "simple" seafood and other bounty from their "terrific raw bars"; N.B. they're BYO, and no reservations are taken.

Heart of Portugal | ∇ 17 | 14 | 16 | $27 |
Plaza 2775, 2781 Rte. 9 N. (W. 4th St.), Howell, 732-370-0003
The Pinto family has "brought the tastes of Newark's Ironbound" to their unassuming Howell BYO – which means plan on "huge portions" and "a lot of good", "tasty" meat options" on the Portuguese menu; it's a "casual and friendly" place where "the owner will stop at your table to see if your meal is satisfactory" and, chances are, "you'll be pleased."

Heatwave Cafe | 23 | 23 | 21 | $46 |
530 Main Ave. (bet. Howe & Mount Sts.), Bay Head, 732-714-8881; www.heatwavecafe.com
"Locals" who want to entertain their "out of town guests" know to "book early" if they want a table on a summer weekend at this "pricey" Bay Head New American, where the "wonderful" dishes cooked with an "elegant simplicity" are matched by a "quiet", "romantic" ambiance; truth be told, though a minority muses about the BYO's "inconsistencies", most of the area "gentry are happy with the results."

Helmers' Cafe ⌿ | 19 | 14 | 17 | $27 |
1036 Washington St. (11th St.), Hoboken, 201-963-3333; www.helmerscafe.com
If you believe in bratwurst and Wiener schnitzel, you can "fill your belly" with these and other "hearty", "heavy" German "delights" at this "warm" and "wonderfully old-fashioned" Hoboken septuagenarian, a "no-nonsense" tavern with "real character" that stocks the "best" (and "most extensive") selection of beers "anywhere"; so, withstand "the cigarette smoke" and let the "friendly waitresses" take you "back to Düsseldorf."

| F | D | S | C |

HIGHLAWN PAVILION | 24 | 28 | 24 | $55 |
Eagle Rock Reservation, Eagle Rock Ave. (Prospect Ave.), West Orange, 973-731-3463; www.highlawn.com
"Oh, that view" of the "stunning" Manhattan skyline alone is "worth the drive" to this "remote" destination sitting "pretty" "atop a mountain ridge" in West Orange that also has enthusiasts insisting that the "palate pleasing" New American fare, "elegant" decor and "excellent" service also merit the mileage; it's "first class" on all fronts, so bring that "special" someone and "fall in love again."

H.I. Rib & Co. | 17 | 14 | 17 | $24 |
145 Rte. 31 N. (Pennington-Hopewell Rd.), Pennington, 609-466-8088; www.hirib.com
Ignore your "cholesterol count" for a while and "bring your appetite" and a "wet nap" to this "no-frills" Pennington barbecue joint for "good", "greasy", "messy" "guilt"-inducing ribs and the like that comes at you in "hearty" portions; as "lively" as it may be, some say the grub's on the "average" side.

Hobby's Deli ⊠ | 24 | 7 | 17 | $16 |
32 Branford Pl. (Halsey St.), Newark, 973-623-0410
The "last of the old-time Newark delis", this 90-plus-year-old "jewel" is a "favorite" breakfast and "lunch stop" with the "courthouse crowd" and known for its "enormous", "terrific" corned beef and pastrami sandwiches and other "classic" kosher and non-kosher fare; there's "no decor to speak of", but you get "service with a smile" and "sour pickles at every table"; N.B. no dinner.

Ho-Ho-Kus Inn, The | 20 | 22 | 20 | $52 |
(aka Marcello's at The Ho-Ho-Kus Inn)
Ho-Ho-Kus Inn, 1 E. Franklin Tpke. (Sheridan Ave.), Ho-Ho-Kus, 201-445-4115; www.hohokusinn.com
Located in a "beautiful" Dutch Colonial from the 1790s, this Continental-Italian in Ho-Ho-Kus "welcomes" diners to "enjoy" its "good" food, "gracious" service and "warm" ambiance ("it feels like you're at your rich grandmother's house"); even if some find the goings on here "inconsistent", most think that what goes on is "wonderful."

Homestead Inn ⊄ | ▽ 23 | 9 | 18 | $45 |
800 Kuser Rd. (bet. Hamilton & Whitehorse Aves.), Trenton, 609-890-9851
Your experience at this "old-world", cash-only Italian-American (known as Chick & Nello's to local insiders) in a "creaky old house" may "vary" "depending on if they know you"; "like a private club", it's a "favorite" "hangout" for Trenton's "movers and shakers" who dig into "top-notch" fare; P.S. though there are "no menus", the "waiters" will "tell you what's for dinner."

| F | D | S | C |

Hot Dog Johnny's
▽ | - | - | - | I |

Rte. 46 (Rte. 31), Buttzville, 908-453-2882; www.hotdogjohnny.com

A Warren County institution for over 60 years now owned by Johnny's daughter, Patricia Fotopoulos, this reliable retro roadside stop in rural Buttzville is famed for its signature dogs made even more satisfying when washed down with a frosty mug of birch beer or buttermilk (talk about a blast from the past!); N.B. extras include swings for the kids and a view of the Pequest River.

Hunan Chinese Room
| 23 | 20 | 21 | $24 |

255 Speedwell Ave. (W. Hanover Ave.), Morris Plains, 973-285-1117

"Standout" cuisine, a "full bar" and a "cool" interior design put this Morris Plains Chinese "a notch above" its competitors; the Wen family "makes everyone feel welcome", and their staff has "mastered the art of fine and cordial service"; it's a "sure winner" that offers "good value" to boot.

Hunan Spring
| 21 | 12 | 17 | $21 |

288 Morris Ave. (Caldwell Pl.), Springfield, 973-379-4994

This "tried and true" "standby" in Springfield (sister of Morris Plains' Hunan Chinese Room) prepares "delicious" Chinese goodies and "creative" "seasonal specials"; what the BYO "lacks" in the looks category, it makes up for with "reasonable" prices that make it "worth trying."

Hunan Taste
| 22 | 24 | 22 | $28 |

67 Bloomfield Ave. (Broadway), Denville, 973-625-2782; www.hunantaste.com

"Opulent to say the least", this Denville Chinese leaves patrons feeling like they've "eaten in the emperor's palace" where "all eyes are on the fish tanks", but where most "mouths water" from the kitchen's "superb" treats matched by "napkin-on-the-lap" service; if the decor's "hokey" to you, consider that many find it "bold" and "beautiful."

Hunt Club Grill
| 17 | 18 | 18 | $43 |

Grand Summit Hotel, 570 Springfield Ave. (Morris Ave.), Summit, 908-273-7656

Backers of this hotel establishment in Summit consider it a "nice place to relax" and dine on "good" items from its surf 'n' turf menu that includes "delicious", "juicy" steaks; many, however, are not too tantalized with the decor even after a spring 2004 renovation, noting a space that "still reeks of sleepy conservatism."

Huntley Taverne
| 21 | 23 | 19 | $44 |

3 Morris Ave. (bet. Broad St. & Springfield Ave.), Summit, 908-273-3166; www.thehuntleytaverne.com

You'll feel like you're "in Vermont" once you visit this "beautifully appointed" "mountain chalet" (and Trap Rock

vote at zagat.com

| F | D | S | C |

sib) in Summit, say those who enjoy the "chic" "ski lodge setting", "well-prepared" New American fare and "young" crowd; with a fireplace for "cold nights" and a "porch in the summer", "they cover all the bases"; P.S. the "wonderful" wine list is "another sure bet."

Hurricane House ▽ 21 | 16 | 15 | $23
688 E. Bay Ave. (Rte. 9), Barnegat, 609-698-4401
The "old-fashioned" "soda fountain" and "checkered tile floor" at this former ice cream parlor turned New American BYO in Barnegat provides a "unique" setting for "delicious", "gourmet" fare on an "extensive" menu that offers "sandwiches to filet mignon"; the prices are "fair", and, yes, you can get sundaes for dessert too.

Iberia ● 20 | 16 | 19 | $32
63-69 Ferry St. (bet. Prospect & Union Sts.), Newark, 973-344-5611
80-84 Ferry St. (bet. Congress & Prospect Sts.), Newark, 973-344-7603
www.iberiarestaurants.com
These Iberians in Newark offer a "parade" of "good" food that involves "mountains of meat" and a "lobster special" that "can't be beat"; "wash it all down" with "sangria that hits the spot", and let the "friendly" service and "festive" atmosphere offset the "unattractive" decor.

Ichiban 18 | 12 | 15 | $27
66 Witherspoon St. (bet. Hulfish St. & Paul Robeson Pl.), Princeton, 609-683-8323
Proponents propose trying this Japanese BYO in Princeton for food that may be "basic", but "does the job"; it's the "only game in town" of its kind, assert adversaries, who take aim at the "antiseptic" ambiance, "service without a smile" and "standard issue" fare.

Il Capriccio 24 | 24 | 24 | $56
633 Rte. 10 (Whippany Rd.), Whippany, 973-884-9175;
www.ilcapriccio.com
It's "always a delight" to dine on "superb" food at this "wonderful" Whippany Italian, where "terrific" service and "truly elegant" ambiance combine to help explain why regulars hold "lots of family celebrations here"; though "a little over the top", as in "awfully fancy" to some, it's the sort of place that makes you "forget the world outside."

Il Forno 16 | 14 | 16 | $27
King Shopping Ctr., 68 Mountain Blvd. (Warrenville Rd.), Warren, 908-755-3336
This "strip-mall" Southern Italian in Warren "popular with families" aims to please with "reasonable" prices and "excellent brick-oven pizza" that may be the "best value" of the BYO; a split decision leaves it "comfortable" and "reliable" to its protectors, and "run of the mill" to critics.

| F | D | S | C |

Il Mondo Vecchio
24 | 20 | 19 | $47

72 Main St. (Central Ave.), Madison, 973-301-0024;
www.scalinifedeli.com

Devotees descend on Michael Cetrulo's Madison relative of Scalini Fedeli that delivers a "special experience" to patrons primed for "memorable", "outstanding" Northern Italian cuisine "from start to finish"; don't be shocked if you encounter a "wait", since the BYO is "always packed" and, ultimately, "always excellent."

Il Mulino
∇ 21 | 22 | 22 | $34

32 Fulper Rd. (Main St.), Flemington, 908-806-0595;
www.ilmulinonj.com

Fans are happy to report such a "reliable" option in Flemington's "outlet land", with this "warm" and "cozy" Northern Italian cooking up "very good" food that arrives via "friendly" service; though BYO, it offers diners the option of purchasing wine from NJ wineries.

Il Pomodoro
20 | 15 | 19 | $38

1 W. High St. (N. Bridge St.), Somerville, 908-526-4466

Bring your "memory" to this subterranean Somerville eatery where the waiters "recite" an "incredible number of specials" apart from a menu made up of "good" Italian specialties; carpers critical of decor in demand of a face-lift "can sit outside in the summer."

Il Porto
∇ 19 | 15 | 17 | $30

7 Boardwalk Pl. (Winona Pkwy.), Sparta, 973-729-9901

A "spectacular view" of Lake Mohawk moves this Sparta BYO with "good", "basic" fare away from other Italians in its league; the dining room "gets packed", but "when weather permits" you can "treat" yourself to alfresco dining on the boardwalk.

Il Tulipano
23 | 22 | 23 | $51

1131 Pompton Ave. (bet. Lindsley Rd. & Stevens Ave.),
Cedar Grove, 973-256-9300; www.iltulipano.com

The setting's "fancy schmancy" and the food's "lovely" at this "refined" Cedar Grove Italian that provides a venue for a "dress-up night"; chances are you'll find "top-notch" service amid all the "elegance", and perhaps a "wedding" or "party" in full swing upstairs, since, to the dismay of some, the place "has swung too much to the catering" side.

Il Villaggio
22 | 16 | 22 | $44

651 Rte. 17 N. (Passaic Ave.), Carlstadt, 201-935-7733

This "reliable" Carlstadt Italian "accommodating" to both "families" and "business" people alike whips up "delicious", "hearty" renditions of fare from The Boot that shares a stage with an "excellent" staff; though the decor may need to go into "retirement", all in all, "it's a pleasure to eat here."

vote at zagat.com

| F | D | S | C |

Il Villino 23 | 22 | 24 | $47
53 Franklin Tpke. (E. Prospect St.), Waldwick, 201-652-8880
"Hospitality" reigns at this "classy" "old-world" "favorite" in Waldwick featuring a "thoroughly professional" staff serving "wonderful " Med–Northern Italian food to raving reviewers; if you're up for "impressing someone", take them here and they'll leave "well fed" and "smiling"; P.S. live piano music on weekends "adds to the charm."

India on the Hudson 22 | 15 | 19 | $24
1210 Washington St. (bet. 12th & 13th Sts.), Hoboken, 201-222-0101; www.indiaonthehudson.com
A "home delivery" "standby", this Hoboken Indian is host to a "great variety" of "tasty and traditional" dishes served with a side of "warmth" from the staff; while deflated diners discover fare that's "reliable but unexciting", many maintain there's "naan better", especially considering an $8.95 lunch buffet that "can't be beat."

Indigo Moon 23 | 19 | 21 | $42
171 First Ave. (Garfield Ave.), Atlantic Highlands, 732-291-2433; www.indigochef.com
"Locals" would prefer to keep this Atlantic Highlands French bistro with "charm" a "secret" on account of its classic specialties "cooked to perfection" and "attentive", "sincere" staff; "bring a bottle of Burgundy" and celebrate the Gallic's BYO status, which helps folks "afford" a sojourn to this piece of the "French countryside."

Indigo Smoke ▽ 24 | 19 | 20 | $28
381 Bloomfield Ave. (Willow St.), Montclair, 973-744-3440
"Bring a six-pack" and hope your tummy's ready for "indulgence" at this "hip", "upscale" BBQ BYO, a "perfect addition to the culinary variety" in Montclair that has fans fired up over "sinful" Kansas City–style stuff that includes a host of "authentic" sides (the bacon hash browns are "a must"); P.S. stop by for its "great" Sunday brunch.

Inn at Millrace Pond 19 | 25 | 19 | $47
313 Johnsonburg Rd. (Rte. 611), Hope, 908-459-4884; www.innatmillracepond.com
It's an "ambiance" thing at this "romantic", "relaxing" American-Continental in Hope set in a "beautiful" converted 18th-century mill that provides an excuse to make a trip "to the boondocks"; though hard to deny the spot's "gorgeous" looks, ornery opponents seem bent on registering their disapproval of "unpolished" service and "adequate" food.

Inn of the Hawke 18 | 18 | 16 | $26
74 S. Union St. (Mount Hope St.), Lambertville, 609-397-9555
"Have a good burger" or some fish 'n' chips "before a stroll around Lambertville" at this New American "neighborhood" "hangout" with the "atmosphere of a British pub", where

| F | D | S | C |

locals are heady over the "great" selection of hops and "comfort food" priced "reasonably"; P.S. the "selling point is the outdoor patio seating" when it's warm.

Irish Pub & Inn ●⊄ | 17 | 16 | 18 | $17 |
164 St. James Pl. (Pacific Ave.), Atlantic City, 609-344-9063; www.theirishpub.com
"Pints up"! at this 24/7 Atlantic City "boardwalk institution" that has "decent" American grub and "friendly bartenders" who serve the "coldest beer in town", making it "the place to go" after the slots "tap you out"; it's the prices, though, that "no one can believe": with "$1.25 burgers" and "$2.50 suds", "you'll be hard pressed to find cheaper in the area."

Isohama | ▽ 22 | 16 | 11 | $31 |
516 Arnold Ave. (Rte. 35), Point Pleasant Beach, 732-899-9927
"Fresh" and "delicious" fare means you'll "satisfy your yen" for sushi and hibachi at this new entry in Point Pleasant Beach; some, though, have bitten into something less pleasant, as in service that inspires comments ranging from mild ("could use a bit more education on Japanese cuisine") to scorching ("rude").

Italian Bistro | 18 | 18 | 18 | $25 |
1509 Kaighn Ave. (Chapel Ave.), Cherry Hill, 856-665-6900
590 Delsea Dr. (Holly Dell Dr.), Sewell, 856-589-8883
www.italianbistro.com
Backers of this Italian duo in Cherry Hill and Sewell say they're a "cut above the chains" and deliver "what you'd expect": "large portions" of "reliable" fare at "good prices" in a "homey" atmosphere; those who give them a whirl let it be known that they're "nothing special."

Italianissimo | 20 | 15 | 17 | $33 |
Broadway Square Mall, 40 Clinton Rd. (Passaic Ave.), West Caldwell, 973-228-5158; www.italianissimo-food-art.com
This "casual", "lively" Italian BYO in West Caldwell, famous for its cameos on "*The Sopranos*", is "always crowded" thanks to the "consistently good", "straightforward" fare and, perhaps, the "Tony" factor; there's "confusion" in the floor ranks at times, but pluses include "easy parking" and a "great" on-site deli where you can "pick up a freshly made sandwich or salad for lunch."

It's Greek To Me | 19 | 11 | 16 | $21 |
352 Anderson Ave. (bet. Jersey & Morningside Aves.), Cliffside Park, 201-945-5447
36 E. Palisade Ave. (bet. Dean & Engle Sts.), Englewood, 201-568-0440
1636 Palisade Ave. (Main St.), Fort Lee, 201-947-2050
538 Washington St. (6th St.), Hoboken, 201-216-1888
2128 Hwy. 35 (Banyan Blvd.), Holmdel, 732-275-0036
(continued)

vote at zagat.com

| | | | F | D | S | C |

(continued)
It's Greek To Me
21 E. Ridgewood Ave. (bet. Broad & Chestnut Sts.), Ridgewood, 201-612-2600
487 Broadway (Westwood Ave.), Westwood, 201-722-3511
www.itsgreektome-taverna.com
Those who like their stuff "fast" and "fresh" go to this "growing" Greek chain that's "sure to please" most for their "well-prepared", "wholesome" fare such as gyros and Greek salads; though "semi authentic" to some and certainly "nothing fancy" to look at, down-to-earth prices means it's "good" for many.

Ivangie Tea House 20 | 11 | 17 | $22
54 Chestnut St. (bet. Franklin & Ridgewood Aves.), Ridgewood, 201-251-8686
"Plain" may sum up the decor but not the food at this Chinese BYO in Ridgewood whose "long list" of "healthy" options on an "imaginative" menu puts it "a step ahead" of its competitors; here's a tip: "make sure" you try the "unusual bubble fruit tea" from its "excellent" selection.

Ivy Inn, The ⊠ 22 | 23 | 22 | $42
268 Terrace Ave. (bet. Kipp Ave. & Washington Pl.), Hasbrouck Heights, 201-393-7699; www.ivyinn.com
"Fireplaces", "rustic" decor and a "warm" ambiance abetted by live piano music (weekends) set the mood for a "quiet, romantic dinner" at this "delightful" "little woodland retreat" in Hasbrouck Heights that's also lauded for its "wonderful", "creative" Continental fare; head over heels groupies wish they could "keep the place for themselves."

Ixora 25 | 21 | 23 | $51
407 Hwy. 22 E. (Rte. 523), Whitehouse Station, 908-534-6676; www.ixoranj.com
This Whitehouse Station "strip-mall" "sleeper" may not be one of New Jersey's "best-kept secrets" for long, not after an across-the-board jump in its ratings this year, a testimony to its "pristine sushi" and other "outstanding" items on the "innovative" Japanese-French fusion menu, as well as the "elegant, modern" decor and "helpful, unobtrusive" staff; P.S. sample some of the BYO's "wonderful teas and coffees."

Jack Cooper's Celebrity Deli 19 | 9 | 16 | $17
Tano Mall, 1199 Amboy Ave. (Rte. 1), Edison, 732-549-4580; www.celebritydeli.com
Though you'll still "find all the classics you would at the Carnegie in NYC" here, a recent ownership change at this deli may mean it's "too soon to know" whether this Edison "institution" will maintain its reputation for "excellent" "corned beef and pastrami sandwiches" and "great latkes"; a few, though, feel caught in the middle of what they claim are "rising prices" and "skimpier portions."

| F | D | S | C |

Java Moon | 20 | 14 | 16 | $21 |
1022 Anderson Rd. (Rte. 537), Jackson, 732-928-3633
345 Hwy. 9 S. (Rte. 520), Manalapan, 732-294-1675
431 Broad St. (Rte. 520), Shrewsbury, 732-530-0141
2420 Hwy. 35 (bet. Church St. & Lakewood Rd.), Wall, 732-292-4592
www.javamoon.com
Known for its "inventive" "salads and sandwiches" and, "of course, good coffee", this expanding chain "gets special props" from "vegetarians" for its "healthy choices" on a "wonderfully creative" Traditional American menu; many thank their lucky stars this one is open all day; N.B. Jackson has a no alcohol policy but the others are BYOs.

Jerry & Harvey's Noshery | 19 | 10 | 15 | $20 |
96 Rte. 9 (Rte. 520), Marlboro, 732-972-1122
"Chicken soup", "chopped liver" and whatnot are there for the noshing at this Marlboro mainstay that's "maintained its consistency" of serving "good" "heartburn" favorites for over 20 years; "shopworn" decor notwithstanding, it's "just like a deli should be" and "fills its role admirably."

Je's | ▽ 24 | 10 | 17 | $18 |
34 Williams St. (Hallsie St.), Newark, 973-623-8848
The few surveyors who know about this "friendly place" located in a nondescript "storefront" in Newark declare it meets their "high standards" with "down-home" soul food including "delicious" ribs and peach cobbler and the "best mac 'n' cheese" around; AM gourmets like that they serve "breakfast items all day", but they say be prepared to line up on a "Sunday."

Jimmy's | 23 | 13 | 18 | $38 |
1405 Asbury Ave. (Prospect Ave.), Asbury Park, 732-774-5051
"A long-standing" "red-sauce" staple of the Asbury Park dining scene, the "veal Marsala" alone packs 'em in to this Italian decked out like a "late '70s" "banquet hall", where diners get ready for "fabulous" Southern Italian fare; "you gotta know someone", some surmise, since "regulars" "feel the warmth" of the "old-school staff", and others sometimes wish for a "smile."

JOCELYNE'S | 27 | 21 | 24 | $47 |
168 Maplewood Ave. (Baker St.), Maplewood, 973-763-4460; www.jocelynesrestaurant.com
"Sweet and petite", this French BYO in Maplewood "has it all": "outstanding" fare, "wonderful" service, a "cozy", "elegant" ambiance and the "great team" of chef-owner Mitchell Altholz and his wife, Jocelyne, "whose friendly and steadying presence is an added bonus"; P.S. "make reservations" "weeks in advance"; dinner only, and closed Mondays and Tuesdays.

vote at zagat.com

	F	D	S	C

Joe & Maggie's Bistro   − | − | − | E
591 Broadway (bet. Bath & Norwood Aves.), Long Branch, 732-571-8848; www.joeandmaggiesbistro.com
The guard's changed at this beloved Long Branch New American, with new owners Peter Fischbach (the chef) and sommelier Dennis Tafuri (both ex Metropolitan Cafe) at the helm; for minglers, there's a new hammered copper bar, TVs and beefed-up wine list, while for munchers, there's a menu evolution afoot, with accents of Asia and Spain.

Joe's Peking Duck House ⊄   20 | 8 | 18 | $20
Marlton Crossing Shopping Ctr., 145 Rte. 73 S. (Rte. 70), Marlton, 856-985-1551
Duck into a "hole-in-the-wall" and sample a host of "terrific" Chinese food including a "spicy salt and pepper squid to die for" at this cash-only Marlboro BYO; the staff's "enthusiasm" may help compensate for the cosmetically challenged digs.

John Henry's Seafood   23 | 16 | 21 | $34
2 Mifflin St. (bet. Franklin & Washington Sts.), Trenton, 609-396-3083; www.johnhenrysseafood.com
First-timers who aren't from Chambersburg sometimes feel like "outsiders" at this Trenton seafooder, but there's a simple remedy for that: "become a regular"; perhaps that's easy for most given the "fresh and imaginatively prepared" fare including "classic" Italian entrees; the hard part may be the "wait on weekends."

Jonathan's on West End   24 | 18 | 21 | $39
672 N. Trenton Ave. (West End Ave.), Atlantic City, 609-441-1800
An "ambitious" Eclectic menu of "well-executed" "designer food" via chef-owner Jonathan Karp sends surveyors to his eatery in the Chelsea section of AC; it's "a Shore-dweller must" that's "worth leaving the casinos" for; P.S. the Sunday–Thursday "early-bird" is a "best buy."

Jose's Mexican Cantina   20 | 15 | 18 | $24
24 South St. (Springfield Ave.), New Providence, 908-464-4360
Quail Run Ctr., 125 Washington Valley Rd. (Morning Glory Rd.), Warren, 732-563-0480
www.josescantina.com
You can either "pay for a plane ticket to Mexico" or visit one of these BYOs cooking up "tasty" treats sent out to "tackily" "festive" dining rooms; though dissenters decry them as "nothing to write *abuela* about", the majority insists they offer "great value for this level of food."

Juanito's   22 | 17 | 19 | $24
714 Main St. (Lareine Ave.), Bradley Beach, 732-502-0025
3830 Rte. 9 S. (Aldrich Rd.), Howell, 732-370-1717
159 Monmouth St. (West St.), Red Bank, 732-747-9118
"Bright and busy", this "casual" BYO chain has fans from all corners of Jersey lining up for its lineup of "cheap"

| F | D | S | C |

Mexican "delights" ("the burritos are the size of footballs"), salsa "that'll open your sinuses" and other "excellent" goodies, many of which come "covered" "in a pound of cheese"; if you're looking for something "lively" and "authentic", this one "hits the spot."

Karen & Rei's ⊉ ▽ 28 | 23 | 26 | $45

1882 Rte. 9 N. (1 mi. north of Avalon Blvd.), Clermont, 609-624-8205; www.karenandrei.com

The lucky few surveyors who've experienced this Clermont BYO heap praise on "super" chef and co-owner Karen Nelson's "outstanding", "interesting" and "amazingly consistent" New American food; enthusiasts add that "everything else is wonderful" too, from the "warm and personable" service, "lovely" atmosphere and even husband/maitre d' Rei Prabhakar's "tantalizing" descriptions of his wife's creations; indeed, "summer isn't complete without a visit here."

Karma Kafe 22 | 18 | 18 | $25

505 Washington St. (bet. 5th & 6th Sts.), Hoboken, 201-610-0900; www.karmakafe.com

Chances are you'll fall for India on the Hudson's "pretty" Downtown Hoboken "sister", a "hip" Indian eatery that "puts out a delectable assortment" of "interesting twists" on favorites and delivers a "bang for the buck" with an $8.95 buffet lunch that's "a steal"; P.S. "sit outside when it's warm" and watch the Washington Street throngs go by.

Kibbitz Down the Shore ▽ 25 | 11 | 13 | $16

846 Central Ave. (bet. 9th & 10th Sts.), Ocean City, 609-398-0880

Although it seems like only a handful have discovered this year-old deli, those who have are confident it makes a "great addition to Ocean City"; expect "loads of" Jewish "comfort food" including "excellent" "sandwiches" and matzo ball soup; do note that there are other things to consider about this enigmatic newcomer, namely that it's seasonal, "small" and has a tendency to "close at odd times."

Kibitz Room 24 | 9 | 15 | $15

Shoppes at Holly Ravine, 100 Springdale Rd. (Evesham Rd.), Cherry Hill, 856-428-7878; www.kibitzroom.net

Get ready to sit "elbow to elbow" at this "take-out mainstay" in Cherry Hill and try to get a handle on and a mouth around "belly-busting servings" of "excellent" deli staples, and a bonus of an "awesome" "pickle bar"; the service is "brisk" – and "brusque", making some wish the folks behind the counter would lose "'tude."

Kiku 20 | 18 | 19 | $37

5-9 Rte. 9 W. (1 mi. south of Closter Dock Rd.), Alpine, 201-767-6322
120 Rte. 4 E. (Spring Valley Rd.), Paramus, 201-845-8008

The "knife acrobatics" on display at these hibachi "faves" (that also serve "good sushi") in Alpine and Paramus make

vote at zagat.com

them "fun for the whole family"; even those who find the fare "so-so" acknowledge that "the kids love" the tableside "entertainment", though some note that the caliber of "the show" "depends on the chef you get."

Kinchley's Tavern ●⊄ | 22 | 8 | 15 | $17 |
586 N. Franklin Tpke. (Spring St.), Ramsey, 201-934-7777
You'll find "treasure" in Ramsey at this "dilapidated old landmark" dating to 1937, according to adoring fans who suggest "holding your breath" since the "super", "thin-crust" pies are accompanied by "smoke, smoke and more smoke"; it may be "always crowded" and often "noisy", but this cash-only spot turns out the "stuff pizza dreams are made of."

King of India | - | - | - | M |
Tower Mkt., 37 Rte. 35 N. (Rte. 71), Eatontown, 732-389-5747; www.kingofindia.net
Those schooled in savory spices feel like moguls at this value-priced Eatontown Indian sleeper where regulars go for the $7.95 lunch buffet and locals who hail from the Bombay 'burbs wax nostalgic over the BYO's biryanis and "great blendings" of "authentic" flavors; P.S. "you won't be sorry" if you chomp on the chile-licked chicken.

Klein's Fish Market & Waterside Cafe | 20 | 13 | 16 | $29 |
708 River Rd. (Main St.), Belmar, 732-681-1177; www.kleinsfish.com
If you see a "long line" in Belmar in the summer, it may just be leading to this fish shack whose setting sets an "unpretentious" stage for "satisfying" seafood specialties served in a variety of venues, from the "casual" cafe, to a more "formal" room (i.e. no "paper plates"), to a sushi bar; P.S. "take a table on the dock" and "enjoy the view of the Shark River."

K.O.B.E. | ∇ 23 | 22 | 21 | $32 |
The Commons at Holmdel, 2132 Rte. 35 S. (Laurel St.), Holmdel, 732-275-0025; www.kobecuisine.com
"Fabulous sushi" and a "modern, serene" setting have turned this two-year-old Japanese BYO in a Holmdel shopping plaza into a "favorite"; though a few frown on "pricey" tabs, fans fond of "fresh" rolls find they want to "go back."

Komegashi | 22 | 16 | 20 | $31 |
103 Montgomery St. (Warren St.), Jersey City, 201-433-4567
99 Pavonia Ave. (bet. River Ct. & Washington Blvd.), Jersey City, 201-533-8888
www.komegashi.com
Roll into either one of this Jersey City sushi duo and dig into "dynamite", "creative" examples of fin fare "so fresh" "you'd think it jumped into the place by itself"; the Japanese

| F | D | S | C |

twins "aren't identical", though: reviewers regard the Montgomery spot as "cozy" and offering "more traditional" fare, while right-on-the-water Pavonia features "more fusion options" and a "beautiful view" of Downtown NYC.

Konbu ▽ 21 | 15 | 17 | $29

Design Ctr., 345 Rte. 9 S. (bet. Gordon's Corner & Taylor Mills Rds.), Manalapan, 732-462-6886

Chef-owner James Tran is always coming up with "new ideas" at his Japanese BYO in Manalapan, which is why fans of his "excellent sushi" focus on the daily specials such as the oft-encored Tokyo Grapefruit, a scintillating sevichelike standout; the stellar standards work well for diners too.

Krogh's 16 | 13 | 16 | $24

23 White Deer Plaza (Seminary Ln.), Sparta, 973-729-8428; www.kroghs.com

The "great" house beers make this "rustic" brewpub opposite Lake Sparta "worth the trip" to Sparta, unless, of course, you already live there and know it to be a "Hobbit"-size "hangout" with "good" New American grub; "noise" lovers go on a weekend "when the bands play", and all should keep in mind that the "bar scene rules the show" here along with the "smoke."

La Bahia ▽ 21 | 19 | 23 | $37

507 Rte. 9 (Dock Rd.), Stafford, 609-978-0550; www.labahiarestaurant.com

This "festive" new Stafford Southwestern BYO comes "highly recommended" by the "happy" few surveyors who've discovered its "large" portions of "delightful" fare served by a capable staff that take its cue from the husband-and-wife team of Chris (chef-owner) and Karen Plecs; P.S. it's "exciting" to have such an "upscale" spot "in the neighborhood."

Labrador Lounge ▽ 24 | 16 | 21 | $34

3581 Rte. 35 N. (Peterson Ln.), Normandy Beach, 732-830-5770; www.kitschens.com

Awarded an "A+" for its "cleverly" cobbled comestibles that include a "unique" range of options (sushi too), this Eclectic in Ocean County will "inspire you to try something" other than the "usual shore fried fish fare"; the BYO policy helps "suppress the cost."

La Campagna ☒ 24 | 18 | 21 | $41

5 Elm St. (South St.), Morristown, 973-644-4943; www.lacampagnaristorante.com

"Consistency" is the middle name of this "terrific" Italian BYO in Morristown outputting "marvelous", "creative" takes on standards; "tight quarters" and "crowds on most nights" don't seem to deter devotees who seem down with being packaged "like sardines."

vote at zagat.com 85

| **F** | **D** | **S** | **C** |

La Campagne
24 | 21 | 22 | $47

312 Kresson Rd. (bet. Brace & Marlkress Rds.), Cherry Hill, 856-429-7647; www.lacampagne.com

It's in Cherry Hill, but a trip to this "charming" BYO will "feel like a brief sojourn in the French countryside" where the "delicious" Gallic fare and "relaxing" "farmhouse setting" are like "a dream come true"; go ahead and "celebrate a special occasion" here because it's "excellent in all respects", "from beginning" *jusquà la fin.*

Laceno Italian Grill
23 | 16 | 21 | $35

Echelon Village Plaza, 1118 White Horse Rd. (Rte. 561), Voorhees, 856-627-3700

The "marvelous" Italian-seafood cooking at this "upscale" strip-mall "crowd"-pleaser in Voorhees that's home to "serious food buffs" has advocates hailing the BYO as "the best of its kind in South Jersey"; "clubby" to some, those who "feel like outsiders" oppose service they see as "lacking" – especially "if you're not a regular."

La Cipollina
22 | 21 | 21 | $41

16A W. Main St. (South St.), Freehold, 732-308-3830; www.lacipollina.com

A "terrific" prix fixe "value" ($19 three-course lunch, $39 four-course dinner) is one reason why "you can't go wrong" at this "refreshing" Italian BYO "hidden" in a "nook" off Freehold's main drag; it may be hard not to appreciate "excellent" cooking from a place diners deem "refreshing."

La Couronne ⌧
18 | 14 | 18 | $34

23 Watchung Plaza (Park St.), Montclair, 973-744-2090

"More classic than au courant", this "unpretentious" BYO in Montclair "popular" with the "post-Bingo crowd" crowns guests with "personal attention" from the owner and feeds "regulars" ready for some "good", "simple" Italian food; true, the decor "could be updated", but, overall, most think it's still "pleasant."

Lada Cafe
– | – | – | I

520 Anderson Ave. (Edgewater Rd.), Cliffside Park, 201-840-8088; www.ladacafe.com

Regional Russian rings true at this Cliffside Park BYO where borscht, pelmeni and other stick-to-your-ribs dishes prevail with panache; though the storefront space piloted by the Borisov family is modest, the prices are too, making the easygoing eatery right for casual-dining nights as well as big-group fetes.

Lafayette House
14 | 14 | 15 | $29

Old Lafayette Village (bet. Rtes. 15 & 94), Lafayette, 973-579-3100; www.thelafayettehouse.com

Bargain-hunters on a brunch binge head for the "great" $15.95 Sunday special at this Traditional American in

| F | D | S | C |

Lafayette that offers fare in its "casual" downstairs pub or in the main room; though the goods here may be "basic", it "meets the needs" of shoppers in the Village.

La Focaccia 22 | 16 | 19 | $37
523 Morris Ave. (Aubrey St.), Summit, 908-277-4006
"Upscale", "loud" and "popular" and not surprising given that this Summit BYO cooks "delicious" Northern Italian for an audience who've endured "long waits" to snare a table; the "friendly" service's been known to turn "frenzied" when stretched, and the no-rezzies policy is "an annoyance" to some; N.B. a refurb scheduled for completion at press time includes the addition of a 30-seat private room.

La Fontana 22 | 22 | 24 | $56
120 Albany St. (bet. George & Spring Sts.), New Brunswick, 732-249-7500; www.lafontanaristorante.com
Some feel like they're in "Louis XIV's living room" when they visit this "special-occasion" Italian opposite the train station in New Brunswick that treats its customers like "visiting dignitaries" as they enjoy the "exceptional" fare; see-sawing surveyors, however, see the decor as either "sophisticated" or "overwrought."

Laguna Grill ∇ 21 | 23 | 21 | $35
1400 Ocean Ave. (14th St.), Brigantine, 609-266-8367; www.lagunagrill.com
The "ocean view from the deck" of this American-Eclectic in Brigantine might be "wonderful" enough to drown out the "casino insanity" of neighboring Atlantic City all by itself, but the "upscale" fare and "great martinis" also chip in; if a few fault "high prices" and "inconsistent" output from the kitchen, in the end, most say this spot's "worth it."

Lahiere's ☒ 22 | 19 | 21 | $51
11 Witherspoon St. (Nassau St.), Princeton, 609-921-2798; www.lahieres.com
Don the "family crest" when visiting this "elegant" Princeton "classic" where the "delicious" French fare, "attentive" service and "excellent" wine list keep the "old guard" coming back; its "frayed-around-the-edges" atmosphere could use a "good kick", but stalwarts stand by the "grande dame", noting with pride that she "has survived" virtually "unchanged" since "the beginning of modern times."

LA ISLA 27 | 10 | 19 | $19
104 Washington St. (bet. 1st & 2nd Sts.), Hoboken, 201-659-8197; www.laislarestaurant.com
"Ridiculously small" but packing the energy of a supernova, this "festive", "diner-esque" Hoboken BYO cooks up "the best Cuban food you've ever had" that arrives via a "quick" and "busy, busy" floor crew; the "multitudes" willing to wait for a table is evidence of its "popularity"; N.B. no reservations taken, and brunch-only on Sundays.

vote at zagat.com

| F | D | S | C |

Lambertville Station 17 | 20 | 18 | $34
11 Bridge St. (Delaware River), Lambertville, 609-397-8300; www.lambertvillestation.com
"Walk around Lambertville" then hop on over to this "steady" Traditional American set in a "beautifully restored old railroad station" that's a destination for "day-trippers" drawn by the "great view" of the Delaware River; not everyone's aboard this one, though, with some citing "just ok" fare and seeing signs of a "tourist trap."

La Mezzaluna 19 | 17 | 19 | $42
25 Witherspoon St. (Nassau St.), Princeton, 609-688-8515; www.lamezzaluna.com
Devotees of this Princeton Italian appreciate its "hearty", "very good" food on an "interesting" menu; though "gown and town" returnees to the BYO see little reason for debate over the quality of the fare that includes "superb specials", some civic-minded sorts just want to let others know the whole package is "a bit expensive."

Lana's ▽ 22 | 16 | 15 | $45
1300 Raritan Rd. (bet. Central & Walnut Aves.), Clark, 732-669-9024; www.lanasfinedining.com
Relatively "undiscovered" and improbably located adjacent to a public golf course, this year-old addition to the Clark dining scene is a "rare find" considering its "creative", "artfully presented" New American dishes and "solid" wine selections; truth be told, some surveyors tell tales of "unprofessional" service, which means this newbie has some "kinks" to work out.

La Nonna Piancone's 20 | 18 | 19 | $34
800 Main St. (McCabe Ave.), Bradley Beach, 732-775-0906; www.piancone.com
Piancone's South
110 Union Ave. (Higgins Ave.), Brielle, 732-528-7833
You "won't go home hungry" if you surrender to one of these Italians that turn out "extra large portions" of "consistently good" food; naysayers note the fare's a tad "heavy", and service is trending "downhill"; P.S. those in-the-know suggest "stick with the Bradley Beach original."

La Pastaria 19 | 15 | 17 | $28
6 Linden Pl. (Broad St.), Red Bank, 732-224-8699
327 Springfield Ave. (Summit Ave.), Summit, 908-522-9088
www.lapastaria.com
For an "affordable" meal out, fans of these "popular" Italian BYOs in Red Bank and Summit "don't mind waiting" for "basic", albeit "delicious" fare including "terrific" pastas served by "friendly" and, frankly, "not-always-on-the-ball" personnel; small-stomached surveyors like that they offer "half-size portions."

| F | D | S | C |

La Petite France   24 | 20 | 22 | $48
7 E. Front St. (Wharf St.), Red Bank, 732-936-0640
"Quaint" and "cozy" and sure to "remind you of a Parisian cafe", this French bistro lures lovers ready for some "romance" in Red Bank and others simply wishing to savor "outstanding" cooking; the BYO's small stature means you should "make a reservation on weekends"; N.B. closed Mondays and Tuesdays.

La Scala   23 | 16 | 22 | $38
117 N. Gaston Ave. (bet. Bartine & William Sts.), Somerville, 908-218-9300; www.lascalafineitalian.com
"Personable" chef-owner Omar Aly scores with his Northern Italian BYO in Somerville whose "imaginative" menu of "impressive" selections feature undeniably "exotic" eats ("where else can you find kangaroo in central Jersey?"); if you believe the decor is "bland", service that's "just right" may help you see things differently.

La Spiaggia   24 | 18 | 22 | $47
357 W. Eighth St. (Rte. 72 W.), Ship Bottom, 609-494-4343; www.laspiaggialbi.com
This "formal" Ship Bottom Italian BYO is a "longtime" LBI "favorite" known for its "wonderful" fare, "professional" service and "old-world elegance"; while it may be an "expensive" option, devotees value a place that "honors your reservations and tries to make your night special."

La Strada   23 | 18 | 22 | $38
1105 Rte. 10 E. (bet. Canfield & Eyland Aves.), Randolph, 973-584-4607; www.lastradarestaurant.com
A "fabulous" choice for an "intimate night out", this "upscale" Randolph Italian "delivers" a "pretty", "dimly lit" setting matched by a "comprehensive" lineup of "excellent traditional" dishes; "phenomenal" service and nightly piano music caps what for many is an "enjoyable" experience.

La Tartuferia   25 | 19 | 23 | $48
1405 Grand St. (14th St.), Hoboken, 201-792-2300; www.latartuferia.com
You may have to dig around a bit to find it, but once you do, plan on a culinary trip to "heaven" via the "amazing" theme ingredient (the truffle) that pops up in every corner of the "modern" menu at this "divine" Hoboken Northern Italian "hidden" under the 14th Street viaduct; add in "friendly" service, remember that "high-quality" food justifies "high prices" and you'll likely conclude it's "well worth the hunt."

La Terraza   20 | 16 | 22 | $35
47B Rte. 206 N. (Cherry Hill Rd.), Princeton, 609-497-2774; www.laterrazarestaurant.com
The "old strip-mall" setting of this Med-Spanish combo in Princeton is offset by "consistently good fare" (including

vote at zagat.com

| F | D | S | C |

"fabulous paella") and "the friendliest service in town"; though the regular dishes are "very good", others put their money "on the specials."

LATOUR
| 26 | 22 | 24 | $49 |

6 E. Ridgewood Ave. (Broad St.), Ridgewood, 201-445-5056
Chef-owner Michael Latour's "fabulous" French-American cuisine matched by "consistently top-notch" service and "elegant", "lovely and low-key" setting have put this "quaint storefront" "by the train station" in Ridgewood on many a "must" list; it is "popular", "small" and utterly "charming" – and thus "tough to get a reservation" at.

La Vecchia Napoli
| 19 | 14 | 19 | $39 |

2 Hilliard Ave. (River Rd.), Edgewater, 201-941-6799; www.lavecchianapoli.com
Fans of this "intimate", "tiny" Edgewater "old-worlder" run by a husband-and-wife team praise the "homey" and "true" Italian cooking brought to table by a staff that considers clients "family" (in a *good* way); expect a "no-frills" look and "good" food some deem a tad "pricey."

Lawrenceville Inn
| 21 | 20 | 21 | $47 |

2691 Main St. (Gordon Ave.), Lawrence Township, 609-219-1900; www.lawrencevilleinn.com
"Imaginative" New American cuisine crafted with "local organic produce" is the hallmark of this "charming", "up and coming" Lawrence Township two-year-old set in a "renovated" Victorian inn; though detractors detect "scrawny" portions and deem the operation "pretentious", defenders "love it" and say it's "special."

Le Fandy ☒
| 24 | 16 | 21 | $45 |

609 River Rd. (Hance Ave.), Fair Haven, 732-530-3338
Sated surveyors who've sampled new chef and owner Luke Peter Ong's fare consider it "some of the best-executed" stuff in Fair Haven and beyond; indeed, folks fawning over the "tiny" BYO's "scrumptious" French bistro food "can't wait to go back"; don't be surprised if this "secret" gets out.

LEGAL SEA FOODS
| 21 | 17 | 18 | $37 |

1 Garden State Plaza (Roosevelt Ave.), Paramus, 201-843-8483
Short Hills Mall, 1200 Morris Tpke. (Rte. 24), Short Hills, 973-467-0089
www.legalseafoods.com
The "crowds" catch on quick to this "smooth-sailing" duo in Paramus and The Short Hills Mall "you'd never know were part of a larger chain" on account of their "outrageously large" slate of the "freshest" seafood items around; they're "crazy busy", and the "harried staff" "does a good job dealing with it"; P.S. "great for kids", and parents appreciate that even their shortest of shorties "love it."

| F | D | S | C |

Le Petit Chateau | 25 | 22 | 24 | $59 |
121 Claremont Rd. (Rte. 202), Bernardsville, 908-766-4544
Some feel this "lovely, little" "special-occasion" French in Bernardsville "doesn't get the buzz it deserves", citing the "phenomenal" $65 prix fixe menu, "impeccable" service and "romantic", "cozy" ambiance; go ahead and "take your best girl or boy" – or at least someone with deep pockets to cover the "large" tab.

Le Plumet Royal | 19 | 21 | 16 | $50 |
The Peacock Inn, 20 Bayard Ln. (Nassau St.), Princeton, 609-924-1707; www.peacockinn.com
Princeton's "beautiful", historic Peacock Inn provides the nest for this New French "occasion" spot that for fans is "tasteful in every way"; the fare, however, "fluctuates from excellent to average", and the same flock find their feathers ruffled over service reminiscent of "Fawlty Towers."

Le Rendez-Vous | 26 | 18 | 23 | $46 |
520 Boulevard (21st St.), Kenilworth, 908-931-0888; www.lerendez-vousnj.com
"An oasis" in an "unlikely" town, this French "wonder" in Kenilworth "charms" patrons in a space so "small" that you "might eat off someone else's plate", and perhaps that wouldn't be so bad given the BYO's "magnificent" food brought to table by a "friendly" staff; N.B. an ownership change a year ago appears to sit quite well with surveyors.

Liberté | 17 | 20 | 17 | $35 |
428 Bloomfield Ave. (bet. Seymour St. & S. Fullerton Ave.), Montclair, 973-746-8840; www.liberterestaurant.com
Many mention that if you get a chance, "sit in the courtyard" that offers the "best outdoor seating" in Montclair at this "cute", "pretty" French-Eclectic; though a few free-speech supporters reason that "lovely decor is poor compensation" for "uneven" fare, the majority expresses its will "to return" to a BYO it finds "dependable" and "pleasant."

Liberty House Restaurant | 19 | 23 | 19 | $44 |
Liberty State Park, 76 Audrey Zapp Dr. (Freedom Way), Jersey City, 201-395-0300; www.libertyhouserestaurant.com
A "spectacular view" of NYC has the lead role at this "upscale" Traditional American in Jersey City inside Liberty State Park dispensing food (if anyone can remember it) that's "quite good"; P.S. if you "don't like the fact that you have to pay for parking", a "great" Sunday "jazz brunch" may help shift your mood.

Light Horse Tavern, The ◐ | – | – | – | E |
199 Washington St. (Morris St.), Jersey City, 201-946-2028; www.lighthorsetavern.com
Beer-lovers are among those leading the charge to this "beautifully restored" Jersey City tavern, whose sterling

Lila ▽ 23 | 19 | 21 | $38

National Hotel, 31 Race St. (Rte. 12), Frenchtown, 908-996-4871; www.frenchtownnational.com

Those who've stopped in to this "lovely" two-year-old Frenchtown New American set in the "historic" and newly refurbed National Hotel agree its "interesting" food includes "creative" "tapas"-style dishes and "outstanding" burgers; if you notice a staff "learning on the job", proponents preach patience, saying "give this place a little time."

Lilac 22 | 21 | 20 | $47

National Hotel, 194-196 Essex St. (Main St.), Millburn, 973-564-9600; www.lilacrestaurant.com

This "pretty", "polished" and petite performer's "delicious" French cooking, "intimate" ambiance and proximity to the Paper Mill Playhouse make it a "good choice" for pre-curtain "fine dining" in Millburn; just consider that service, though "gracious", has been known to "get bogged down" before a show.

Lilly's on the Canal 20 | 20 | 18 | $34

2 Canal St. (Bridge St.), Lambertville, 609-397-6242

A "factory"-"chic" space is home to this bi-level Eclectic in Lambertville, where supping on "well-prepared" dishes in the "homey"-meets-"exotic" vein and monitoring the action in the open kitchen keep things "interesting"; while its fans "delight" in the setting "overlooking the canal", others notice "servers that could be more attentive."

Limestone Cafe 23 | 17 | 17 | $40

89 Main St. (Holland Ave.), Peapack, 908-234-1475

Take a ride to this "homey" Peapack BYO that's "off the beaten track" "in the heart of horse country" and offers "outstanding" Traditional American "comfort food" as well as more "adventurous" dishes; if "spotty" service "mars the gastronomic experience" for a few, most warm to a "menu that should please anyone."

Lincroft Inn 20 | 18 | 19 | $38

700 Newman Springs Rd. (Middletown Lincroft Rd.), Middletown, 732-747-0890; www.lincroftinn.com

When people call this "historic" eatery in the Lincroft section of Middletown an "old standby", they mean it (the building dates to 1697); what's also obvious is the "significant improvement" this Continental has made over the past few years, from the "fresh", "interesting" menu that's moved "to a higher league" to the "excellent" "new wine list"; N.B. look for a scheduled upgrade of the interior this year.

| F | D | S | C |

Little Café, A
25 | 17 | 23 | $37

Plaza Shoppes, 118 White Horse Rd. E. (Burnt Mill Rd.), Voorhees, 856-784-3344

This "perky", pint-sized player tucked away in a strip mall in Voorhees is a "pleasure" for those who've fallen for its "terrific" Eclectic food on a "varied" yet somewhat "small" menu; yes, "elbow room" in the BYO may be at a premium, but fare that's "big on flavor" and "friendly" service means it's a "great find."

Little Tuna
21 | 14 | 20 | $30

403 N. Haddon Ave. (Hawthorne Ave.), Haddonfield, 856-795-0888
Seaview Harbor Marina, 301 Longport-Somers Point Blvd. (Anchorage Dr.), Longport, 609-823-8989

"Popular with locals", this "small" storefront BYO in Haddonfield purveys "excellent" eats from the sea to patrons pleased with the "very reasonable price/quality" ratio; "unimpressive" in the looks department as it may be, it's still "paradise" for fish lovers; N.B. a new Longport satellite caters to diners who've docked boats at the Seaview Harbor Marina.

Lobster House
21 | 18 | 18 | $35

Fisherman's Wharf, 906 Schellenger's Landing Rd. (Rte. 109 S.), Cape May, 609-884-8296; www.thelobsterhouse.com

"Generations" of neighborhood locals and "tourists" have made a pilgrimage to this Cape May mainstay for, quite simply, "great fresh fish" and "good and fast service"; outdoor types eat up the edibles at the "raw bar" and the "wharfy ambiance", while others savor the atmosphere of the more "formal" indoor option; P.S. if you want to bypass the "waits" in the summer do take out from the "excellent market."

Lodos
– | – | – | I

690 River Rd. (Henley Ave.), New Milford, 201-265-0004; www.lodosrestaurant.4t.com

Flowing purple fabrics divide the exotic bi-level storefront space that's home to this appealing Turkish BYO in New Milford; instant regulars often make a meal of the myriad appetizers and point to the stuffed grape leaves, kebabs and rotating seafood specialties as reasons why they've warmed to this newcomer; another enticement is a bill that won't bite.

Look See
19 | 14 | 15 | $27

295 N. Franklin Tpke. (Rte. 17), Ramsey, 201-327-1515

It's "a cut above" others in its genre, pronounce proponents of this Chinese offering a "crowd" "good", "tasty" items for prices on the "reasonable" side; opponents opine that "fast" and "rude" service may, quite sensibly, make the BYO "better for takeout."

vote at zagat.com

F	D	S	C

Los Amigos 23 | 19 | 19 | $26
1926 Atlantic Ave. (bet. Michigan & Ohio Aves.), Atlantic City, 609-344-2293 ☽
461 Rte. 73 N. (Franklin Ave.), West Berlin, 856-767-5216
www.losamigosrest.com
There's "always a party" at these "busy" Mexican-Southwestern *hermanos* in West Berlin and Atlantic City, where the festivities feature "exciting", "innovative" fare and "mesmerizing margaritas"; so "keep the salsa and chips coming", say supporters, since this duo's "as good as gold."

Lotus Cafe 25 | 14 | 21 | $21
Home Depot Shopping Ctr., 450 Hackensack Ave. (Rte. 4), Hackensack, 201-488-7070
Food that's "excellent any time of day" baits backers of this Chinese BYO to its strip-mall home in Hackensack; enthusiasts endorse service as "fast" and "friendly" "as you can imagine", and prices on the low side means this town's got a "winner" in its midst.

LouCás 23 | 19 | 20 | $36
Colonial Village Shopping Ctr., 9 Lincoln Hwy. (Parsonage Rd.), Edison, 732-549-8580; www.loucasrestaurant.com
Chef and co-owner Loucás Sofocli's "fabulous" Italian seafood specialist in Edison is a "tried and true favorite" with "excellent" cooking teaming up with a "well-trained" staff; add in "modest prices", and it's easy to figure out why this BYO's "always jumping."

Lua – | – | – | E
1300 Sinatra Dr. N. (Independence Ct.), Hoboken, 201-876-1900
A shoo-in for coolest contender around, this slick, new and super-hot 7,000-sq.-ft. Pan-Latin number in Hoboken sitting hard on the Hudson offers a panoramic view of the Manhattan skyline from either the dining space or the glowing amber resin-topped oval bar; foodwise, those tapping into tapas are lining up to be well-fed by Ricardo Cardona, an NYC transplant.

Luchento's 20 | 12 | 17 | $33
520 Hwy. 33 W. (Dugans Grove Rd.), Millstone, 732-446-8500; www.luchentos.com
Expect "good" Cajun/Creole/Italian vittles served in "abundance" at this "crowded", "family-style" Millstone BYO where the "complimentary salad and bread is a meal in itself" in a "picnic"-like atmosphere; head scratchers, however, seek an explanation about "spotty" service.

Luigi's 19 | 15 | 19 | $33
Berkeley Plaza, 434 Ridgedale Ave. (McKinley Ave.), East Hanover, 973-887-8408; www.luigisitalianrestaurant.com
For a "dependable" deal, supporters cite Luigi Viola's "homey" East Hanover Italian and its "flavorful" fare

| F | D | S | C |

coupled with "pleasant" service; if it's not terribly exciting ("doesn't set the world on fire"), at least the bill "doesn't break the bank."

Luka's ☒ | 22 | 12 | 19 | $32 |
238 Main St. (Park St.), Ridgefield Park, 201-440-2996; www.lukasitaliancuisine.com

"Even if it's not in your neighborhood", you may wish to pay a visit to this "deservedly popular" BYO operation in Ridgefield Park that dispenses Italian goods that arrive via an "efficient" staff; aesthetes advise that you "ignore the decor" and keep your eyes on the prize – "delectable", "reasonably priced" food.

Lulu's Bistro ☒ | 22 | 17 | 22 | $37 |
498 S. Livingston Ave. (Northfield Ave.), Livingston, 973-994-0150

Supporters of this "adorable" two-year-old BYO in a Livingston strip mall praise the culinary craft of chef-owner Michael Dilonno, whose "creative" New American "delights" are sure to satisfy a crowd; lickety-split service from an "exceptionally attentive" and "warm" staff completes the package.

LU NELLO ☒ | 26 | 19 | 24 | $50 |
331 Union Blvd. (Rte. 46), Totowa, 973-790-1410; www.lunello.com

It pays to "become a regular" of Louis Seger's "top-notch" Northern Italian spot in Totowa, since the "superb" specialties shine and the "skilled" staff "treats you like royalty"; if commoners complain about feeling on the outs (it's "cliquish"), focus on what you put in your mouth, sit back and be "amazed."

Madame Claude ⌀ | – | – | – | M |
364 ½ Fourth St. (Newark Ave.), Jersey City, 201-876-8800; www.madameclaudecafe.com

Surreally situated between a gas station and a mini parking lot, this pocket-size surprise run by a husband-and-wife team brims with charm and kitsch and gives Jersey Cityites a reason to cram into its remarkably bright, sunny space to sample French bistro classics morning, noon and night; it's strictly BYO *bouteille*.

Mad Batter | 20 | 18 | 19 | $31 |
Carroll Villa Hotel, 19 Jackson St. (bet. Beach Dr. & Carpenter Ln.), Cape May, 609-884-5970

"Get in line" for a "seat on the porch" at this Cape May American, a "perennial favorite" where the "aroma of great breakfast" fills the air and early-risers toast the "terrific pancakes" while others tout the merits of weekend brunch and dinner; though a few bat around "inattentive service" and "shopworn" decor, most are mad about its "old-world charm."

F	D	S	C

Madeleine's Petit Paris   23 | 19 | 21 | $47
416 Tappan Rd. (Paris Ave.), Northvale, 201-767-0063;
www.madeleinespetitparis.com
Très, très big on hospitality, Madeleine and Gaspard Caloz's Northvale standby is "lovely, quiet and very, very French" and where gourmets who go for the Gallic cite "superb" standards, including "first-class" desserts; despite a contingent of contrarians still smarting about a years-ago move from Bergenfield ("it's lost its touch"), this ode to the Left Bank, for many, remains a "class act."

Madison Bar & Grill   20 | 20 | 19 | $34
1316 Washington St. (14th St.), Hoboken, 201-386-0300;
www.madisonbarandgrill.com
"Location, location, location" keeps this "interesting mix" of a "hip watering hole" and "family-friendly" New American in north Hoboken "always busy"; you may encounter "spotty" service, but the "daily specials" and "seasonal menu" make it "worth the parking" ordeal – just arrive early if you want to "avoid the trendoids."

Magic Pot   ∇ 18 | 14 | 18 | $38
934 River Rd. (bet. Dempsey and Hilliard Aves.), Edgewater, 201-969-8005; www.themagicpotfonduebistro.com
"Fondue finds New Jersey" at this DIY, BYO "interactive food experience" in Edgewater, where patrons don't just say cheese since there's everything from fish to chocolate to dunk in the tabletop pots; it's "kind of pricey" but "fun" "with a group" – now, if only the place could "get some help from an interior decorator."

Mahogany Grille   24 | 22 | 20 | $48
142 Main St. (Parker Ave.), Manasquan, 732-292-1300
"Celebrate any occasion" by tucking into "inventive" takes on "traditional favorites" at this "popular" New American with "cosmopolitan flair in the seaside town" of Manasquan; regulars rate it "first class", but some protest "NYC prices", while others wish it would "take reservations."

Mahzu   22 | 16 | 19 | $30
Aberdeen Plaza, 1077 Rte. 34 (Lloyd Rd.), Aberdeen, 732-583-8985
"A very extensive menu" showcases "great sushi" including "creative rolls" at this "family-friendly" Japanese BYO in Aberdeen that's worth "many repeat trips" for "the freshest fish in town"; cooked eats can be sampled at the segregated hibachi bar; P.S. fans "can't believe" the shopping center space once housed an auto parts store.

Main Street Bistro   22 | 19 | 19 | $38
30 E. Main St. (Spring St.), Freehold, 732-294-1112;
www.bistro1.com
The "New American menu that changes with the seasons" comes as a "wonderful surprise in the middle of Freehold's

| F | D | S | C |

pizzerias" to surveyors seeking "a special night out in the neighborhood"; indeed, there's "wonderful", "masterfully presented" provisions from the BYO's kitchen, joined by "inconsistent" service on the floor.

Main Street Cafe | 16 | 14 | 17 | $26 |
54 Main St. (bet. Central Ave. & Waverly Pl.), Madison, 973-966-0252
Find "non-fancy food at non-fancy prices" at this Madison New American that's "one notch up from TGI Friday's – but a significant notch"; with a "standout beer selection" and sports perpetually on the tubes, it's a sure bet this "solid standby" attracts a "large college crowd" as well as "young professionals" ducking in for "a quick bite."

Main Street Euro-American Bistro | 19 | 15 | 19 | $31 |
Princeton Shopping Ctr., 301 N. Harrison St. (Valley Rd.), Princeton, 609-921-2779; www.mainstreetprinceton.com
"There's always something new to try" on the "interesting" menu at this "homey, unpretentious" Princeton New American in a "convenient shopping center"; where some see an "ordinary" experience, others offer it's the "best everyday restaurant in town."

Maize ●☒ | 20 | 21 | 17 | $43 |
Robert Treat Hotel, 50 Park Pl. (bet. Center & E. Park Sts.), Newark, 973-639-1200; www.maizerestaurant.com
"A bright spot in the overly Iberian offerings of Newark" is this "slightly different" Traditional American that "can get seriously crowded when there's an NJPAC performance"; the "little" lounge is "extremely romantic", leading lovers to dub it an "excellent date spot" even as detractors try to "forget it's in a hotel" and decry service that's the "slowest north of the Mason-Dixon line."

Makeda | 23 | 24 | 20 | $33 |
338 George St. (bet. Bayard St. & Livingston Ave.), New Brunswick, 732-545-5115; www.makedas.com
"Great Ethiopian is not an oxymoron" assert acolytes of this "rare treat" in New Brunswick where the "elegant atmosphere" and "well-spiced, unique" cuisine prompt a plethora of praises; some "dance between courses" to the live music while others shrug off the fact that this fork-free spot may "lack some organization"; N.B. there's an African arts shop next door.

Makoto Japanese Steakhouse | ▽ 18 | 15 | 19 | $31 |
Stafford Square Shopping Ctr., 297 Rte. 72 W. (bet. Rtes. 9 & 554), Stafford, 609-978-9986
Kimono-clad waitresses present "original" sushi at this Japanese BYO in Stafford that's seen as a "welcome eatery in a town dominated" by chains; the handful who know it claim "the hibachi show is fun" and note there's "lots of value" to be found.

vote at zagat.com

| F | D | S | C |

Málaga
20 | 16 | 20 | $32

511 Lalor St. (Rte. 129 S.), Hamilton, 609-396-8878;
www.malagarestaurant.com

"The well-prepared" food at this "classic" Iberian in Hamilton proves "good" Spanish fare "can be found outside the Ironbound"; "charming" service and sangria that "leaves everyone happy" make it a "great place to host a party", even if it's "not in the prettiest part of town."

Manhattan Steakhouse
22 | 19 | 20 | $51

2105 Rte. 35 N. (W. Park Ave.), Ocean Township, 732-493-6328

It's "better than schlepping into the city" confirm followers of this "carnivore heaven" in Monmouth County where "steak is king"; while beef eaters boast of the "worthy effort", a Cab-conscious committee claims "the wine list leaves something to be desired", and others fear this animal has fallen prey to "Manhattan prices."

Manon ⌽
23 | 20 | 22 | $40

19 N. Union St. (Bridge St.), Lambertville, 609-397-2596

"*Très bien*" tout bistro lovers of this "delightful escape" in Lambertville that's the "ultimate end to a work-weary week"; "let yourself be transported to Arles" ("love the 'Starry Night' mural on the ceiling") and forget that the "quarters are a bit cramped" while you tuck into the "traditional Provençal" fare, but do remember this BYO says a firm *non* to credit cards; N.B. closed Mondays and Tuesdays.

Manor, The
23 | 25 | 24 | $58

111 Prospect Ave. (Woodland Ave.), West Orange, 973-731-2360; www.themanorrestaurant.com

You may find the "antithesis of an intimate setting" at this Traditional American "grand old dame" in West Orange that remains a "legend", with "fountains and opulent gardens" paving the way to a lobster-padded "seafood buffet" that "can't be missed"; factor in a service crew that "caters to all needs" and you'll understand why many wish their "wallet and waist could afford this treat every week."

Mansion on Main Street, The
20 | 24 | 22 | $44

3000 Main St. (bet. Evesham & Kresson Rds.), Voorhees, 856-751-6060; www.mansiononmainstreet.com

"They make every occasion special" at this Voorhees Continental open to the public only for holiday dinners and for Sunday brunches that are "feasts"; you can count on "white-glove service", but some note that the "elegance elevates" "overpriced" food to "something more."

Marakesh
∇ 20 | 21 | 20 | $31

321 Rte. 46 E. (Edward Rd.), Parsippany, 973-808-0062; www.marakesh.com

You just might feel as though "you were whisked away to Marrakesh and that Bogart and Bergman will step right in"

| F | D | S | C |

to this Moroccan BYO in Parsippany that's "fun for a group" and known for "authentic, delicious, exotic" dishes; "eat with your fingers", watch the "belly dancers in the aisles", and call it a "satisfying adventure" "in a strip mall."

Marcello & Dino Roman Cafe   21 | 19 | 21 | $40
12 Tappan Rd. (Schraalenburgh Rd.), Harrington Park, 201-767-4245; www.romancafe.com
"The service is doting, yet unobtrusive" at this "classic" Italian in Harrington Park with "top of the line" selections and where the namesake "father and son" proprietors "can't do enough to help you enjoy your meal"; indeed, it's a "neighborhood favorite", albeit in an area without an *abundanza* of choices.

Marco & Pepe   – | – | – | M
289 Grove St. (Mercer St.), Jersey City, 201-860-9688; www.marcoandpepe.com
Casual and chic without trying to be, this jazzy Jersey City storefront proffers a foodie-friendly menu confident enough to swing toward France and Spain without losing its New American identity; small-plate options and a concise, well-edited wine list have helped make it a hit since the day it opened; N.B. open for brunch on Saturdays and Sundays.

Margherita's   23 | 12 | 18 | $24
740 Washington St. (8th St.), Hoboken, 201-222-2400
"Definitely" a place to "eat, eat, eat", this "homestyle" Italian BYO is "the neighborhood standby" and known throughout Hoboken for "huge portions" of "very good" food and waits for tables that last "forever"; pass the time "sipping a drink next door", then "cram into" the "tight quarters", where there may be a few doubters who feel "duped by free bruschetta" and, despite a high Food score, some claim the fare is "marginal."

Mariques French Cuisine   23 | 18 | 21 | $42
25 E. Main St. (Rte. 124), Mendham, 973-543-9571
"A personal visit" from chef-owner Eric Sellin "will enhance your experience" at this French BYO in Mendham, where the "wonderful", "changing menus" inspire asides of "*c'est magnifique*"; though some find it all "just fair" and feel the "cozy" spot "needs some sprucing up", it remains for most "one of the best-kept secrets in the area."

Market Roost   ▽ 21 | 16 | 15 | $21
65 Main St. (Bloomfield Ave.), Flemington, 908-788-4949; www.marketroost.com
For "consistently good" Eclectic eats, park yourself into this Flemington BYO that's a "good" buy for a pre- or post-outlet shopping meal; longtime chef-owners Carol and Norman Todd purvey "interesting combinations" that folks count on for their midday repasts; N.B. closed Mondays and Tuesdays, and dinner not served.

vote at zagat.com

| F | D | S | C |

Marra's | 21 | 17 | 17 | $38
16 S. Broad St. (E. Ridgewood Ave.), Ridgewood, 201-444-1332;
www.marrasrestaurant.com
"Small, quaint" and Italian, this Ridgewood BYO with "wonderful specials" has been "a family favorite for decades"; it's "always crowded for a reason" most say, and some want to make it clear that the fare's "designed for those" who think "abundance" is the "goal."

Marsilio's Ⓢ | 21 | 17 | 20 | $37
541 Roebling Ave. (Chestnut Ave.), Trenton, 609-695-1916
Take a "step back to the Rat Pack days" at this "classic red-gravy" Italian in Trenton's Chambersburg where pols from the nearby Statehouse give the "see-and-be seen" scene their vote; ah, sigh some, "it feels like going to Nonna's for Sunday dinner."

Martino's | 20 | 10 | 18 | $23
212 W. Main St. (Doughty Ave.), Somerville, 908-722-8602
"Energetic" chef-owner Martino Linares "may sing or do a little dance" for you at this "authentic" Cuban BYO in Somerville with "down-home" specialties; there's "nothing fancy" here, but the "Christmas lights" and "memorabilia" in a room that evokes the "pre-Castro" era is one of this place's "special treats."

Masala Grill | 21 | 14 | 14 | $25
19 Chambers St. (Nassau St.), Princeton, 609-921-0500
Princetonians eat up "tummy-pleasing takes" on "spicy" "delicacies" on the "interesting menu" at this BYO Indian that's a "haven for vegetarians"; but it needs to season an "uninspired ambiance", critics contend, and should do something to wake up "slow service."

Mastoris ◐ | 20 | 13 | 19 | $22
144 Hwy. 130 (Rte. 206), Bordentown, 609-298-4650;
www.mastoris.com
Bordentown is home to this "big old landmark diner" with a menu that "stretches into eternity" and dining spaces "cavernous enough for the Elks, Lions and Rotary to hold weekly meetings simultaneously"; despite detractors quick to point out that "quantity and quality really aren't interchangeable", this "classic" remains a "survivor."

Matisse Ⓢ | 22 | 21 | 19 | $45
1300 Ocean Ave. (13th Ave.), Belmar, 732-681-7680;
www.matissecatering.com
"Fabulous ocean views with food to match" make this Belmar New American BYO piloted by chef-owner Anthony Wall a "destination" for a "totally pleasing experience"; it may be "pricey", but locals know it's best to "satisfy your taste buds" "when the tourists go home", and add that "the beach never looked so good in winter."

| F | D | S | C |

Mattar's
▽ 25 | 20 | 25 | $44

1115 Rte. 517 (Ridge Rd.), Allamuchy, 908-852-2300;
www.mattars.com

"Out of the way, but worth the trip", this Warren County stalwart exists in a "culinary wasteland", though the "excellent" Continental fare, "charming owner" and "elegant style" make it "great for a special occasion."

Max's Fine Dining
21 | 23 | 17 | $43

602 Burlington Pike (bet. Highland & Riverton Rds.), Cinnaminson, 856-663-6297

A revolving door of chefs has surveyors chattering about ups and downs at this "expensive" French-Italian in Cinnaminson; the decor is "lovely" and fans find "flashes of brilliance" in the fare, but "poor" service adds to a feeling that this BYO has "fallen from grace."

Mazi
▽ 23 | 17 | 21 | $35

401 Main St. (4th St.), Bradley Beach, 732-775-8828

"Where to start?" ask die-hard devotees of this "bistro-like" seasonal Bradley Beach Med BYO whose "creative" menu (with Greek and Portuguese dishes thrown in) includes "perfect piri-piri chicken" and "desserts in a league of their own"; it also helps that it's "charming" and "cute."

McCormick & Schmick's
19 | 19 | 18 | $38

Bridgewater Commons, 400 Commons Way
(Prince Rodgers Ave.), Bridgewater, 908-707-9996
Riverside Square Mall, 175 Riverside Sq. (Hackensack Ave.), Hackensack, 201-968-9410
www.mccormickandschmicks.com

"You'll be hooked" on this "chain-operated" piscine pair in Bridgewater and Hackensack that make surveyors swim after "fabulous fish" that's "fresh, fresh, fresh" and served by a "friendly" staff; but a mutinous crew of (outvoted) landlubbers advise fans not go overboard, saying these seafooder's are just "serviceable."

McLoone's Riverside
18 | 22 | 19 | $39

816 Ocean Ave. (Beach Way), Sea Bright, 732-842-2894;
www.mcloones.com

"Tim McLoone is a witty host" who helps this Sea Bright American be "the best place on the Jersey Shore in the summer"; its location (where the Navesink and Shrewsbury rivers meet) makes for a "near-perfect setting" and, given the "billion-dollar views" of the mansions across the water, most get past the "indifferent service."

Mediterra
19 | 21 | 18 | $40

29 Hulfish St. (bet. Chambers & Witherspoon Sts.), Princeton, 609-252-9680; www.terramomo.com

This "landlocked" Princeton Mediterranean is "a safe bet in a town short on great restaurants", where fare that's

vote at zagat.com

| F | D | S | C |

"sometimes excellent" and a "premier location" "within walking distance" of Nassau Street's "popular shops" are reasons to consider it for an "informal night out"; but "uneven service" causes some to dock it points.

Meemah | 23 | 10 | 18 | $19 |
Colonial Village Shopping Ctr., 9 Lincoln Hwy. (Parsonage Rd.), Edison, 732-906-2223
"Specials elevate the food out of its environment" at this "always packed" Malaysian-Chinese BYO in Edison; though it's "name means prettiness", the "decor lacks it", and "service can sometimes be spotty or snooty", but perhaps it's the "fantastic", "creative" dishes that mesmerize the masses.

Meil's ⌿ | 23 | 13 | 18 | $25 |
Bridge St. (Main St.), Stockton, 609-397-8033
"Like an upscale Alice's Restaurant of yore", this "friendly" Stockton BYO is a "great escape from everyday chain restaurants" and a "place to enjoy" "eclectic" American "gourmet comfort food"; do as locals do and go "when you want a big, wonderful, old-fashioned breakfast"; N.B. it's open for lunch and dinner too.

Mela | 19 | 15 | 16 | $26 |
47 E. Ridgewood Ave. (Chestnut St.), Ridgewood, 201-445-6060; www.melarestaurant.com
Ridgewoodites back their neighborhood BYO Indian by saying "it ain't your typical bowl of curry"; but since "the place looks tired" and the "lame" service "hinders enjoyment of the meal", it's no wonder minds are mixed: is it "consistently good" or "consistently disappointing"?

Mélange Cafe | 25 | 15 | 21 | $33 |
1601 Chapel Ave. (Rte. 38), Cherry Hill, 856-663-7339; www.melangecafe.com
There's a "loyal following" of this Cherry Hill "oasis", where chef Joe Brown "pulls off" a "sensational", "not-mainstream" menu that's a "true mélange" of Cajun and Italian; while the "change-of-pace" provisions please, some take umbrage with the "cramped" BYO's look, and conclude that a "makeover" would "make the whole experience enjoyable."

Melissa's Bistro | ▽ 21 | 15 | 20 | $37 |
9307 Ventnor Ave. (bet. Jefferson & Washington Aves.), Margate, 609-823-1414
"Almost an institution", this Margate Traditional American is "heavy on the seafood, and rightly so" given its nearby beach locale; expect to dine at a BYO with "yummy food", and "if you love Victoriana" and "funky decor", this "is your place"; so ignore those who call it "claustrophobic" or claim it "needs some updating" and put it "on your to-visit list."

| F | D | S | C |

Melting Pot, The   20 | 22 | 21 | $45
Galleria, 2 Bridge Ave. (W. Front St.), Red Bank, 732-219-0090
190 W. Main St. (Doughty Ave.), Somerville, 813-881-0055
250 Center Ave. (Westwood Ave.), Westwood, 201-664-8877
www.meltingpot.com

"All the fun of a '70s fondue party" means these hot-pot specialists are "great spots to hang with friends"; the "cook-it-yourself concept" works whether "you are a cheese, meat or chocolate lover" – though a vocal faction stew over prices and claim the place has "mastered how to make you run up the check."

Memphis Pig Out   19 | 12 | 17 | $25
67 First Ave. (Center Ave.), Atlantic Highlands, 732-291-5533

"Cheap and cheerful", this Atlantic Highlands 'cue specialist has "the best pulled pork in the 732 area code", not to mention "pig in more ways than you can imagine" – and that includes the "bizarre *pig*-abilia" slathering every inch of this rib-tickler that rubs some the wrong way.

Merion Inn, The   21 | 22 | 22 | $43
106 Decatur St. (Columbia Ave.), Cape May, 609-884-8363;
www.merioninn.com

"Feel like you're in the late 19th century" at this "quaint", "quintessentially Cape May" eatery with "dollhouse" decor and "just-right" service, and where surveyors "welcome the restaurant's effort" to update the "good" (albeit '50s country-clublike) American menu; a "soothing" bar with "live piano music", though, keeps it in the "traditional" class.

Meritage   22 | 23 | 20 | $46
1969 Hwy. 34 (Allaire Rd.), Wall, 732-974-5566;
www.meritagerestaurant.com

With a "happenin' bar", "elegant" dining room and (surprise!) a sushi area, this Wall New American seems to cover every base imaginable; oh, and it also has an "inventive" menu, a staff that "makes you feel like a star" and a "great after-work bar scene"; anything else?; yes, amped-up, "loud" live jazz on some nights.

Meson Madrid   18 | 12 | 15 | $34
343 Bergen Blvd. (Palisades Blvd.), Palisades Park,
201-947-1038; www.mesonmadridrestaurant.com

Denizens descend on this Iberian "treat" in Palisades Park for "generous portions of hearty fare"; though a "favorite", critics comment that there's neither bustle to the service ("when you're not in a rush, the staff isn't either") nor "charm" to the decor.

Metropolitan Cafe   21 | 20 | 19 | $39
8 E. Main St. (South St.), Freehold, 732-780-9400

It's "dark and swanky" and jam-packed with "beautiful people" trying to "hook up" at the bar of this Freehold

vote at zagat.com

F D S C

Asian-Eclectic that's as "close to NYC hip as you get" in this area; while the "imaginative" food's "on the pricey side", the reward is "a great night out" – just don't mind the "staff with attitude."

Metuchen Inn
23 | 21 | 19 | $48

424 Middlesex Ave. (Linden Ave.), Metuchen, 732-494-6444
You'll feel cosseted by the "cozy", "old-world atmosphere" at this Metuchen New American that's a "nice change from the local restaurant scene" thanks to "delicious" dishes, a "romantic environment" and "historic" (circa 1843) setting; surveyors, however, cite a disparity between the "creative" "gourmet" cooking and "amateurish" service.

Mexicali Rose
17 | 15 | 16 | $24

10 Park St. (Bloomfield Ave.), Montclair, 973-746-9005
"Screaming toddlers" don't stand a chance of being heard above the din at this "raucous" Montclair BYO serving "basic", "American-style" Mexican standards in a "kitschy" setting; it's a "good alternative" for kids "tired of ordering chicken fingers", but purists peg it as akin to "a chain restaurant in Iowa"; N.B. tote your tequila and they'll whip up a margarita for you.

Mexican Food Factory
21 | 15 | 16 | $24

601 Rte. 70 W. (Cropwell Rd.), Marlton, 856-983-9222
Voters vouch for this "popular", "reasonably priced" Marlton "roadside shack" where you'll find "*not*-assembly-line" Mexican eats (including "terrific fish specials"), Frida Kahlo reprints that "plaster the walls" and tequila "by the tons" at the bar.

Mexico Lindo
▽ 23 | – | 19 | $19

1135 Burnt Tavern Rd. (Sage St.), Brick, 732-202-1930
An "unexpected pleasure" awaits off the parkway via this BYO Mexican "treasure" in Brick that prepares "authentic", "authentically delicious" fare for just a few *pesos*; P.S. a recent "colorful" redecoration puts some "in the mood for a fiesta."

Mia Sorella
19 | 13 | 18 | $30

337 N. Main St. (Dukes Pkwy.), Manville, 908-595-1599;
www.miasorellaristorante.com
Supporters say this Manville Italian "deserves more credit" for its "good", "homestyle" cooking and "personable service"; it's "nothing special", note naysayers, and a picky pool of people add that they've "lost the incentive to go" since the place "stopped being a BYO."

Midori
25 | 16 | 21 | $30

Stanfield Commons Mall, 3130 Rte. 10 W. (bet. Franklin & Hill Rds.), Denville, 973-537-8588; www.midorirestaurant.com
There's "no better place" for "expertly prepared" sushi than at this Japanese in Denville, where "the photo-ready"

| F | D | S | C |

presentations on the plate are "spectacular" enough for all to appreciate; "try to ignore" the BYO's "diner" looks as you ponder a menu with "plenty of choices", advise advocates who give a nod to the "friendly" staff and "excellent value."

Mie Thai | 24 | 16 | 20 | $21 |
34 Main St. (Berry St.), Woodbridge, 732-596-9400; www.miethai.com

The digs may be "dull", but stalwarts shrug them off and state that this "delicious and affordable" Thai's "terrific" staff serves "the best food in Woodbridge"; the "fresh" specialties "pack a punch", and it's up to your taste buds whether this BYO's spices "require a fire truck" or merely register as "mild."

Mignon Steakhouse | 23 | 19 | 20 | $44 |
72 Park Ave. (Franklin Pl.), Rutherford, 201-896-0202

Slab lovers dig digging into "tender" hunks o' beef and "incredible sides" at "lower prices than the big-bucks", big-name places at this BYO steakhouse in Rutherford; there's an "NYC feel" to this "cozy" meat mecca, though fans confess they "wish no one else would find" it.

Mikado | 24 | 15 | 20 | $27 |
2320 Rte. 70 W. (S. Union Ave.), Cherry Hill, 856-665-4411
Mikado II ●
9210 Ventnor Ave. (S. Decatur Ave.), Margate, 609-822-4759

The "word is out" on these BYO Japanese sibs in Cherry Hill and Margate that present "lots of original roll combos", not to mention some of South Jersey's "freshest sushi" served by a "friendly" and "efficient" crew; no wonder that it's "fun for everyone", including raw-fish "newbies."

Mile Square, The | 16 | 16 | 15 | $25 |
221 Washington St. (bet. 2nd & 3rd Sts.), Hoboken, 201-420-0222; www.themilesquare.com

A "bar first, restaurant second", this American with a "big menu" "smack dab in the middle" of the action in Hoboken draws "a college crowd" and "the recently graduated" who toil in New York City; while "service leaves a lot to be desired", the "amazing beers on tap" keep the minions coming back for more.

Mill at Spring Lake Heights, The | 19 | 23 | 20 | $43 |
(fka Old Mill Inn)
101 Old Mill Rd. (Ocean Rd.), Spring Lake Heights, 732-449-1800; www.themillatslh.com

This Spring Lake Heights surf 'n' turf–centric American "on a picturesque lake complete with swans" is a "lovely spot" for a "special occasion"; though a "professional" staff and "impressive digs" do little for the disillusioned who dis "average" food at "inflated prices", it's still "a real asset to the community."

vote at zagat.com

| F | D | S | C |

Ming
| 24 | 22 | 19 | $32 |

Oak Tree Shopping Ctr., 1655-185 Oak Tree Rd. (bet. Grove & Wood Aves.), Edison, 732-549-5051; www.mingrestaurants.com
An "exotic combination of heavenly delights" makes this Asian BYO in Edison a "fantastic find" "like nothing else in the area", with fare that "borrows spices and flavors" from myriad Eastern cuisines; add a "tastefully decorated" interior and an "informative" staff, it's no wonder you may have to "wait too long" for a table.

Misto
∇ | 22 | 21 | 20 | $40 |

Village Walk Shopping Ctr., 1990 Rte. 70 E. (bet. Old Orchard & Springdale Rds.), Cherry Hill, 856-751-1711
Chef Alex Capasso (ex Max's Fine Dining) is running the kitchen show at this new "sleek, sophisticated" French-Italian BYO in Cherry Hill that's for those looking for "something a little out of the ordinary"; while it may be "too trendy" for the 'hood, fans say "it shines."

Mixx
| 23 | 24 | 19 | $42 |

Borgata Hotel, Casino & Spa, 1 Borgata Way (Atlantic City Expwy., exit 1), Atlantic City, 609-317-7249; www.theborgata.com
Big Apple vets Edwyn Ferrari and Aaron Sanchez (ex Nobu and Paladar, respectively) import a "terrific" Asian fusion mix to the Borgata's "sushi bar-cum-restaurant-cum nightclub" that's populated by "hot, young" types in a "cool", "cavernous" setting; sure, the service can be "slow", but that doesn't keep AC'ers from asserting "this is a very sexy" spot.

Moghul
| 24 | 19 | 20 | $30 |

Oak Tree Shopping Ctr., 1655-195 Oak Tree Rd. (bet. Grove & Wood Aves.), Edison, 732-549-5050
35 Morris St. (bet. Dumont & Spring Sts.), Morristown, 973-631-1100
www.moghul.com
"Fantastic discoveries of top-notch" dishes await at this pair of Indians in Edison and Morristown, where the "succulent" fare is "served with a smile"; loyalists laud the "exceptional curries", "best breads around" and "extensive" lunch buffet, and maintain the place is "unmatched outside of New Delhi"; N.B. Edison is BYO, while Morristown sports a full bar.

Mojave Grille
| 22 | 19 | 19 | $34 |

235 North Ave. (bet. Central & Elm Sts.), Westfield, 908-233-7772; www.mojavegrille.com
"Nouveau" Southwestern cooking "works well in Westfield" where cowpokes who crave the "absolutely yummy" seasonal food feel like they've "been transported" from the "suburbs to Santa Fe"; it's "dress-down fun", and the fact that it's BYO and the staff is "attentive" keep the partisans powwowing.

| F | D | S | C |

mojo   23 | 24 | 21 | $47
223 N. Washington Ave. (bet. Amherst & Monmouth Aves.), Margate, 609-487-0300; www.mojonj.com
Calling all beautiful, young things: report to this "hip" and oh-so-"trendy" eatery that's "*the* spot" in Margate for a menu of "excellent" Eclectic dishes, a "mojito and martini list that's a menu in itself", and, as you probably figured, an "ultra-cool atmo"; P.S. "romantics" may find that the "funky", "islands-meets-NYC" decor casts a spell.

Molly Pitcher Inn   22 | 25 | 22 | $45
Molly Pitcher Inn, 88 Riverside Ave. (W. Front St.), Red Bank, 732-747-2500; www.mollypitcher-oysterpoint.com
"A special day place" with a "fantastic brunch", Red Bank's "luxurious" New American overlooks the Navesink – and "the river is all the decor this place needs"; "treat out-of-towners", but don't forget this "quiet, subdued" historic inn with "right-on" service is "a Shore tradition with mom."

Moon Street   14 | 13 | 16 | $25
11 N. Dean St. (Palisade Ave.), Englewood, 201-541-0086
There's "nothing to write home about" at "family-central" in Englewood, a Traditional American whose "*un*-feng shui'd" digs feature "comfy banquettes that can hide a gaggle of boisterous kids"; critics see the sun setting on a place with "uneven service" and claim the menu, though "ok", still "needs an overhaul."

MOONSTRUCK   24 | 25 | 22 | $45
517 Lake Ave. (bet. Main St. & Ocean Ave.), Asbury Park, 732-988-0123; www.moonstrucknj.com
Diners are "awestruck" by this "beautiful" "superstar" in Asbury Park, a "high-class" Mediterranean with "superb" fare and a "romantic" vibe – even "on a Saturday night", when it's as "busy as a cruise ship dining room"; "the light-footed staff stays afloat", a fine feat amid hosts who can be "standoffish" and patrons who may be miffed about the no-reservations policy.

Morton's, The Steakhouse   24 | 22 | 23 | $59
Riverside Square Mall, 274 Riverside Sq. (Hackensack Ave.), Hackensack, 201-487-1303; www.mortons.com
Carnivores wish their "cholesterol counts were lower" and the number "of dollars" in their "wallets higher" so they could eat at this Hackensack outpost of a national chain "at least once a week"; the "terrific" cuts are backed by an "exceptional" wine list and a staff that "treats you like royalty."

M-R Chefs Café   – | – | – | M
526 Main St. (Sylvania Ave.), Avon-by-the-Sea, 732-774-4200
The ever-changing menu keeps regulars intrigued at this warm-toned seasonal New American BYO in Avon-by-the-

vote at zagat.com

F | D | S | C

Sea that's decidedly un-glitzy but bold in its interpretations of both classics and more trendy temptations; the husband-and-wife team in charge keeps things charming.

Mr. Chu 20 | 13 | 18 | $23
44 Rte. 10 W. (Ridgedale Ave.), East Hanover, 973-887-7555
"High-quality ingredients" highlight dishes from the "simple to the exotic" at this BYO that's a "little bit of Chinatown in East Hanover"; though the "staff can be a bit brusque", at least "you'll get a smile" from the host – which may or may not make up for quarters that "could use some sprucing up."

Mud City Crab House 25 | 14 | 19 | $26
1185 E. Bay Ave. (Rte. 72 E.), Manahawkin, 609-978-3660
Folks "elbow-deep" in crabs "smash and bash" their way through a meal here at this seasonal Manahawkin BYO, a "family fave" that's "a must on the mainland" (it's minutes inland from LBI); expect "a big line in the summer", an "amiable" floor crew and "appropriately low-rent" setup.

Mustache Bill's Diner ⊄ – | – | – | I
Broadway & Eighth St. (Central Ave.), Barnegat Light, 609-494-0155
To devotees, this diner in Barnegat Light is the "best bang for your buck on Long Beach Island"; it's more than just "a great place for coffee after a morning of fishing", say locals who tout fat sandwiches of fried fish caught by customers and are proud to call it their "hangout" for breakfast "the way it's supposed to be."

Nag's Head ⊄ ∇ 24 | 15 | 16 | $23
801 Asbury Ave. (8th St.), Ocean City, 609-391-9080
"A great seashore delight", this "tiny" place in the heart of Ocean City's shopping district is an "unbelievable value", offering "creative" American dishes made with the "freshest ingredients"; open year-round, it's become a "repeat occurrence" for many, despite "unimpressive" looks and "crowded" conditions in high season; N.B. this Shore burg's a dry town.

Namaskaar 20 | 16 | 17 | $31
The Shops at IV, 275 Rte. 4 W. (Johnson Ave.), Paramus, 201-342-8868; www.namaskaar.com
"If you miss India, come here", boast boosters of this Paramus Indian whose "good" (albeit "unadventurous") menu includes "lots of vegetarian options"; most forgive the "spartan" appearance and head straight for the "first-rate", "reasonably priced" lunch buffet.

Nanni Ristorante 24 | 20 | 25 | $51
53 W. Passaic St. (Rte. 17 N.), Rochelle Park, 201-843-1250; www.nanni.com
"Perfect service" from a "tuxedoed" staff and "top-notch" food prompt partisans to profess that this "classy" Rochelle

| F | D | S | C |

Park Italian's "a cut above the rest"; but before you come for that "special-occasion feast", "rent or borrow a BMW or Mercedes", since you may see some of the "old-timer customers" arrive in one.

Napa Valley Grille | 22 | 22 | 20 | $42 |
Garden State Plaza, 1146 Garden State Plaza (Rtes. 4 & 17), Paramus, 201-845-5555; www.napavalleygrille.com
Add some sunshine to your shopping day by "skipping the food court" in favor of a "California dining experience" in a Paramus shopping mall; "eat, drink and be merry", for its virtues include "wonderful" New American fare and a "fantastic" 400-label Golden State–strong wine list; since the "staff doesn't hurry guests", many count on it when seeking a "civilized" setting.

NAUVOO GRILL CLUB | 16 | 27 | 16 | $38 |
121 Fair Haven Rd. (River Rd.), Fair Haven, 732-747-8777
The "elegant", "ski lodge"-like design (think "Aspen" meets "Frank Lloyd Wright") is a "delight" at this New American in Fair Haven that's a bastion of "yuppies who come to suburbia" looking for "everything from burgers" to a "great bar scene"; while the decor attains the heights of "grandeur", it's a slippery slope from there on – from "disappointing" food to "ill-prepared" service.

Navesink Fishery | 23 | 9 | 16 | $32 |
A&P Shopping Ctr., 1004 Rte. 36 S. (Valley Dr.), Middletown, 732-291-8017
Though it may "not be big on atmosphere", supporters say of this BYO Middletown seafooder that it's a "local treasure", and its "quirky thrift-shop decor" cannot detract from the "fresh", "well-prepared" fare; so be prepared for "long, chaotic waits" and remember: "for the dollar, it can't be beat."

Neelam | 19 | 13 | 17 | $23 |
Village Mall, 1178 Rte. 35 (New Monmouth Rd.), Middletown, 732-671-8900
115 South Orange Ave. (Irvington Ave.), South Orange, 973-762-1100
These suburban BYOs serve a "decent selection" of Indian dishes in "Moghul-baroque" settings that some say may "need a freshening up" – though regulars don't spend much time absorbing the digs since the duo's "take-out business seems to overshadow" the eat-in trade; expect "fairly standard" stuff, though their lunch buffets will leave you "happily stuffed."

Nero's Grille | 16 | 15 | 17 | $41 |
618 S. Livingston Ave. (Hobart Gap Rd.), Livingston, 973-994-1410; www.neros.com
"A fixture in the area for years", this stuccoed steakhouse is "a neighborhood hangout" of the "Livingston social set"

vote at zagat.com

| F | D | S | C |

"who want to be seen"; they also go since "the most generously sized drinks on the East Coast" might ease the pain of "the high bill" and "erratic service", especially since the "menu needs an uplift" and the interior an "update."

New Main Taste Thai | 23 | 15 | 18 | $32 |
225 Main St. (bet. Hillside & S. Passaic Aves.), Chatham, 973-635-7333
"Everything seems made-from-scratch perfect" at this "quiet" Thai BYO in Chatham, where your "patience" with sometimes "slow" service is "rewarded" with "distinct", "exciting" cooking that "pleases both the eye and palate"; even acolytes admit, though, that the place could use a "fresh ambiance."

Nha Tranh Place | ∇ 21 | 7 | 13 | $17 |
(fka Pho Thanh Hoai)
249 Newark Ave. (bet. Cole & 2nd Sts.), Jersey City, 201-239-1988
Get ready for "incredible food at prices that are hard to believe" at this "gem" in Jersey City that's the closest you may come to finding "amazingly" "authentic Vietnamese"; yes, it's "off the beaten path", but since it's "usually packed on weekends" and "not too pretty", you may want to "get takeout and gorge in the privacy of your own home."

NICHOLAS | 28 | 24 | 28 | $79 |
160 Rte. 35 S. (bet. Navesink River Rd. & Pine St.), Middletown, 732-345-9977; www.restaurantnicholas.com
Though the setting is "sophisticated" and "calm", the "tasting menu delivers a roller-coaster" ride "for the taste buds" at Melissa and Nicholas Harary's "spectacular" Middletown New American (No. 1 for Food and Service in this *Survey*); you may have to "mortgage the Shore house" to experience its "culinary masterpieces", but it's a "place to celebrate" offering a "Mercedes meal" complete with an "impeccable", "unobtrusive" staff: just call it "perfect."

Niecy's | ∇ 18 | 15 | 16 | $26 |
65B South Orange Ave. (Valley St.), South Orange, 973-275-1770
"Come hungry" and dig in to "down-home cooking" at this Southern BYO in South Orange with a "charming owner" who "comes to the table" to ensure all that "comfort food" goes down just right; N.B. a recent post-*Survey* move to new digs has this veteran in transition and locals hoping that it becomes full service soon.

Nikko | 22 | 15 | 20 | $35 |
881 Rte. 10 E. (Rte. 287), Whippany, 973-428-0787; www.nikkonj.com
"Check out the rolls and the daily specials" at this Whippany Japanese with "dependably delicious" sushi and "really friendly service" that almost make up for an "aging"

| | | | F | D | S | C |

Ninety Grand Grille   24 | 23 | 22 | $53
90 Grand Ave. (Palisade Ave.), Englewood, 201-568-5959; www.90grandgrille.com
You'll "feel like a million bucks" at this "upscale" New American "hot spot" in Englewood that acolytes avow is "head and shoulders above all competition in the area"; the place can "get loud", but little can drown out a host of "dazzling choices" on the menu that help make for a "fantastic experience" – though one that feels like it costs "90 grand."

Nobi   ▽ 22 | 13 | 19 | $27
T.J. Maxx Plaza, 1338 Hooper Ave. (Rte. 37), Dover Township, 732-244-7888
Notwithstanding the strip-mall, "no-atmosphere" digs, Ocean County locals swarm this BYO for sushi that's "fresh", "inventive" and offered at "decent prices", and for cooked items such as "light, crispy" tempura; add "friendly" service that makes raw-fish fanatics feel like they're "with family", and it's little wonder that you'll find it "always crowded."

No. 9   25 | 15 | 21 | $38
9 Klines Ct. (Bridge St.), Lambertville, 609-397-6380
A "diamond" in Lambertville, the smitten say this BYO makes up for its "lack of space" and "average decor" with "marvelous" New American food that "never disappoints" and an "attentive" staff; if you want to compliment chef-owner Matthew Kane, however, you'll have to speak over the "din."

Noodle House, The   ▽ 19 | 21 | 18 | $24
2313 Rte. 1 S. (bet. Aaron Rd. & Commerce Blvd.), North Brunswick, 732-951-0141
There's "nothing bland except the name" at this North Brunswick BYO that presents "unique" Asian fusion fare in a "contemporary", "vibrant" setting that includes lots of "cloths, candles and plants"; place your order on "notepads" and the "attentive" crew will bring "a wide variety of noodles" to your table, then top off your time with one of the "great teas."

Norma's Middle Eastern   21 | 11 | 18 | $19
Barclay Farms Shopping Ctr., 132-145 Rte. 70 E. (Kings Hwy.), Cherry Hill, 856-795-1373
"Have a feast for only a few bucks" at this "authentic" Middle Easterner in a Cherry Hill strip mall; the decor may be "modest", but the food is "delicious" and the back room "romantic", and if you "go with a group" you can chatter about the "entertaining" dancing (yes, belly dancing, but only on weekends).

| F | D | S | C |

Northstar Café   20 | 19 | 18 | $39
25 Liberty St. (bet. George & Neilson Sts.), New Brunswick, 732-846-0700 ☻
Zimmerli Museum, 71 Hamilton St. (George St.), New Brunswick, 732-246-3071
Expect a "trendy scene" at this New Brunswick Med, a small-plate specialist serving "tasty" "American-style" tapas to a pre- and post-theater crowd in "intimate" digs; even though the high-minded feel it's "not good enough to break into the elite", the "great" wine list and "lively" live jazz (weekends) help make it a "favorite"; N.B. there's a limited-menu offshoot in the nearby Zimmerli Museum.

Nova Terra   22 | 23 | 21 | $40
78 Albany St. (Neilson St.), New Brunswick, 732-296-1600; www.terramomo.com
"Not a place for quiet conversation", this "stylish, upbeat" Nuevo Latino in New Brunswick with "lots of energy" is a "place for post-grads" to go for "unique" food and "yummy" drinks; recently renovated and overall "much improved", its added attractions include "spicy" live music on weekends to shake your bon-bons to and a staff that's "easy on the eyes."

Nunzio Ristorante Rustico   24 | 24 | 20 | $36
706 Haddon Ave. (Collings Ave.), Collingswood, 856-858-9840; www.nunzioristoranterustico.com
Philly import Nunzio Patruno is "leading the Collingswood revival" with his Italian arrival showcasing "simple", "well-done" dishes ferried by a staff that's "more than helpful" in decor reminiscent of a "Tuscan courtyard"; so "reserve well in advance" for an experience "a cut above the typical South Jersey" homage to the red, white and green.

Nusantara   ∇ 17 | 15 | 18 | $26
Powder Mill Plaza, 2920 Rte. 10 W. (bet. Parks & Powder Mill Rds.), Morris Plains, 973-889-1608; www.nusantararestaurant.com
An "overlooked gem hidden in a strip mall", this Indonesian-Malaysian in Morris Plains puts a "twist" on Asian cuisine and strikes some as a "real find" "for the money"; and where fans find inspiration in touches such as the "solid wood" appointments, detractors are deflated by its "ordinary" food.

Ocino   – | – | – | M
289 Rte. 31 S. (bet. Rymon & Springtown Rds.), Washington, 908-689-9400; www.ocinorestaurant.com
Impressing folks in Warren County is this Italian set in a dramatic wood-accented space anchored by a grand fieldstone fireplace, where chef Brian Spagnola turns out brick-oven pizzas for the after-soccer crowd and grilled steaks for couples lingering over a bottle of Barbera; N.B. at press time, owners Gloria and Carl LaGrassa were putting the finishing touches on their second restaurant, the posh Pluckemin Inn, in Bedminster.

| F | D | S | C |

Oddfellows Rest Louisiana Bar & Restaurant
20 | 17 | 18 | $26

80 River St. (bet. Hudson Pl. & Newark St.), Hoboken, 201-656-9009
111 Montgomery St. (Warren St.), Jersey City, 201-433-6999
www.oddfellowsrest.com

There's a "taste of old N'Awlins" at these "affordable" Cajun-Creoles where it's "noisy" from "folks having fun" – especially "frat boys" (Hoboken) and "happy workers" (both spots) who "shoot some pool and eat some awesome Southern-style catfish"; while the fare's "good", critics caution it's not "knockout"-quality stuff.

Old Bay, The ⓩ
18 | 17 | 17 | $32

61-63 Church St. (Neilson St.), New Brunswick, 732-246-3111;
www.oldbay.com

If you "crave a little Southern charm from the bayou", scope out this Cajun-Creole with "an extensive menu of microbrews" "in the middle of New Brunswick"; regulars reveal that the "pub grub" is a "worthy accompaniment" to the "festive and lively" scene that comes complete with "live" rock or jazz on weekends, while others bay at "shortcomings in the kitchen and service."

Olde Corner Deli
– | – | – | M

22 Central Ave. (Ocean Ave.), Island Heights, 732-288-9098

Step from the nondescript deli into the adjacent dining room and you'll find the most knowledgeable foodies in Ocean County delighting over chef-owner Greg Manning's (ex Jeffrey's) soulful New American fare at his beloved BYO, where the menu's short but sweet and the desserts well-traveled classics; N.B. limited hours means it may be best to call ahead.

Old Homestead
24 | 25 | 23 | $68

Borgata Hotel, Casino & Spa, 1 Borgata Way (Atlantic City Expwy., exit 1), Atlantic City, 866-692-6742; www.theborgata.com

"Beef is what it's all about" at this NYC import in the heart of the Borgata where "if you can afford the Kobe beef", you may have "one of the best meals of your life"; "*Flintstone-size portions*" of steak and an "extensive and expensive" single-malt scotch menu (not to mention a 400-bottle vino list) lure diners "from the loud gaming floor" into a "fabulous", bi-level setting.

Old Man Rafferty's
18 | 16 | 17 | $25

284 Rte. 206 (Triangle Rd.), Hillsborough, 908-904-9731
106 Albany St. (George St.), New Brunswick, 732-846-6153
www.oldmanraffertys.com

These Americans in Hillsborough (with "more of a family atmosphere") and New Brunswick ("a favorite for Rutgers' folks and execs alike") offer "diverse menus" that allow diners to "keep to a budget or splurge"; "skip the amazing

vote at zagat.com

array of cheesecake choices" and "you deserve to have your taste buds divorce you" dare the denizens devoted to the ol' gals' "nothing fancy" persona.

Olive
18 | 21 | 17 | $32

Short Hills Farm, 482 Evesham Rd. (bet. Rtes. 73 & 561), Cherry Hill, 856-428-4999; www.olive-restaurant.com

A "nice, subdued" "upscale hangout" for the "yuppie and Gen-X crowd", this Cherry Hill Med-American is "perfect for after-work or dinner with friends" – especially with an upstairs bar and dance floor at the ready; though the fare's "better than expected", it's made a tad "less appealing" by the "young staff that's more eager to mingle than serve."

Ombra
24 | 26 | 23 | $50

Borgata Hotel, Casino & Spa, 1 Borgata Way (Atlantic City Expwy., exit 1), Atlantic City, 866-692-6742; www.theborgata.com

"Don't be surprised" if you spot "superstars from sports and entertainment" tuning into chef Luke Palladino's "marvelous" cooking at this "classy", "grottolike" Italian in the Borgata; the "unique" decor makes you "feel like you're in a cellar" since "bottles surround you" (literally), so try a "terrific" wine flight paired with a "nice cheese selection" – and try not to take umbrage at the "high" tabs.

Onieal's
19 | 17 | 18 | $27

343 Park Ave. (4th St.), Hoboken, 201-653-1492; www.oniealshoboken.com

Couples on a date may appreciate that this "lively" Hoboken pub doubles as an "intimate" New American eatery sporting an "unlikely" "white-tablecloth" menu supplemented by "nightly specials" that are, insiders insist, "the way to go."

Opa Bar & Grille ●
∇ 19 | 19 | 18 | $31

1743 Boardwalk (Indiana Ave.), Atlantic City, 609-344-0094; www.opa1.com

This "jewel" right on Atlantic City's Boardwalk offers a "real touch of Greece" – and not just because it sports a "great view of the ocean": indeed, those seeking something authentic go and "enjoy a fine meal and some wine", not to mention conversations with "flying plates" in a rare "outside of casino" setting.

Opah Grille
24 | 22 | 22 | $45

12 Lackawanna Ave. (Main St.), Gladstone, 908-781-1888; www.opahgrille.com

Reviewers are emphatic about this seafood specialist "tucked away" in Gladstone, a "hidden treasure" where "new fish" preparations are "discovered" daily; it may be "landlocked", but the "creative" dishes, "impeccable" service and "casual", "comfortable" surroundings ("ask to sit in the aquarium room") prompt a plethora of piscatorians to "feel the sea breeze."

| F | D | S | C |

Orbis Bistro
20 | 14 | 17 | $40

128 Watchung Ave. (N. Fullerton Ave.), Upper Montclair, 973-746-7641; www.orbisbistro.com

Upper Montclair is home to this "interesting little boutique" BYO with a "rotating menu" of "delicious" New American fare bolstered by a "great variety of specials" incorporating the "freshest ingredients"; it's the orbit of chef-owner Nancy Caballes, but even her talent "doesn't trump the need for a little interior design" or help a "wait staff that can be overwhelmed."

ORIGIN
27 | 20 | 20 | $34

10 South St. (Morris St.), Morristown, 973-971-9933
25 Division St. (Main St.), Somerville, 908-685-1344
www.originthai.com

You may ask yourself if "the flavors are from France, Thailand or heaven"? admit those awed by these paeans to fusion fare in Morristown (the new sibling) and Somerville (the older, but recently expanded original); no matter, exult those who dub these BYOs "a delight for all five senses" and a "true adventure in eating", and even if the crowds often "overwhelm" the staff, diners are "transported by the first bite."

Orleans
∇ 19 | 19 | 18 | $38

128 Bay Ave. (bet. Cornwall & Jackson Sts.), Highlands, 732-872-2400

Don't be surprised if "you think you're in the Big Easy" "the second you walk in" and find "a great liquor selection at the bar" and "inventive Creole cuisine" courtesy of chef-owner Michael Duplantis; "nice touches throughout" lend a "cool, jazzy" tone to this Highlands spot that "should be more popular than it is", but may be "pricey" for what it is.

Osteria Dante
19 | 17 | 17 | $39

91 Broad St. (Linden Pl.), Red Bank, 732-530-0602; www.osteriadante.com

Converts of this BYO in Red Bank claim the brick-walled Italian is an "enjoyable" detour if in town, with an "authentic", "very good" lineup of eats; lamentably, though it "started out with a bang", a vocal minority, however, has turned on it, moaning that the "sour" service has "driven" them away.

Ota-Ya
24 | 14 | 20 | $31

21 Ferry St. (S. Union St.), Lambertville, 609-397-9228; www.ota-ya.com

The lucky in Lambertville know this Japanese BYO's "spicy tuna roll is uniquely delicious" and the "very fresh sushi" is "artistically presented"; since it's the "only game in town", you'll frequently see "a crowd" of raw-fish fans lined up outside despite what is seen as "trapped-in-the-'80s" decor on the inside.

vote at zagat.com

Pacific Grille | 22 | 15 | 19 | $30 |

Village II Shoppes, 1200 S. Church St. (Academy Dr.), Mount Laurel, 856-778-0909; www.pacificgrill.com

"An underrated find" in Mount Laurel is this "strip-mall" Pacific Rim–accented American with a "wide variety" of "delicious" items that are both "healthy" and "attractive"; the floor crew "aims to please", and many seem to have taken a shine to the BYO's "eclectic", if not "wacky", setting.

Pad Thai | 23 | 11 | 18 | $20 |

217 Raritan Ave. (bet. 2nd & 3rd Aves.), Highland Park, 732-247-9636; www.pad-thai.com

Bring your own firehose to this Thai "gem" in Highland Park, where the "spiciness" quotient on dishes is through "the roof" (of your *mouth*, that is) and where it might be wise to "order mild" "if you cherish your taste buds"; though "better than its competitors", fans hope renovations relieve the "claustrophobic", "cramped" interior.

Palazzo | 20 | 21 | 19 | $36 |

11 S. Fullerton Ave. (Bloomfield Ave.), Montclair, 973-746-6778; www.palazzonj.com

Expect cuisine that's "more imaginative than your typical Italian" laud locals who land at this "charmer" in Montclair that's decked out in an "inviting" "blue-and-yellow" motif; sporting a list of NJ wines, it's also "worth remembering" you can BYO vino and catch "live jazz" some nights.

Palm, The | - | - | - | E |

The Quarter at the Tropicana, 2801 N. Pacific Ave. (Iowa Ave.), Atlantic City, 609-344-7256; www.thepalm.com

Putting its carnivorous imprimatur on the Tropicana's brand-new, Old Havana–themed complex, The Quarter, this legendary heavyweight of a national chain brings its tried-and-true signatures to Atlantic City – steaks, chops and lobsters scaled-up to feed outsize appetites – amid dining rooms embellished with celebrity caricatures; look out for the A-list crowd of regulars that you may be seated next to.

Pamir | 22 | 16 | 18 | $28 |

85 Washington St. (bet. Cobb Pl. & Phoenix Ave.), Morristown, 973-605-1095; www.pamirrestaurant.com

The "flavorful" fare bodes well in this "quirkily decorated" Afghan BYO in Morristown "near the courthouse" and, as a result, is "pretty busy during lunch"; reviewers rave there are "no other" in its class (and, incidentally, no others of its kind around).

Panevino | 17 | 16 | 17 | $28 |

637 W. Mt. Pleasant Ave. (bet. Okner Pkwy. & River Rd.), Livingston, 973-535-6160; www.restaurantassociates.com

"Popular with families", this Livingston Italian with "good" and "plentiful" "Tuscan-style" food is "at its best on sunny

| F | D | S | C |

days" when you can dine alfresco or in the "airy" confines of its dining room; for a vocal minority, however, the experience proves a bit too "deafening" and merely "pedestrian."

Panico's 23 | 22 | 24 | $53
103 Church St. (Neilson St.), New Brunswick, 732-545-6100; www.panicosrestaurant.com
"Filled with fine old regulars" ("see if you can spot the J&J executives"), this "high-end" New Brunswick Italian with "excellent" food features "polished service", "subdued lighting" and a "quiet bar"; take some green, since it's ripe for a "splurge night out", but if your boss isn't picking up your tab, you may see red.

Paramount Steakhouse – | – | – | E
(fka Paramount Restaurant, The)
130 Main St. (Parker Ave.), Manasquan, 732-223-2581
Recently rehabbed from a diner-style Downtown eatery to a serene dining space, this Manasquan American BYO now sports a lineup of steaks to tempt locals into its storefront; expect to find hunky meats, including a portly porterhouse studded with blue cheese, and an eager-beaver floor crew keeping watch.

Park, The 22 | 19 | 20 | $51
151 Kinderkamack Rd. (bet. Grand & Park Aves.), Park Ridge, 201-930-1300; www.theparksteakhouse.com
"Dreamworld" for carnivores, this Park Ridge steakhouse serves up a "deliciously" beefy, "creative" menu that includes surf even loyalists "love"; though naysayers nix "NYC prices without the goods" to back them up, supporters sense "tremendous strides" on all fronts.

PARK & ORCHARD 23 | 14 | 19 | $36
240 Hackensack St. (Union Ave. W.), East Rutherford, 201-939-9292; www.parkandorchard.com
This "healthy and heavenly" East Rutherford Eclectic "crowd-pleaser" that's known as "one of the best places for innovative comfort food" around also allows you to "stop your wine magazine subscriptions", since a review of the "extraordinary" and utterly "reasonably priced" 2,400-label list can educate even the most committed vino geek; the modern warehouse look, though, "could use" a "touch-up."

Passage to India 24 | 19 | 20 | $28
Lawrence Shopping Ctr., 2495 Brunswick Pike/Rte. 1 (Texas Ave.), Lawrenceville, 609-637-0800
Step into this "peaceful" Lawrenceville Indian whose "bright colors" enliven the dining room and where its "wonderful" food (check out the "really good" buffet) "served in copper pots" adds to an "authentic" air; and given the "friendly", "efficient" staff, it's no wonder it's seen as a "destination."

vote at zagat.com

| F | D | S | C |

Pasta Fresca Café   23 | 14 | 16 | $27
The Grove, 637 Rte. 35 (Shadow Brook Rd.), Shrewsbury, 732-747-5616
While daytime types dub this BYO a "great place to grab a bite while shopping at The Grove" in Shrewsbury, those who wish to "avoid the carriage parade of babies" know to "go at night for serenity"; no matter the time of day, there's "fresh", "seasonal" New American fare to be had, though the "uncomfortable chairs" and "austere atmosphere" prompt the picky to "get it to go."

Pastels   20 | 18 | 18 | $37
119 Franklin Tpke. (bet. Cedar Hill Ave. & Stephens Ln.), Mahwah, 201-529-1700
"Wait to hear the specials" implore surveyors who swear by the "imaginative food" at this "strip-mall" New American BYO; there's "not much else in Mahwah", but at least it's "interesting" to dine amid decor (featuring "large plastic vegetables" hanging from the ceiling) that's "quirky" to some and "'80s" "cheese" to others.

Pearl of the Sea   ∇ 22 | 13 | 19 | $28
46 S. Broadway (Ocean Ave.), Long Branch, 732-263-1050
Smitten surveyors say this Iberian might be the "best-kept secret in Long Branch", a pearl in the Ocean Place Hilton parking lot that's "as Portuguese as you can get"; fans focus on "garlic prawns that can't be beat" and an "awesome" tandem – sangria and a "helpful" staff.

Pelican Club   22 | 23 | 21 | $47
Marquis de Lafayette Hotel, 501 Beach Ave. (bet. Decatur St. & Ocean Ave.), Cape May, 609-884-3995; www.pelicanclubcapemay.com
"Reserve in advance" advise those swooning over this Cape May New American whose enviable perch on the sixth floor of the Marquis de Lafayette affords diners a "spectacular ocean vista"; "more relaxed" than its sister, The Washington Inn, it's considered by many to be "a parent's dream" for "great wine", "interesting" food and a "kid-friendly atmosphere"; N.B. open Fridays and Saturdays in winter, and every day in summer.

Penang   20 | 15 | 14 | $23
200 Rte. 10 W. (River Rd.), East Hanover, 973-887-6989
505 Old Post Rd. (bet. Rte. 1 & Vineyard Rd.), Edison, 732-287-3038
Nassau Park Pavilion, 635 Nassau Park Blvd. (Brunswick Pike/Rte. 1 S.), West Windsor, 609-897-9088
"Tasty" Malaysian with a side of Thai keeps this "holy trinity" in East Hanover, Edison and West Windsor "always hustling and bustling" with a "clientele that goes for the real deal"; the BYOs are a "culinary adventure" so even if the service might be a little "gruff", the "cheap" eats leave only a handful "staying home."

| F | D | S | C |

PERRYVILLE INN 26 | 24 | 24 | $52
167 Perryville Rd. (I-78, exit 12), Union Township, 908-730-9500; www.theperryvilleinn.com
"A country classic" in Hunterdon County is this "perfect getaway" in a "historic" 1813 Colonial building where "consistently" "well-executed and creative" New American fare courtesy of chef-owner Paul Ingenito "hits a homer"; it makes for an "exquisitely romantic" dinner, prompting partisans to brag it's a "find off Route 78."

Peter Shields Inn 24 | 26 | 24 | $50
1301 Beach Dr. (Trenton Ave.), Cape May, 609-884-9090; www.petershieldsinn.com
Sit back and "enjoy being pampered" (and take in the "cool breezes" on the veranda) at this "absolute delight" in Cape May set in a "spectacular oceanfront" Georgian Revival mansion, where the "top-notch" New American cuisine and "superlative service" make it a "hands-down favorite at the Shore"; N.B. though it's BYO, the restaurant offers a short selection of Garden State wines.

P.F. Chang's China Bistro 22 | 22 | 20 | $28
The Quarter at the Tropicana, 2801 N. Pacific Ave. #101 (Iowa Ave.), Atlantic City, 609-348-4600 ●
Promenade at Sagemore, 500 Rte. 73 (Rte. 70), Marlton, 856-396-0818
10 Port Imperial Blvd. (Halfmoon Ct.), West New York, 201-866-7790
www.pfchangs.com
"Chain dining at its best" brings plaudits to this "high-decibel" Asian trio whose "delicious" food and "reasonable prices" ensure that fans leave "shaking heads" and "wondering how they pull it off"; the few who quip about "Americanized" "fast food in disguise" are overruled.

Pheasants Landing 19 | 18 | 19 | $35
311 Amwell Rd. (Willow Rd.), Hillsborough, 908-281-1288; www.pheasantslanding.com
There's a Continental smorgasbord of favorites at Heinz Keller's "unpretentious" "find" in Hillsborough where chef Andrea Gross cooks "hearty", "authentic" Austrian, German and Swiss specialties; others opt to settle into the more casual downstairs pub featuring weekend live music.

Pierre's 23 | 23 | 22 | $44
995 Mt. Kemble Ave. (bet. N. Maple Ave. & Tempewick Rd.), Morristown, 973-425-1212; www.pierresbistro.com
It's "packed for a reason" boast those who frequent Michael Peter's bistro in Morristown and find it "as close to dining in a French country inn as you can get" in Jersey; expect "terrific" food, an "intelligently edited" wine list, service that's "deferential", and what's more, you'll "dine like an emperor for a pittance" at the $13.95 lunch buffet.

vote at zagat.com

| F | D | S | C |

Pietro's Coal Oven Pizzeria   18 | 15 | 16 | $23
140 Rte. 70 W. (Rte. 73), Marlton, 856-596-5500;
www.pietrospizza.com
"Portions are large, so bring your appetite" – and the kids – to this "family-style" pizza joint in Marlton that's "always crowded and loud"; though the service "needs improvement", as long as you like a "thin-crust" pie, "it's worth a visit if you're nearby."

Pilot House   17 | 22 | 17 | $32
799 Rte. 70 (bet. Brick Blvd. & Rte. 88), Brick, 732-920-8900;
www.pilothouserestaurant.com
Frequented by the "boating crowd", this Brick American is the kind of place where "you'll feel like you're on vacation in a seaport town"; though the service may be "slow", and the fare drifts from "excellent" to "standard", its "edge-of-marina" locale on the Metedeconk River helps make it a "fabulous place to take someone out for a birthday."

Pine Tavern   21 | 14 | 19 | $34
151 Rte. 34 (Cottrell Rd.), Old Bridge, 732-727-5060;
www.pinetavern.net
"Knotty pine paneling" and "un-stylish booths" belie other things in store at this Asian-influenced New American in Old Bridge, where the "delicious" food and "knowledgeable" crew "pleasantly surprise" first-timers; old-timers here know you "better make reservations" or be prepared to wait at "the tightly packed bar"; N.B. listen to live blues and jazz on weekends.

Plantation   20 | 22 | 19 | $40
7908 Long Beach Blvd. (80th St.), Harvey Cedars, 609-494-8191;
www.plantationrestaurant.com
You'll think you're "in the Hamptons" at this "island"-like "getaway" in Harvey Cedars with an "innovative" New American selection offering an "escape" from "traditional summer Shore fare", and where "happy hour is a must-do"; fans state with confidence "this one should last."

Ponzio's ◐   17 | 11 | 17 | $20
7 Rte. 70 W. (Kings Hwy.), Cherry Hill, 856-428-4808;
www.ponzios.com
"The Le Bec Fin of South Jersey diners" is this Cherry Hill staple where "local movers and shakers meet" over "a power breakfast" or anything from the bakery; "if you believe more is more, this is your place" say skeptics who know not to let anything labeled 'small' on the "endless" menu fool 'em; though "typical", it's still "the benchmark."

Portobello   19 | 17 | 17 | $35
155 Ramapo Valley Rd. (Long Hill Rd.), Oakland, 201-337-8990
There's likely "something for everyone" given that the "daily specials" augment an already "huge menu" filled with

| F | D | S | C |

"good" stuff at this Oakland Italian; though critics quibble about "inconsistent" service and the "Italianate" backdrop that "leaves something to be desired", others muse that at least prices are "low."

Portofino's

| 18 | 12 | 17 | $26 |

29 Mills St. (Washington St.), Morristown, 973-540-0026;
www.portofinosrestaurant.com

"Cheap" dates take note: though the digs at this "red-sauce" BYO are "nothing to write home about" and detractors declare the place "no big deal", you'll realize that the "laughter in the air" may be a result of this Italian's "solid" food and "reasonable prices" that keep it a "favorite."

Porto Leggero

| – | – | – | E |

Harborside Financial Plaza 5 (Pearl St.), Jersey City, 201-434-3200;
www.portoleggero.net

The Scalini Fedeli team (Cetrulo, Marandola and Stella) has unveiled this ambitious, heralded new destination in Jersey City whose colorful, spirited modern-meets-medieval setting provides a stark contrast to the cool glass and steel towers that surround it; expect to navigate an Italian menu that's evenly divided between traditional dishes and those offerings pointing toward a slightly-more-adventurous spectrum.

Portuguese Manor

| 21 | 14 | 19 | $30 |

310 Elm St. (bet. Fayette & Smith Sts.), Perth Amboy,
732-826-2233

Longtimers not bound to the Ironbound have been heading to this Perth Amboy Iberian since day one to feast on its "tasty" fare; sure, the decor's "drab", and a handful deem the place "average", but this "busy, noisy spot" is where you go when you "don't have a lot of cash" and "need leftovers for a week" or a lift from "a pitcher of sangria."

Posillipo

| 20 | 16 | 21 | $37 |

715 Second Ave. (Main St.), Asbury Park, 732-774-5819;
www.posilliporestaurant.com

A "bastion of old-world dining" in Asbury Park, this Italian is "an underrated gem in an unassuming building" where the "accommodating staff" comes bearing gifts of "well-executed classics" and Wednesday opera night is a "pleasure"; a tad "stuffy" to some and "dated" to others, pundits ponder how it's "going to compete" in the local "dining wars"; but remember, this "landmark's" seen a lot come, and a lot go.

Primavera

| 22 | 18 | 19 | $43 |

Wilshire Grand, 350 Pleasant Valley Way (Eagle Rock Ave.),
West Orange, 973-731-4779

"Better than ever", this West Orange Italian has gained some "elbow room" in its new Wilshire Grand home, remaining a "reliable option" for "excellent" food; regulars

| F | D | S | C |

may be happy to know that servers still "rattle off" a "long list" of "sublime specials", in a somewhat "boisterous", sometimes "chaotic" atmosphere.

Pronto Cena | 21 | 18 | 19 | $35 |
87 Sussex St. (Washington St.), Jersey City, 201-435-0004
The Legal Ctr., 1 Riverfront Plaza (McCarter Hwy.), Newark, 973-824-8999

These sibs in Jersey City and Newark offer a "wide range" of "consistently good" Italian specialties on noticeably consistent menus (they've remained the "same for years"); depending on your mood or perspective, the decor at this pair either "lacks warmth" or is "charming" and "cozy."

Pub, The | 18 | 13 | 16 | $29 |
Airport Circle, 7600 Kaighn Ave. (Rte. 130), Pennsauken, 856-665-6440; www.thepubnj.com

A "decades-old standby" (make that 1951), this Pennsauken perennial steakhouse is a "throwback to yesteryear when dinner clubs ruled"; if you don't mind dining in a room "the size of Grand Central", the "relic" that seats 600 suits those who shrug off "indifferent service" and the "Knights of the Round Table theme" for a "good" hunk of beef.

Puccini's | 22 | 20 | 22 | $41 |
1064 Westside Ave. (Broadway), Jersey City, 201-432-4111; www.puccinisrestaurant.com

"Avoid the trek to Little Italy" and opt for this "old-style", "over-the-top" bedecked Jersey City Italian that caters to palates on the lookout for "authentic", "well-prepared" food; the crew, you should note, will "do anything to make patrons happy"; P.S. the valet parking is a "big bonus."

Quiet Man, The | 23 | 17 | 19 | $29 |
64 E. McFarlan St. (Hudson St.), Dover, 973-366-6333; www.quietmanpub.com

"You've just entered John Wayne zone" at this "dimly lit" American-Irish pub in western Morris County whose moniker is a "tribute" to the film but where the fare is anything but quiet; indeed, the ayes are smiling on "the best food in any tavern east of the Mississippi", chow that's boosted by a "warm welcome" and "prompt service"; "all in all, the Duke would be proud."

Raagini | 22 | 20 | 21 | $29 |
1085 Rte. 22 E. (Mill Ln.), Mountainside, 908-789-9777; www.raagini.com

"A delectable feast fit for a maharajah" awaits at this "superb" Indian in Mountainside, where the staff "treats you like royalty" and "gladly guides your selections"; it's "sophisticated", "without the typical Bollywood decor", and the weekend sitar player and "bargain" buffet lunches ($10.95–$12.95) are further enticements.

subscribe to zagat.com

| F | D | S | C |

Radicchio   22 | 17 | 18 | $45
32 Franklin Ave. (bet. Chestnut & Oak Sts.), Ridgewood, 201-670-7311
"Specials, specials and more specials" are given "creative treatment" at this Italian "delight" in Ridgewood that's seen as a "consistent winner" in a town "filled with newcomers that don't always hit the mark"; it can be "loud" and the service "could be better", but it's still a "favorite."

Raimondo's   24 | 17 | 20 | $40
1101 Long Beach Blvd. (11th St.), Ship Bottom, 609-494-5391
"Italian the way mama used to make it" brings in the "early-bird crowd" and amps up "the din" to "incredible" levels at this Ship Bottom BYO where diners are known to make "reservations weeks ahead"; "off-season" rules, insiders say, when it's easier to enjoy the "ocean-fresh" seafood and other "delicious" dishes.

Ram's Head Inn   25 | 24 | 24 | $51
9 W. White Horse Pike (Garden State Pkwy., exit 40), Galloway, 609-652-1700; www.ramsheadinn.com
This Galloway American is a "diamond" of "leisurely dining" and "worth the short trek from AC" for "first-class" fare, "white-glove service" and an "idyllic", "relaxing" setting; toast a "special occasion", but just bring "someone else to pick up the check"; N.B. jackets required at dinner.

RAT'S   24 | 28 | 24 | $60
Grounds for Sculpture, 16 Fairgrounds Rd. (Sculptor's Way), Hamilton, 609-584-7800; www.ratsrestaurant.org
A "fantasy" in every sense of the word, this piece of "magic" within a "wondrous" re-creation of Monet's fabled Giverny ranks No. 1 once again for Decor in our *Survey*; "prepare for an unrushed evening of culinary and sensory delight", starting with a stroll through the "spectacular" Grounds for Sculpture (thanks, Mr. Johnson) and continuing with a "phenomenal" New French repast enhanced by "superb service"; simply put, it's "breathtaking inside and out."

Rattlesnake Ranch Café   14 | 14 | 14 | $24
Foodtown Shopping Ctr., 559 E. Main St. (Station Rd.), Denville, 973-586-3800; www.rattlesnakeranchcafe.com
If you're looking for something "interesting", look no further than this Denville strip maller that really puts a "twist" on Southwestern by offering a virtual zoo of "game" meats, including "bison, ostrich and rattlesnake" ("it really does taste like chicken!"); it's "fun" for some, though others want to do a 180 and "run away."

RAVEN AND THE PEACH   24 | 27 | 23 | $57
740 River Rd. (Fair Haven Rd.), Fair Haven, 732-747-4666
"Feel like you stepped onto the set of *Casablanca*" as you enter this "sophisticated and sublime" New American in

vote at zagat.com   **123**

| F | D | S | C |

Fair Haven where an "attentive and educated staff" is "always on top" of the "classy" floor show and where chef Artie Keenan's creations are so "wonderful" he "should run for mayor"; a committee of critics, though, register their disapproval by voting down the "way-too-expensive" tabs.

Raymond's
| 22 | 19 | 17 | $21 |

28 Church St. (bet. Fullerton Ave. & Park St.), Montclair, 973-744-9263

This "popular", "deliciously" "hip" Montclair New American courtesy of co-owner Raymond Badach is where "kids in soccer uniforms" are right at home with the "lunchtime Kate Spade handbag ladies"; fans fawn over the BYO's "reinvented" space and chef Matthew Seeber's (ex NYC's Gramercy Tavern) cooking.

Ray's Little Silver Seafood ∌
| 23 | 11 | 18 | $32 |

Markham Place Plaza, 125 Markham Pl. (Prospect Ave.), Little Silver, 732-758-8166

"Cozy" and "unpretentious", this "storefront" is where you're likely to spot "friends and neighbors" noshing on "inventive" gifts from the sea that are "always fresh"; the BYO policy helps reel in the costs, so it's no wonder Little Silver denizens deem this a "great" place to go.

Rebecca's
| 23 | 19 | 21 | $42 |

236 Old River Rd. (bet. Gorge Rd. & Thompson Ln.), Edgewater, 201-943-8808; www.rebeccasedgewater.com

"Charming" and "intimate" sums up the sentiments of most for this "small" Cuban-Caribbean BYO in Edgewater where "well-conceived" dishes "prepared with panache" "transport you to the islands"; choose between a "romantic garden" in back or an indoor scene "surrounded by mirrors and brick walls", and since "service is not rushed", "bring several" bottles of wine to this "hideaway."

Red ●
| 20 | 24 | 19 | $45 |

5 Broad St. (W. Front St.), Red Bank, 732-741-3232; www.rednj.com

"Taking the Shore by storm", this "chic", "glitzy" address in the heart of Red Bank's "red-hot" Downtown is "the place" to check out a "beautiful crowd" and a staff that's a "remarkable assortment of eye candy"; expect cuisine of the New American persuasion, and if you're a "staid" type, "don't let" the "sexy upstairs lounge" "scare you away."

Red Hen Cafe
| ∇ 26 | 18 | 23 | $33 |

Ironstone Village Shopping Ctr., 560 Stokes Rd. (bet. Jackson & Skeet Rds.), Medford, 609-953-2655; www.redhencafe.freeservers.com

"Delectable dishes" from Central and Eastern Europe make this "tiny", "unassuming" BYO in Medford "the best-kept secret in the land" to fans hungry for chef Tracey Slack's "superb" creations such as Wiener schnitzel with spaetzle

subscribe to zagat.com

| F | D | S | C |

and sweet and sour cabbage; "exceptional", "attentive" servers boost the storefront to "better-than-grandma's" status for many.

Red Hot & Blue | 15 | 12 | 14 | $24 |
Holiday Inn, 2175 Old Marlton Pike (Sayer Ave.), Cherry Hill, 856-665-7427; www.redhotanblue.com

"The ribs are good but the music is the real reason to go" say those who dig the "smoky bar and blues" at this Cherry Hill BBQ specialist; "hit-or-miss service" and "average" eats make sticklers stay away, insisting "any resemblance to barbecue is purely coincidental."

Red's Lobster Pot | 23 | 14 | 18 | $33 |
57 Inlet Dr. (Ocean Ave.), Point Pleasant Beach, 732-295-6622; www.redslobsterpot.com

It's got the "perfect beach-bum atmosphere", a "great dockside raw bar" on the inlet, and to top it off, the Point Pleasant Beach BYO "shack" will float your boat with "the best down and dirty" seafood in the 'hood; the outdoor patio makes the "inevitable wait" at this "little bit of Maine" "more enjoyable"; you'll see the only thing "missing is Jimmy Buffett."

Reef Club, The | 20 | 21 | 17 | $48 |
228 New Ocean Ave. (Joline Ave.), Long Branch, 732-229-6004; www.thereefclub.com

"Huge tropical fish tanks" add to the allure of the "jam-packed bar scene" at this Long Branch Eclectic reef-sider where it's advisable not to be "put off by the noise" (you may have to "read lips") or a staff that may throw some "'tude" since there's "creative" seafood about, including sushi that's "quite good"; N.B. dinner only.

Renault Winery | 21 | 23 | 23 | $43 |
72 N. Bremen Ave. (Moss Mill Rd.), Egg Harbor, 609-965-2111; www.renaultwinery.com

Set on the grounds of a "beautiful" winery, this Egg Harbor City New American is "worth the trip" for both "special occasions" and for a " brunch that's not to be missed"; while the "blueberry wine" may be "a unique guzzle", there are others who don't hesitate to praise this place's "romance"; P.S. the adjacent hotel and new golf course make it "a weekend hideaway delight."

Reservoir Tavern ☒ | 24 | 8 | 17 | $22 |
90 Parsippany Blvd. (Rtes. 202 & 287), Boonton, 973-334-5708

If you're on a "quest" in search of NJ's best pizza, look no further, say pie hounds who boast this Boonton Italian turns out "the best in the state"; fans of the "amazing thin crust", "zesty" sauce and "terrific" toppings contend it's worth "fighting the crowd" to gain entry into the "busy little tavern" – even if it "looks like a cafeteria."

vote at zagat.com

| F | D | S | C |

Restaurant, The   21 | 24 | 21 | $51
160 Prospect Ave. (bet. Beech St. & Central Ave.), Hackensack, 201-678-1100; www.therestaurant.net
"A hot place" for a "mature" crowd, this Hackensack New American "screams first class" even though it sits "in the middle of high-rise condo purgatory"; "the ceilings are vaulted and so are the prices", but that doesn't keep it from being a "Friday night 'meat' market."

Ria's Café   – | – | – | I
24 Mercer St. (Grove St.), Jersey City, 201-915-0045
This wee BYO opposite City Hall in Jersey City turns out Dominican fare for those who turn up for authentic specialties in the way of tripe soup and chicken stew; a pleasant setting's a fitting accompaniment to its down-home cuisine; N.B. open for brunch on weekends.

Rice   ∇ 21 | 24 | 19 | $41
300 Shore Dr. (Waterwitch Ave.), Highlands, 732-708-1190; www.ricefusion.com
"Trendy" and packing an "exotic aura" in Highlands, this Thai–Asian fusion newbie lures locals with its "knockout" decor (featuring a "beautiful" outside area complete with "waterfalls" and koi pond) and "great" bar scene; as for the food, converts "savor memories of intense flavors for days."

Richard's ⊄   21 | 10 | 15 | $17
155 Brighton Ave. (Ocean Ave.), Long Branch, 732-870-9133
Diehards decree that "there's no better" of its kind in the area than this Long Branch deli; think "huge, delish" sandwiches and "good" matzo ball soup and don't think too hard about its look and service "that could be friendlier."

Ristorante da Benito   24 | 21 | 22 | $51
222 Galloping Hill Rd. (Walton Ave.), Union, 908-964-5850; www.dabenito.com
A haunt for "deal-makers, politicians" and regular folks alike, this "showstopper" in Union rewards patrons with "beautifully prepared" examples of Italian cooking that come in "big portions" and a "thoughtfully selected" wine list that "adds to the experience"; with "service at your service", only a few mind the "unrelenting din."

Ritz Seafood   24 | 15 | 18 | $34
Ritz Shopping Ctr., 910 Haddonfield-Berlin Rd. (White Horse Rd.), Voorhees, 856-566-6650
"Inspired", "exquisite" seafood with Asian accents bumps up reviewers' overall impressions of this "peaceful", "unpretentious" BYO to the level of "magnificent little gem"; with a "hands-on owner" and "fabulous" confections, it's no wonder locals look to the Voorhees "favorite" "before, after or instead of" the flicks at the nearby cinema; N.B. tea-timers are wooed by the 30 varieties at the sipping bar.

| F | D | S | C |

RIVER PALM TERRACE   24 | 18 | 20 | $53
1416 River Rd. (Palisade Terrace), Edgewater, 201-224-2013
41-11 Rte. 4 W. (bet. Paramus & Saddle River Rds.), Fair Lawn, 201-703-3500
209 Ramapo Valley Rd. (off Rte. 202), Mahwah, 201-529-1111
www.riverpalm.com
North Jersey's capitals for carnivores "would give any NYC steakhouse a run for its money", staunch supporters state; find a "powerhouse crowd of sexy people" at this trio where the chops "don't come any better", but bring some patience with you, since you may have a beef with "record-breaking waits", sometimes "even with reservations."

Rivoli's   15 | 11 | 16 | $24
781 Fischer Blvd. (bet. Bay Ave. & Rte. 37 E.), Dover Township, 732-270-3634
Carb-aholics will be quite pleased with the "obscene" quantities ("a pound of pasta covered in sauce") set in front of them at this Dover Township Italian; those with revved-up appetites label the BYO a "great value", though others brand it "generous mediocrity."

Roberto's Dolce Vita   21 | 20 | 21 | $36
12907 Long Beach Blvd. (E. New Jersey Ave.), Beach Haven, 609-492-1001
A "must" on Long Beach Island is this Italian BYO whose "recent renovations are a step up" and well suited to the "sweet" owners who "go out of their way to make guests comfortable"; to those who have seen a slew of tributes to the red, white and green, there are "no surprises", just "good, solid" food.

Roberto's II   21 | 13 | 19 | $39
936 River Rd. (Dempsey Ave.), Edgewater, 201-224-2524
"Down home, hearty Italian" cooking allows this Edgewater standby to "thrive" in a region with many competitors; though the "friendly and attentive" staff gets a thumbs-up, even supporters wish the "closed-in, windowless setting" would get a "serious face-lift" to take it out of "the '50s."

Robin's Nest   22 | 21 | 20 | $27
2-4 Washington St. (High St.), Mount Holly, 609-261-6149
"Slowly reviving" Mount Holly is home to this "charming" American "in a lovely neighborhood of boutiques" that offers "imaginative" savories and "magnificent desserts"; now that a little bird has tipped you to the "little-known treasure", "take an elderly aunt" to the "genteel" yet "homey" spot.

Robongi   24 | 16 | 19 | $27
520 Washington St. (bet. 5th & 6th Sts.), Hoboken, 201-222-8388
In a town not known for raw fish, champions of this Japanese believe it serves the "best in Hoboken", with "competitive prices" that make it easier to overlook the

vote at zagat.com

| F | D | S | C |

"bland" decor; it's become a "happening" quite quickly, but despite a high food score, a minority wonders if the BYO can "satisfy a sushi snob."

Rocca — | — | — | E

203 Rock Rd. (bet. Glen Ave. & Main St.), Glen Rock, 201-670-4945
Now playing in the space once belonging to Mezzaluna is this Glen Rock Italian where ricotta gnocchi with a sausage ragu and lusty lasagne rule; the BYO's comfy divided dining area mirrors the rustic nature of its menu, the creation of chef-owner Craig Levy (ex NYC's Gotham Bar & Grill).

Rod's Olde Irish Tavern 18 | 16 | 17 | $28

507 Washington Blvd. (Rte. 71), Sea Girt, 732-449-2020; www.rodstavern.com
Start with "classic" "Irish tavern" decor, add a menu of American "pub grub" and "fast, friendly" service and you've got "a home away from home" for many, including "middle-aged surfers" and those "crowding around the bar" to watch sports on the tube; yup, "it's noisy, fun" and "nothing spectacular", but it's a "staple" in Sea Girt.

Rod's Steak & Seafood Grille 20 | 23 | 20 | $43

The Madison Hotel, 1 Convent Rd. (Madison Ave.), Convent Station, 973-539-6666; www.rodssteak.com
"Stick to the steak and you'll do very well" at this example of "high Victoriana" in Convent Station that also proffers "fresh" seafood in a "bygone-era" setting; though it may not be the "Orient Express", most are happy to "indulge that low-carb diet"; P.S. "dine in the restored train car."

Rooney's Ocean Crab House 17 | 21 | 17 | $40

100 Ocean Ave. (Cooper Ave.), Long Branch, 732-870-1200; www.rooneysocean.com
Surveyors seduced by this Long Branch seafooder surmise that the "sea breezes on the patio" and "commanding ocean views" may be the "best part" of this beachfront bastion; though the "huge" menu of fin fare's "fair" to "very good", "uneven" service "trips up the quality" of the experience.

RosaLuca's Italian Bistro ▽ 24 | 16 | 20 | $42

1114 Rte. 173 (Rte. 78, exit 11), Bethlehem, 908-238-0018
Chef-owners Carmine and Jill Castaldo make it "worth the trip" to this "rural" part of western Hunterdon County, where seasonal Italian specialties are "delicious – from entree to dessert"; sure, it's a "little out of the way" and the decor is "minimalist", but with "professional" service and dishes "receiving raves", it's considered a welcome "surprise."

ROSEMARY AND SAGE 26 | 19 | 23 | $50

26 Hamburg Tpke. (I-287, exit 53), Riverdale, 973-616-0606; www.rosemaryandsage.com
"All you seek is here" at this 60-seat Riverdale home for "foodies", where "new items are added regularly" to an

"outstanding" New American menu and the "lovely owners" "pay attention to details"; with "interesting, affordable" wines and a five-course prix fixe dinner that's a "great value", "you won't be disappointed"; N.B. Wednesday–Sunday, dinner only.

Ruga 23 | 19 | 22 | $47
4 Barbara Ln. (W. Oakland Ave.), Oakland, 201-337-0813; www.rugarestaurant.com
Faithful followers of this "elegant" Oakland New American go for the "creative" New American creations, "superb" service and "romantic" piano bar; though the sound shocked throw up their arms and say "abandon all hope for quiet conversation" once the place fills up, overall, it's still "as good as ever."

RUTH'S CHRIS STEAK HOUSE 25 | 21 | 23 | $54
Hilton Hotel, 1 Hilton Ct. (Rte. 10 W.), Parsippany, 973-889-1400
1000 Harbor Blvd. (19th St.), Weehawken, 201-863-5100
www.ruthschris.com
Feed your inner carnivore at these "powerhouses" in North Jersey that, "chain or no chain", offer "fantastic" cuts "swimming" ("deliciously") "in butter" and a view of NYC (Weehawken) that "can't be beat"; "don't eat all day because you'll definitely binge at night", advise enthusiasts, and steel yourself for a bloated bill, 'cause those "great" sides and wines "add up."

RYLAND INN, THE 28 | 27 | 26 | $87
Rte. 22 W. (Rte. 523), Whitehouse, 908-534-4011; www.rylandinn.com
"The magic of culinary excellence" inspires acolytes to worship at the "granddaddy of NJ restaurants" (No. 1 for Popularity in our *Survey*), a showcase for the "gastronomic wizardry" of "brilliant" chef Craig Shelton; since 1991, devout diners have been making pilgrimages to this country inn in Whitehouse to savor "magnificent" New French fare (bolstered by the on-site organic garden), service that "misses nothing" and a "superbly" selected wine list; all of the above leaves surveyors asking "how can you improve perfection?"

Sabor 24 | 21 | 21 | $44
8809 River Rd. (bet. Bulls Ferry & Gorge Rds.), North Bergen, 201-943-6366
"Exotic, creative" Nuevo Latino prepared by a "chef who knows how to blend flavors" makes this "epicurean delight" in North Bergen "a charming find in an out-of-the-way place"; "sexy, stylish decor" and a staff that "couldn't be nicer" prompt the "jumping, eclectic crowd" to shout "*muy bueno*"; P.S. you might want to "stay upstairs to hear yourself think" should the "lively music" pulsate.

| F | D | S | C |

SADDLE RIVER INN   27 | 25 | 25 | $59
2 Barnstable Ct. (bet. E. Allendale Ave. & W. Saddle River Rd.), Saddle River, 201-825-4016; www.saddleriverinn.com
"Once you open the doors, the enchanted journey begins" at this Saddle River "gem" in a "quaint barn" that "oozes country elegance", a "veteran" creating "exceptional" French–New American food "without novelties", "foams or fussiness"; with a "chef-owner who really cares", and who "understands the subtleties of good service", it shouldn't shock anyone that this BYO "continues to perform at the top of its game."

Saffron Indian Cuisine   ∇ 23 | 23 | 21 | $30
249 Rte. 10 E. (New Murray Rd.), East Hanover, 973-599-0700; www.saffronnj.com
"Everything is tops" at this year-old "upscale" Indian in East Hanover, where zealots zero in on "fantastic", "flavorful" dishes incorporating "noticeably fresh spices"; even though the BYO is in an "easy-to-miss storefront", its "beautiful wooden columns and beadwork" bring "first-class" appeal and make it a "pleasant addition to the scene."

SAGAMI   26 | 15 | 21 | $33
37 W. Crescent Blvd. (Haddon Ave.), Collingswood, 856-854-9773
"Unsurpassed sushi" and "unparalleled commitment" from the owner ensure this Collingswood Japanese remains in the "favorite" category for everyone from "Philadelphia TV news anchors" to locals who dub it their "family's special place for any occasion"; sure, the "location stinks" and its "low-profile look" doesn't titillate, but the BYO's always "worth the trip."

Saigon R   24 | 10 | 20 | $25
(fka Saigon Republic)
58 W. Palisade Ave. (William St.), Englewood, 201-871-4777; www.saigonr.com
It's a "real hole-in-the-wall", but since "everything is sumptuous, savory, tender and exquisitely prepared", Englewood's denizens are quick to forgive the "bare-bones" shortcomings of this Vietnamese BYO; it's "tight" in there, so "squeeze in" and witness some slurping of "exceptional" pho and servers who don't "rush" diners, "even on a busy night."

Sails   19 | 24 | 20 | $52
998 Bay Ave. (Goll Ave.), Somers Point, 609-926-9611; www.njsails.com
Expect a "magnificent view and a stunning room filled with beautiful people" at this Somers Point newcomer featuring "long waits on summer weekend nights" along with its "pricey", yet "appealing" Eclectic bill of fare; the floor crew might "need some training", but for vacationers keen

| F | D | S | C |

on kicking-back, it's the "'in' spot" "to be seen"; P.S. listen to some "great" live music "on the outdoor deck."

Sakura-Bana   23 | 11 | 18 | $31
43 Franklin Ave. (bet. Chestnut & Oak Sts.), Ridgewood, 201-447-6525
This Japanese BYO, a Ridgewood "staple for years", is where fans flock for "first-rate sushi" in a "very unassuming atmosphere" where you sit "cheek by jowl with your neighbors" and watch them down the "freshest fish" in the area; though critics caution there's new competition in town and that the ol' gal may soon be "eclipsed", its champions maintain this "standard" bearer "continues to hold the edge."

Sallee Tee's Grille   20 | 18 | 19 | $32
33 West St. (Beach Rd.), Monmouth Beach, 732-870-8999; www.salleeteesgrille.com
"What a mix" exult eager eaters who descend in droves upon this "very casual" American-Eclectic "on the water" ("well, by the boats") in Monmouth Beach where "most everything is super-sized", from "monster sandwiches" that "could feed a small nation" to "Italian to seafood to steak to sushi"; since there's a "sunset like Key West" and an "upbeat boating crowd" that keeps the bar "hopping", it's no wonder it's as "crowded" as can be.

Sally Ling   18 | 16 | 18 | $28
1636 Palisade Ave. (Main St.), Fort Lee, 201-346-1282
"A bit more pricey than the competition", but delivering "fancier selections" and "fancier surroundings", loyalists look out for this Fort Lee Chinese they consider a "very efficient operation" serving "satisfying" specialties and an "excellent range of vegetarian options"; skeptics, however, skew toward claiming it a "nothing-special suburban" Sino with "average" chow.

Salt Creek Grille   20 | 24 | 20 | $40
4 Bingham Ave. (River Rd.), Rumson, 732-933-9272; www.saltcreekgrille.com
"Rustic coziness", a "big fire pit at the entrance", "beautiful Arts and Crafts–style" decor and a view of the Navesink River "that's one of the tops at the Shore" all serve to make this Rumson American "even busy on a Monday night"; you'll get "everything from hamburgers to filet mignon, casual diners next to shirts and ties" at this "favorite" whose "scenic" scenery tends to outshine the "very good" food.

Samdan   21 | 14 | 18 | $30
178 Piermont Rd. (Union Ave.), Cresskill, 201-816-7343; www.samdanrestaurant.com
Try "tantalizing" Turkish food at this "popular" BYO in Cresskill whose "remarkable variety and authenticity" of fare keeps reviewers flowing in; while the "friendly" service

vote at zagat.com

| F | D | S | C |

and "incredible value" score a hit with those who revel in being "treated like special guests", "the '80s called" and they "want their decor back."

Sammy's Ye Old Cider Mill | 21 | 8 | 15 | $58 |
353 Mendham Rd. W. (Oak Knoll Rd.), Mendham, 973-543-7675; www.sammyscidermill.com
"Bring a wad of cash" to this Mendham "classic" slabhouse that's a "cattle call preppie scene" where locals arrive hungry for hunks of beef and lobster and "greasy fries to die for"; while "interminable" waits are irksome and its basement setup "decorated like a rec room" is "so bad it's good", most love it as a "billionaire's barn" ripe for a "feast."

San Remo | 23 | 15 | 20 | $37 |
37 E. Newman Springs Rd. (Rte. 35), Shrewsbury, 732-345-8200; www.sanremoitaliana.com
Known as a "quiet little treasure trove" you just might "drive by", this "comfortable" Shrewsbury Italian whips up "lots of creative dishes" that happen to be "excellent"; locals know the BYO "may not have a view", but being both "away from the Red Bank hype" and home to "servers who make dining relaxing" help give it "winner" status.

Sapporo Sushi & Steak House | 19 | 15 | 15 | $31 |
375 George St. (bet. Church & Paterson Sts.), New Brunswick, 732-828-3888; sapporo.wtc.net
New Brunswick is where you'll find this Japanese surf 'n' turfer that, on the one hand puts on a "show" (the "hibachi" is "good" "for that dreaded first date"), and rolls, slices and serves sushi on the other; critics, however, cut up fare that leans toward the "exceedingly average" and service on the "slow" or "nonexistent" side.

Savanna | – | – | – | E |
The Galleria, 10 Bridge Ave. (West Front St.), Red Bank, 732-741-6333
Transforming the old House of Coffee space in Red Bank's industrial-chic Galleria shopping complex is this newcomer where Spanish tapas dominate a multifaceted small-plates menu that doesn't ignore classic bits and bites from other domains; the BYO's soaring space softened by low-hung lanterns, lots of warm wood and cushy banquettes transforms it into a date-worthy destination.

Savaradio ⌀ | 25 | 16 | 22 | $39 |
5223 Ventnor Ave. (Little Rock Ave.), Ventnor, 609-823-2110
While it's "booked solid on summer evenings", this Ventnor Eclectic with "out-of-this-world" "fish preparations" makes it "worth being seated like sardines" – that is, if you don't know to "go mid-week or before Memorial Day"; insiders indicate the BYO plans on adding a new location, which "should help" ease the waits here, given that this spot's "always crowded because the food is always good."

132   subscribe to zagat.com

| F | D | S | C |

Sawa Steakhouse & Sushi Bar 24 | 21 | 20 | $30
42 Rte. 36 (Rte. 35), Eatontown, 732-544-8885;
www.sawasteakhouse.com
Head straight for the "great starters, rolls and the bare necessities – sushi and sashimi" at this Eatontown Japanese BYO where "imaginative" raw-fish dishes star on the "extensive" menu; the "beautiful" setting "with lots of wood and a koi pond" complements a floor crew "happy to please"; P.S. the "hibachi" option is "great for kids."

SCALINI FEDELI ☒ 27 | 25 | 24 | $64
63 Main St. (Parrot Mill Rd.), Chatham, 973-701-9200;
www.scalinifedeli.com
"Culinary heaven on earth", this "beautiful", "world-class" Chatham Northern Italian "pampers" patrons lucky enough to get in – what can be a "three-month wait" is forgotten after tasting Michael Cetrulo's "magical" prix fixe "wonders" served by a "staff that knows the right amount of schmooze"; the only issue, for many, is deciding which of the "divine" creations to order.

Scarborough Fair 21 | 23 | 19 | $40
1414 Meetinghouse Rd. (Rte. 35), Wall, 732-223-6658;
www.scarboroughfairnj.com
"Ask for one of the cubicles" along the "spiral stairway" to ensure the most "romance" at this Wall New American with something of a "fairy-tale atmosphere" and "extremely tasty" selections; indeed, the "tiered table seating" "allows for a very cozy and intimate dinner", warming up even those who sense "slow" service.

Scuttlebutt's Pub 20 | 10 | 17 | $24
400 Centre St. (Franklin Ave.), Nutley, 973-661-2026
Expect "a little pizzazz" in your burger at this "family-run", "neighborhood" pub that offers both "typical bar food and eclectic inventions"; rumors abound that locals urge grubbers to go for "wing night" and shrug off the "nothing fancy" decor at "God's gift to Nutley."

Seafood Empire 22 | 14 | 17 | $25
Commerce Plaza, 2205 Rte. 1 S. (Commerce Blvd.),
North Brunswick, 732-398-9090
It's "like a trip to Shanghai" – and "worth driving on Route 1" to arrive at this "authentic" BYO, a Chinese seafood specialist in North Brunswick that "has found its voice"; beyond its "well-executed standards" are "many unique dishes" and "moderate prices."

Sea Shack 20 | 15 | 20 | $41
293 Polifly Rd. (Rte. 17), Hackensack, 201-489-7232;
www.seashack.com
"Not an exciting dining experience", but finatics say "if you like seafood, then go" to this Hackensack "standby" for

vote at zagat.com

| F | D | S | C |

"perfectly prepared" fish; though you may have to go wallet-diving to pay for what some consider one "pricey" shack, the majority thinks this operation "can't be beat."

Segovia | 23 | 13 | 18 | $34 |
150 Moonachie Rd. (bet. Joseph St. & Rooney Pl.), Moonachie, 201-641-4266; www.segoviarestaurant.com
"The king of its kind in the area", this Moonachie Iberian "a stone's throw from Giants Stadium" is where you get "big steaks" that allow you to "leave full and smiling"; "seating can be a little cramped" ("it's too crowded"), so you may receive an inadvertent "shove" at some point, but most give up and can't resist the "smell of garlic a block away."

SERENADE | 27 | 26 | 26 | $66 |
6 Roosevelt Ave. (Main St.), Chatham, 973-701-0303; www.restaurantserenade.com
Hitting all the high notes with surveyors, this "magnificent" New French in Chatham (from the union of "husband-chef" James Laird and "wife-in-front" Nancy Sheridan Laird) is "fabulous from start to finish", with "breathtaking" food, an "incredible wine list" shepherded by a "very user-friendly" sommelier, "understated service" and a "magical setting"; all in all, this one will "impress" "even people from the big city."

Sergeantsville Inn, The | 23 | 26 | 21 | $46 |
601 Rosemont-Ringoes Rd. (Rtes. 523 & 604), Sergeantsville, 609-397-3700; www.sergeantsvilleinn.com
"A roaring fire, stone walls and unusual entrees" allow this "intimate" New American "gem" set in a "charming old farmhouse" in a "lovely" Hunterdon County "hamlet" to be viewed as a "great place for Valentine's Day or special occasion"; there'll be more than romance once you show up, say reviewers, since there's "delicious" food too; P.S. the adjacent tavern is a "less expensive" option.

Settebello ☒ | 23 | 19 | 21 | $35 |
2 Cattano Ave. (Speedwell Ave.), Morristown, 973-267-3355
"Everything is so good" at this Morristown Northern Italian, especially the "imaginative" and "inspired" food and the staff that "goes out of its way to make you feel you're its only customer"; regulars "never get tired" of the BYO's appeal, finding it "a very romantic hideaway" that's "perfect on a cold winter night" and equally alluring "in the courtyard when weather permits."

Seven Hills of Istanbul | 21 | 19 | 20 | $28 |
441 Raritan Ave. (S. 5th Ave.), Highland Park, 732-777-9711; www.7hillsofistanbul.com
"Istanbul on the Raritan" is how fans describe this Highland Park Turkish-Med with "cuisine fit for a pasha"; there's much to adore at this "child-friendly" BYO where you can

| F | D | S | C |

start with "the best hummus this side of the Atlantic" and end with some "awesome coffee."

75 South | 22 | 23 | 21 | $47 |
75 South St. (bet. Lincoln Pl. & McLean St.), Freehold, 732-780-4441

Guests who dine in this "charming, old" "Victorian" BYO with "different decor in each room" feel they've "gone back to another era" and "left the bustling streets of Freehold behind"; in addition, "delicious", "eclectic" New American fare served with an "elegant" touch means it's "always wonderful" for a "special occasion"; N.B. closed Mondays and Tuesdays.

Shadowbrook | 19 | 25 | 20 | $47 |
92 Obre Pl. (Rte. 35), Shrewsbury, 732-747-0200; www.shadowbrook.com

A "gem of a setting" in a "lovely" Georgian mansion lends this "sophisticated" Shrewsbury American suited for "parties" and "weddings" "old-world charm"; critics conclude that the food "needs more creativity" and lives "in the shadow" of its decor, adding the "classic" eatery's "reputation far exceeds the facts."

Shanghai Jazz | 20 | 18 | 20 | $37 |
24 Main St. (Green Village Rd.), Madison, 973-822-2899; www.shanghaijazz.com

"If you are looking for outside-the-box Chinese" with a side of "top-flight live jazz", "look no further" than this Madison restaurant-cum-club where "there's no cover" and "you're always treated like a favorite customer"; and since the "very good", "eclectic" dishes are a veritable "bargain", both chompers and foot-stompers agree "it's a true night out on the town."

Ship Inn, The | ▽ 16 | 16 | 16 | $26 |
61 Bridge St. (Rte. 519), Milford, 908-995-0188; www.shipinn.com

Snag a seat at this Milford hopster and "enjoy" the "closest thing to a real English pub this side of the pond" and all it has to offer – a "wide and changing selection of brews", an "excellent" single malt list and, of course, fish 'n' chips; consider it "England on the Delaware."

Shipwreck Grill | 26 | 18 | 21 | $43 |
720 Ashley Ave. (Evergreen Ave.), Brielle, 732-292-9380; www.shipwreckgrill.com

This "nautically" themed Brielle "beauty has it all", rave reviewers craving the "imaginative", seafood-centric plates on a New American menu; "the open space tends to get noisy" (there's "not much separation between the bar and restaurant"), but since there's a "knowledgeable bar staff" and "friendly" floor crew, you'll need to keep an eye out for "all the preppies" who dock here for a night.

| F | D | S | C |

Shogun   18 | 15 | 18 | $29
Bey Lea Golf Course, 1536 N. Bay Ave. (Garden State Pkwy., exit 82), Dover Township, 732-286-9888
Center 18 Mall, 1020 Rte. 18 N. (bet. Gunia St. & Hillsdale Rd.), East Brunswick, 732-390-1922; www.shogun18.net
166 Rte. 22 (Washington Ave.), Green Brook, 732-968-3330; www.shogun22.net
3376 Rte. 27 (Sand Hills Rd.), Kendall Park, 732-422-1117; www.shogun27.com

"Food as entertainment" keeps the comments coming about these Japanese cousins where surveyors are "not sure about" the "blah" decor but think the "hibachi's a sure thing"; those "looking for thrills" know it's "all about the flames", but purists fire away at the raw-fish dishes, dubbing them "McSushi" and lump the mini-chain in the category of the "mundane."

Shubox Café   19 | 13 | 18 | $27
256 Pompton Ave. (S. Mountain Ave.), Cedar Grove, 973-239-8880; www.shuboxcafe.com

There's "no wait, no dress code, no worries" at this "kitschy", "quirky" Cedar Grove New American that "doesn't try to be more than it is"; yup, the "shoebox decor is a bit worn out", but the service is "gracious" and the "desserts are outrageous", as in "great" – boons to those who wear either Manolos or Merrells.

Shumi   24 | 11 | 19 | $35
30 S. Doughty Ave. (Veterans Memorial Dr. W.), Somerville, 908-526-8596; www.shumirestaurant.com

They like "Ike", the chef who presides over this raw-fish BYO for "purists" in Somerville, where the "awesome" sushi draws the likes of "former Governor Christie Whitman"; sure, the "decor is nothing to write home about" and it's "hard to find", but "put down your menus", "ask for the master's creations" and "you'll be hooked."

Siam ⌿   22 | 9 | 15 | $23
61 N. Main St. (bet. Coryell & York Sts.), Lambertville, 609-397-8128

"No frills is an understatement" in describing this Thai storefront serving "nice twists on curries and noodles", not to mention other "authentic" dishes that strike most as "real bargains"; the Lambertville BYO "puts all its punch into the food", which might explain why a handful of reviewers label service as "slow."

Siam Garden   23 | 20 | 20 | $32
233 E. Main St. (Wyckoff Ave.), Manasquan, 732-292-9909
The Galleria, 2 Bridge Ave. (W. Front St.), Red Bank, 732-224-1233
www.siamgardenrestaurant.com

There's a "touch of Siam" at the Shore within the walls of these Thai siblings in Manasquan and Red Bank that provide

| F | D | S | C |

"delightful" food; even if critics chide the pair for serving "small portions", the "exotically hip" settings and "helpful" service help the BYOs prevail.

Silver Spring Farm ▽ 23 | 15 | 20 | $51

Flanders Drakestown Rd./Rte. 206 S. (Flanders Netcong Rd.), Flanders, 973-584-0202; www.silverspringfarm.com

"Aging gracefully", this Gallic "classic" restaurant has gourmets gushing "ooh-la-la!" and state it still "doesn't disappoint" after 60-plus years; indeed, the Flanders' stalwart (born in 1940) may be a "little long in the tooth" and always "under-crowded", but its "excellent" Country French fare and "European inn" ambiance "transport you out of Jersey."

Simply Radishing 20 | 10 | 17 | $18

Lawrence Shopping Ctr., 2495 Brunswick Pike/Rte. 1 (Texas Ave.), Lawrenceville, 609-882-3760

If you're a "vegetarian working in the Route 1 business corridor", this Lawrenceville Contemporary American that's a "convenient choice" for a "lunch stop" comes "highly recommended" for its "delightful natural and organic options", including "multiple kinds of bread"; the BYO's "yummy salads" "beat the heck out of those from the chains" and since it's "light on your wallet", you might not mind the "dated" decor; N.B. also open for dinner.

Sirin 19 | 17 | 19 | $28

3 Pine St. (South St.), Morristown, 973-993-9122; www.sirinthairestaurant.com

It's a bit "like eating Thai in your grandma's dining room", what with the "floral country wallpaper" ("it feels like being in someone's country home"), but admirers of this Morristown veteran see something else here too: "good" goodies and a "proximity to the Community Theater" that makes the BYO "convenient."

SIRI'S THAI FRENCH CUISINE 26 | 21 | 24 | $36

2117 Old Marlton Pike (bet. Grove St. & Sayer Ave.), Cherry Hill, 856-663-6781; www.siris-nj.com

The change of ownership that took place in 2004 had tongues wagging about this Cherry Hill Thai-French, but it's safe to say the BYO "buried in a strip mall" is still "so much better than" big-city spots in the same genre, presenting "dazzling" specialties that arrive via a "very fine" staff; "excellent on all fronts", the "tremendous value" turns this one into a "must."

Slowly ▽ 24 | 24 | 21 | $46

73 Main St. (Washington St.), Toms River, 732-914-0102

Setting a "new standard" in Toms River dining is this New American addition that takes a tip (and its name) from the Slow Food Movement (think organic local produce, strict attention to seasonal ingredients), creating fare "put

vote at zagat.com

| F | D | S | C |

together with great thought" amid a "hip, New-York-to-the-hilt" setting; factor in "friendly, not stuffy" service, and you'll see why this BYO is seen by locals as "an oasis."

Smithville Inn 19 | 21 | 20 | $36
1 N. New York Rd. (Moss Mill Rd.), Smithville, 609-652-7777; www.smithvillenj.com
Step foot in this Smithville New American eatery and you'll swear it's something out of "Colonial Williamsburg"; the "old-standby's" "old-inn feel" provides shoppers with a "lovely place for a break", while the "food is like mom's" ("some of the best chicken pot pie around") – at least if her stuff was "yummy."

Smoke Chophouse & Cigar Emporium 20 | 17 | 22 | $58
36 Engle St. (Palisade Ave.), Englewood, 201-541-8530; www.thesmokechophouse.com
"Sublime steaks and stogies for the suit-and-tie set" are found at this Englewood steakhouse with a slate of seafood on the side; "no one beats their meats" boast those who revel in the "gentleman's club" scene and find it a "great place to hang with the guys", but "you'd better dry clean" your clothes the next day since "the smoke is a bit much, even for smokers."

Sogno 23 | 19 | 21 | $45
69 Broad St. (Monmouth St.), Red Bank, 732-747-6969
True, a new owner took over a year ago, and another chef is behind the burners, but it seems as if Red Bank has nothing to fear, since this "warm and friendly" Italian still outputs "delicious" "eclectic" eats for "sophisticated palates"; the "wine shop next door" makes it convenient to pick up a bottle en route to the BYO that, quite frankly, "can be the loudest restaurant on earth", especially when it's "fully occupied."

SOHO ON GEORGE 24 | 23 | 22 | $47
335 George St. (Bayard St.), New Brunswick, 732-296-0533; www.sohoongeorge.com
"Part of the George Street renaissance" and undeniably "hip", this "bustling" and "sophisticated" New Brunswick Contemporary American sports "the entire package", which includes "exceptionally prepared" dishes, "accommodating service" and "stylish elegance"; diners dig the "enveloping glass windows" that "feels like you're eating outside", but just be forewarned that tabs may reflect a "New York City" markup.

Soho 33 20 | 15 | 18 | $31
33 Main St. (Waverly Pl.), Madison, 973-822-2600; www.soho33.com
The "worldly menu" at this "neighborhood" Madison American gives it a special appeal among locals looking

| | F | D | S | C |

for "something with a different twist", where the BYO's boosters believe it's bolstered by "top-notch" confections and "fair prices"; depending on your perspective, the "minimalist" setting is either "lacking" or "subdued."

Solari's ⓢ 20 | 17 | 19 | $38
61 River St. (Atlantic St.), Hackensack, 201-487-1969;
www.solarisrestaurant.com
"A third-generation" traditional Italian that's a "favorite for Hackensack lawyers" and "top politicians", chef, host and owner Marco Solari's "out-of-the-way, but worth finding" "special-occasion" spot provides "an intimate venue to eat good food"; they will "make everyone feel welcome", and regular rounds of "live music" keep the "bar scene lively."

So Moon Nan Jip ● ▽ 22 | 12 | 17 | $24
238 Broad Ave. (Brinkerhoff Ave.), Palisades Park,
201-944-3998
This little-known BYO cooks "the best Korean barbecue in the Palisades Park environs – hands down", assert advocates who thrill to "awesome dishes that shine" and to meats "cooked at your table over wood coals" while savoring "side dishes that are better than most"; so, "with everything so great, who cares about decor?"

Sonoma Grill ⓢ 22 | 19 | 20 | $47
64 Hoboken Rd. (9th St.), East Rutherford, 201-507-8989
Find a "piece of California in Jersey" at this East Rutherford "wine lover's dream" where "abundant portions" of "delicious" New American fare abound; the folks in charge have changed, but folks still go for "tasty" provisions, a taste of "friendly, yet unpretentious" service and "neat Friday night jazz."

Sono Sushi 25 | 16 | 20 | $27
Village Mall, 1098 Rte. 35 (New Monmouth Rd.),
Middletown, 732-706-3588; www.sonosushi.com
With the "most unique rolls around", sushi mavens zero in on this Japanese mecca in Middletown, labeling it the area's "best", and describing the master of the raw-fish bar as "a truly gifted artist"; though "tucked away in a shopping center", the BYO's noted for "large turnover" in the "take-out" trade.

Soonja's 17 | 8 | 16 | $25
244 Alexander St. (Faculty Rd.), Princeton, 609-924-9260;
www.soonjasushi.com
A committed core of supporters say the food at this "modest" Princeton BYO for "students and their visitors" includes "surprisingly good sushi" and Korean "specialties"; but protesters pan the Pan-Asian, pronouncing that the "ethnically confused" confluence of all edibles Eastern makes for "mediocrity."

vote at zagat.com

| F | D | S | C |

Sophie's Bistro   23 | 19 | 21 | $34
700 Hamilton St. (Douglas Ave.), Somerset, 732-545-7778;
www.sophiesbistro.net
"Love it! love it! love it"! exclaim fervent fans of this "piece of Paris" with "all the charm and flavors" "true" to a "great bistro"; "unlike any other" in the area, this Somerset French with "reasonably priced food and a wine selection that leaves you smiling" also comes with a "congenial host who "makes everyone feel at home."

Soufflé   22 | 20 | 21 | $45
7 Union Pl. (Summit Ave.), Summit, 908-598-0717;
www.soufflerestaurant.com
Surveyors rise and applaud the "light, fluffy" and "perfect" signature dish at this "quiet", "elegant" Summit French that's one of the town's "better BYOs", where the bill of fare ventures beyond the soufflé to deliver "consistently good classics" to an "older crowd"; it's a "thoroughly enjoyable" change from the "many Italian restaurants in the area."

SOUTH CITY GRILL   24 | 24 | 20 | $45
70 Pavonia Ave. (Washington Blvd.), Jersey City, 201-610-9225
60 Rte. 46 E. (Crane Rd.), Mountain Lakes, 973-335-8585
55 Rte. 17 S. (bet. Essex & Passaic Sts.), Rochelle Park, 201-845-3737
www.southcitygrill.com
"As sleek and chic as it can get", these seafood-strong Americans bringing "NYC to Jersey" are seen as "great" perches for "watching the bar hotties" and "sipping martinis"; don't kid yourself if you think they aren't "meat markets", but don't forget about the food, which happens to be "out of this world"; P.S. strictly conversation-free zones, since they tend to be "extremely loud."

South Street Trattoria   17 | 14 | 16 | $23
90 South St. (Pine St.), Morristown, 973-326-9200
If you're looking for "pretty good" "old-fashioned red-sauce specialties" that "won't put a dent in your wallet", consider this Italian "trattoria" in Morristown where "people-watching on South Street" is a varsity sport; note that "hordes of children" routinely descend on the BYO, "guaranteeing noisiness" in a room with the ambiance of "a high school gym."

Southwinds Grille   ∇ 21 | 21 | 19 | $34
361 E. Lacey Rd. (Rte. 9), Lacey, 609-242-2666
"Bright and cheerful", this New American eatery in the Forked River section of Lacey stands out "from the usual" bill of fare, serving "delicious", "varied" cuisine; a "river"-side marina locale gives it the additional advantage of a "beautiful water view."

| F | D | S | C |

Spain
| 21 | 15 | 19 | $32 |

419 Market St. (Raymond Blvd.), Newark, 973-344-0994;
www.spainrestaurant.com
"Big and tasty" portions reign at this Newark Spanish-Continental that's a "little quieter than others" of its kind in the Ironbound; get past the "shabby exterior" and tuck into standards such as "shrimp with garlic to die for" brought to table by "friendly waiters."

Spain 92
| 16 | 17 | 18 | $34 |

1116 Hwy. 202 (Rte. 567), Raritan, 908-704-9292;
www.spain-92.com
Find a "complete" lineup of "traditional" fare at this Spanish stalwart in Raritan; opinions are decidedly split along party lines, with pros proclaiming it a "good alternative to going to the Ironbound", and cons countering "something's missing in the quality" since the years-ago relocation in a place that now serves "mass quantities of plain food."

Spanish Tavern
| 21 | 16 | 21 | $35 |

1239 Rte. 22 E. (Locust Ave.), Mountainside, 908-232-2171
103 McWhorter St. (Green St.), Newark, 973-589-4959
www.spanishtavern.com
Ardent adherents stress this duo has "no rival" in the Iberian genre in light of their "delicious" food, so "forget the Lipitor and just enjoy" the "bountiful" plates of paella and remember that the tabs won't "crush your wallet"; N.B. the Mountainside branch's recent redo gives it a new look.

Spargo's Grille
| 23 | 18 | 20 | $42 |

Andee Plaza, 130 Rte. 33 W. (Millhurst Rd.), Manalapan, 732-294-9921; www.spargosgrille.com
"A palate pleaser" parked in a strip mall, this "upscale" New American BYO in Manalapan cooks up "creative" fare that's "as good to look at as it is to eat"; though enthusiasts endorse the "above-average" service, some find it wise to "come early" before the personnel get "overwhelmed."

Specchio
| 23 | 24 | 22 | $59 |

Borgata Hotel, Casino & Spa, 1 Borgata Way (Atlantic City Expwy., exit 1), Atlantic City, 866-692-6742; www.theborgata.com
"High rollers" hit Luke Palladino's "elegant" and "stylish" Italian in the Borgata where the "heavenly", "innovative" cooking is enough "to take away the sting of casino losses"; but a "beautiful" atmosphere and "impeccable service" may not soothe those few who decry portion sizes on the plate fit "for a child at prices for a rich man."

Spike's
| 21 | 8 | 16 | $25 |

415 Broadway (bet. Rte. 35 & St. Louis Ave.),
Point Pleasant Beach, 732-295-9400
This "tiny little shack with lots to offer" in Point Pleasant Beach is a "no-nonsense combo" of "fish market and

| F | D | S | C |

restaurant" that draws "long lines in the summer"; if there are whispers about service ("it needs to be improved"), most "aren't disappointed" with "fresh fish."

Spirito Grill | 18 | 19 | 19 | $39 |

Sheraton Suites Hotel, 500 Harbor Blvd. (19th St.), Weehawken, 201-867-0101; www.spiritogrill.com

"Hop off the ferry and check out" this Italian "surprise" in the Sheraton Hotel in Weehawken; to fans, it's a "winner with neat views" of The Big Apple and a "good" bet for "well-prepared" fare, while others notice "slow" service and "uninspired" food.

Squan Tavern | 21 | 14 | 19 | $24 |

15 Broad St. (Main St.), Manasquan, 732-223-3324; www.squantavern.com

The food's the star at this "busy, friendly, neighborhood" Italian "landmark" that's "so popular, you almost always have to wait for a table"; it's Manasquan's unofficial town hall, "an icon" of "good old-fashioned cooking" that's "been the same for years" – "friendly waitresses" included – so "why change the formula if it works?"

Sri Thai | 24 | 7 | 17 | $19 |

234 Bloomfield St. (3rd St.), Hoboken, 201-798-4822

A bona fide "hole-in-the-wall", this "tiny" Thai eatery in Hoboken proffers treats so "fantastic", they'll "make you feel like you're eating from a vendor in Bangkok"; if you find the quarters cosmetically compromised, you may, quite logically, "opt for takeout"; P.S. "cheap prices" keep it on the "must-visit" lists of many.

STAGE HOUSE RESTAURANT & WINE BAR | 26 | 24 | 24 | $62 |

366 Park Ave. (Front St.), Scotch Plains, 908-322-4224; www.stagehouserestaurant.com

Even in the post–David Drake era, "it all still works" at this "romantic" "gem on the sleepy main drag" of Scotch Plains where New French fare is served forth in a "charming" 1737 building; "walk past the herb garden" and dig into the seasonal "market menu", insiders advise, or relax "in front of a roaring fire in the winter" over dishes that are "perfectly refined and ready" for what's on the "incredible wine list."

STAGE LEFT | 26 | 23 | 25 | $61 |

5 Livingston Ave. (George St.), New Brunswick, 732-828-4444; www.stageleft.com

The "love of food, wine and cheese permeates the air" at this New American "adjacent to the popular New Brunswick theater district" whose "impressive staff" delivers the kitchen's "exquisite" culinary creations; it's a vinophile's "paradise", grape geeks gush, so "get ready to spend" and see if you side with those who swear "every dollar's worth it."

	F	D	S	C

Starlite
| | 16 | 11 | 15 | $22 |

993 Pleasant Valley Way (Rte. 10), West Orange, 973-736-9440

"Duded-up" a bit after a recent renovation, this West Orange Italian/pizzeria now sports an enlarged space and a "cozy bar" but still serves what supporters say are "very good" pies; while some claim "visitors from outer space would make this their first stop for pizza", a few believe space brothers "could find better" options if they zoom around the Garden State.

Steve & Cookie's By the Bay
| | 25 | 22 | 23 | $47 |

9700 Amherst Ave. (N. Monroe Ave.), Margate, 609-823-1163; www.steveandcookies.com

"A little piece of Martha's Vineyard on the Jersey Shore", this Margate New American is where surf-catching "loafers and Louis Vuitton lovers" from Philadelphia congregate over "excellent" eats (including a "must-try lobster mac 'n' cheese appetizer") that inspire a "crowd" in summer; you may "need to make your reservations weeks ahead for a Saturday night" or learn what locals know – "winters are best!"

Stony Hill Inn
| | 23 | 25 | 23 | $51 |

231 Polifly Rd. (Rte. 80), Hackensack, 201-342-4085; www.stonyhillinn.com

If you want someone to "love you for life", take them to this "beautiful" "romantic delight" in Hackensack set in an 1818 building and known for "great" Continental-Italian food "with a sophisticated flair"; a plurality of patrons profess it's ideal for "formal, leisurely dining."

Store, The
| | 14 | 14 | 17 | $26 |

55 S. Finley Ave. (Henry St.), Basking Ridge, 908-766-9856; www.growthrestaurants.com

Though you "shouldn't expect The Ritz", this Basking Ridge American is more like "an old friend that comes through in the clutch" "when you're too tired to cook at home"; yes, "it could use a little je ne sais quoi", but it's a place where "families are welcome" and most of them don't mind that it's strictly, decidedly "run of the mill."

Strip House
| | 23 | 22 | 21 | $61 |

Westminster Hotel, 550 W. Mount Pleasant Ave. (bet. Daven Ave. & Microlab Rd.), Livingston, 973-548-0050; www.theglaziergroup.com

Supplicants of all things slablike go to the Livingston brother of Penny and Peter Glazier's NYC original for meat of the "melt-in-your-mouth" variety and "tasty sides"; the "bright red", "velvet"-heavy decor can play tricks on you (like a "jewelry box" or "bordello?"), and some reckon that "high tabs" mean you may have to "strip your wallet" before you leave.

vote at zagat.com

| F | D | S | C |

SUILAN
| 25 | 26 | 24 | $61 |

Borgata Hotel, Casino & Spa, 1 Borgata Way (Atlantic City Expwy., exit 1), Atlantic City, 609-317-7725; www.theborgata.com
Susanna Foo brings her trademark Chinese-French fusion fare to Atlantic City in the form of this "spectacular", "very upscale" entry in the Borgata's all-star lineup; "from potstickers to sashimi to complex preparations of fresh fish", "you'll be in for the experience of a lifetime" and be "doted on" by the staff amid "soothing" surroundings.

Sunny Garden
| 22 | 20 | 18 | $27 |

15 Farber Rd. (Rte. 1), West Windsor, 609-520-1881; www.sunnygarden.net
"This ain't just a take-out joint", maintain mavens who tout the "seasonal selections" at this West Windsor Chinese "tucked behind the hustle and bustle of busy Route 1" a few "minutes from Princeton University"; considering the "calming and serene" setting and "prompt" staff, the BYO's brightly deemed "a find."

Surf Taco
| - | - | - | I |

121 Parker Ave. (Stockton Lake Blvd.), Manasquan, 732-223-7757
1300 Richmond Ave. (Marcia Ave.), Point Pleasant Beach, 732-701-9000
www.surftaco.com
Ride the waves to these Eclectic twins in bustling beach towns and find students of all stripes chowing down on Shore-styled Mexican street fare as surfer videos streak by on screens in the background; as casual and relaxed as a Malibu morning, the BYOs boast some of the biggest seafood-stuffed burritos around, not to mention mile-high salads and rad wraps.

Sushi by Kazu
| ∇ 24 | 11 | 19 | $32 |

2724 Rte. 9 S. (bet. 2nd & 3rd Sts.), Howell, 732-370-2528
Chef "Kazu is king" and his "specials" are "particularly enjoyable" at this Japanese "secret" in a "teeny strip mall" in Howell; "don't be fooled by the off-putting location" and be advised you may experience "a long wait" at the BYO that serves some of the "freshest sushi in the area."

Sushi Lounge
| 23 | 22 | 19 | $34 |

200 Hudson St. (2nd St.), Hoboken, 201-386-1117; www.sushilounge.com
If you like a "scene" with your sushi, one of the "sexiest", "trendiest" venues in Downtown Hoboken may be just the right catch for you, where a "fresh-out-of-college" crowd can be seen supping on "fresh and tasty" raw fare, sipping "martinis" at the bar and "screaming" over the "damn-loud" music from a nightly DJ; BTW, it's cool and correct to "ask to see the chef's special roll list."

| F | D | S | C |

Sweet Vidalia   21 | 16 | 20 | $41
122 N. Bay Ave. (Long Beach Blvd.), Beach Haven, 609-207-1200
"A welcome addition to the Beach Haven gourmet scene" is this seasonal New American BYO with an "ever-changing" bill of fare and, natch, several dishes "featuring Vidalia onions"; its early fans adore the "updated takes" on classics, and appreciate that the "old storefront" has turned into one of the "fancier places" on LBI.

Tacconelli's Pizzeria ⊖   21 | 11 | 15 | $16
450 S. Lenola Rd. (Rte. 38), Maple Shade, 856-638-0338
"One of Philly's best comes across the river" to Maple Shade and is being welcomed by surveyors enamored of the "white with garlic" pizza and pleased to skip the "schlepping" to the Port Richmond, PA, "papa"; divided diners of the dough and sauce deem the "original" "better", but most don't deny this Jersey pie stop its due, considering its "unbeatable" "crisp crust."

Taipei Noodle House   21 | 10 | 19 | $21
483 Cedar Ln. (bet. Elm & Garrison Aves.), Teaneck, 201-836-8230
"Inexpensive, delicious Chinese food, the kind you yearn for on a Sunday night", is the hallmark of this "bright and happy" Teaneck Asian that serves "numerous choices" of "delicious" delights; "be daring when you order", authorities advise, and take advantage of the "friendly and efficient service" at the BYO with a "small town feel."

Tang Dynasty   ▽ 24 | 17 | 18 | $25
Stella Towne Ctr., 1226 Rte. 166 (Bey Lea Rd.), Dover Township, 732-286-1505
A Japanese-Chinese newcomer with an "impressive sushi bar" lures those in-the-know who appreciate the "great variety" of "yummy" Asian dishes at this Dover Township BYO; early birds to the shopping center locale report a spacious scene and eager-to-please service.

Tapas de Espana   20 | 17 | 19 | $35
47 N. Dean St. (bet. Palisade Ave. & Park Pl.), Englewood, 201-569-9999
7909 Bergenline Ave. (79th St.), North Bergen, 201-453-1690
There's "a long and varied list of tapas" at these Bergen County Iberians that make you "feel like you've stepped into Madrid"; "the ever-present crowd" amps up the "sound and smoke level" so that it "rivals a disco", and if the "entrees are too simple and small to justify their high prices", it's wise to "make an entire meal" of the nibbles and bits.

Taro   21 | 23 | 19 | $35
32 Church St. (S. Park St.), Montclair, 973-509-2266;
www.tarorestaurant.com
"Hip" "minimalist decor" sets a "tranquil and lovely" setting at this Montclair multi-Asian with a menu "that juggles

vote at zagat.com

| F | D | S | C |

techniques and ingredients from the different Eastern cultures", and results in cuisine with "that rarest of qualities" – "memorable"; though a minority moans that it's "overpriced" and the food "under-spiced", a "loyal crowd" likes what it sees and concludes the BYO's "impressive."

Taste of Asia, A   22 | 15 | 20 | $28
245 Main St. (N. Passaic Ave.), Chatham, 973-701-8821
54-56 W. South Orange Ave. (bet. Ridgewood & Scotland Rds.), South Orange, 973-378-8818
www.atasteofasianj.com
"Once you've tasted" the "eclectic collection" of dishes at these North Jersey Southeast Malaysian specialists, "you'll never eat neighborhood Chinese again", claim converts to the BYO's "well-prepared offerings" that leave fans "wanting for nothing but more room for more food"; so, bear with the "bare spaces" and flash a smile, since the service is "helpful" and the tabs "reasonable."

Taste of Vietnam   – | – | – | M
Sayreville Plaza, 960 Rte. 9 S. (Garden State Pkwy., exit 123), South Amboy, 732-525-8878; www.tasteofvietnamnj.com
Take a short detour off the parkway to savor some pho and other Vietnamese classics at this South Amboy storefront BYO that may not have good looks on its side, but remains true to its cuisine; the yearling's straightforward style is attracting purists who like its no-nonsense sensibilities.

Tattoni's Cafe ⊠   ∇ 22 | 11 | 20 | $24
800 Chestnut Ave. (Morris Ave.), Trenton, 609-394-1456
"Not your get-dressed-up-to-dinner-Italian" but rather more "like eating in your grandmother's kitchen", insist insiders of this "homey" Trenton "jewel" with "no menus" but with "addictive chicken cacciatore in white wine"; expect "friendly" service and a "smoky", "quirky" scene.

Teak   22 | 24 | 19 | $40
64 Monmouth St. (Broad St.), Red Bank, 732-747-5775; www.teakrestaurant.com
Call it "chic" and wonder if it's "maybe too trendy for the long haul", but know that on "any Thursday, Friday or Saturday night, the bar is three deep" at this "super-cool" Pan-Asian in Red Bank with "Zen-like decor" that includes "huge palm trees" and a Buddha; while most give this "pearl" "high marks" for "creative, beautiful" "fusion" food, disillusioned dissenters" cite "smoke and mirrors service."

Teresa's   20 | 15 | 16 | $28
19-23 Palmer Sq. E. (Nassau St.), Princeton, 609-921-1974; www.terramomo.com
"Perfect for a college town" and "always hopping", this "Princeton hangout" serves up "low-key" Italian selections that "never fail to satisfy"; yup, the "waits are ridiculous" and the "captive audience" sometimes senses a "spotty"

| F | D | S | C |

floor crew, but "when you need a pasta fix" it just might be the "best value in town."

Terrace Restaurant | 22 | 21 | 21 | $45 |
Hilton at Short Hills, 41 JFK Pkwy. (Rte. 24, exit 7C), Short Hills, 973-379-0100; www.hiltonshorthills.com

"Luxury" and "class" meet at this Mediterranean near the Mall at Short Hills that's dubbed the Hilton's "second restaurant", but is an "impressive" venue nonetheless "for business or pleasure"; "an excellent Sunday brunch with unsurpassed variety" "can't be matched", eager eaters enthuse, and since the "surroundings are lovely", it may be easy to lose sight of "expense-account" tabs.

Terra Christa's | 19 | 19 | 19 | $31 |
231 Main St. (Rte. 34), Matawan, 732-441-9292; www.terrachristas.com

"Innovative dishes" and an "amiable chef-owner" boost this New American "in an otherwise unassuming strip mall" in Matawan to "real-find" status; though naysayers note it's a "strictly amateur hour" operation, and cite "inconsistent preparations", locals still look to it as a "nice, intimate" BYO.

Tesauro's | 19 | 17 | 18 | $31 |
401 Broadway (Rte. 35), Point Pleasant Beach, 732-892-2090; www.tesaurosrestaurant.com

Point Pleasant Beach may be a "town of seafooders", but this "good old-fashioned Italian" has long inspired "strong loyalty" among day-trippers and locals; though a few fret over how the "landmark" will fare with the arrival of new owners (who took over more than a year ago), most signs indicate that it's retaining its "friendly" reputation.

Tewksbury Inn | 22 | 20 | 20 | $41 |
55 Main St./Rte. 517 (King St.), Oldwick, 908-439-2641

It's "quintessential country", but ever since the relatively recent arrival of the "new chef", foodies are taking note of this "perfect" New American destination in Oldwick; mingle with "blue bloods in blazers", "yuppies", "gentleman farmers and real farmers" who "meet on common ground" and "dine in a sea of toile and candlelight" or in the "casual" "clubby" tavern; P.S. the no-reservations thing is a "downer."

Texas Arizona | 14 | 12 | 14 | $24 |
76 River St. (Hudson Pl.), Hoboken, 201-420-0304; www.texasarizona.com

PATH proximity makes this Hoboken American with a "college bar feel" a stop for "loud and happy" hordes of happy-hour hounds to "unwind" and sup on all sorts of "decent" vittles and, natch, to slurp down some brew; "don't expect anything fancy here", and if you want four-star service, some say "look elsewhere."

vote at zagat.com

	F	D	S	C

THAI CHEF 22 | 17 | 18 | $30
28A Diamond Spring Rd. (W. Main St.), Denville, 973-983-0800
Palisade Court Shopping Ctr., 63 Nathaniel Pl. (Palisade Ave.), Englewood, 201-227-7487
Riverside Square Mall, 169 Hackensack Ave. (off Rte. 4), Hackensack, 201-342-7257
664 Bloomfield Ave. (bet. Orange & Valley Rds.), Montclair, 973-783-4994
24 E. Main St. (bet. Bridge & Warren Sts.), Somerville, 908-253-8300
www.thaichefrestaurant.com

"Try Thai for the first time" at this expanding mini-chain that boasts "traditional favorites" and "nice surprises" and individualizing nuances among the branches (Somerville sports sushi, while Englewood goes a little Gallic); reviewers regale with tales of "innovative, fragrant, spicy and sweet" dishes and don't mind if the setting's "lackluster" and the service "sometimes overwhelmed"

Thai Kitchen 24 | 14 | 22 | $22
1351 Prince Rodgers Ave. (off I-287, exit 14B), Bridgewater, 908-231-8822
Somerset Shopping Ctr., 327 Hwy. 202/206 (off Rte. 22), Bridgewater, 908-722-8983
Hillsborough Shopping Ctr., 649 Hwy. 206 (Amwell Rd.), Hillsborough, 908-904-8038

A lunch hub that's a "popular" venue for "business" doings and dealings, these Somerset County sibs showcase dining rooms that are "always jam-packed" with those waiting for the "terrific" takes on Thai; with "friendly, friendly, friendly" wait staffs that are "attentive", yet "pleasantly invisible during the meal", the BYOs are "not a well-kept secret."

Thai Thai 25 | 16 | 23 | $25
1168 Valley Rd. (bet. Poplar Dr. & Warren Ave.), Stirling, 908-903-0790

"There's no need for bridges, tunnels or tolls" since this "sleepy-little-strip-mall" Stirling Thai BYO keeps droves of "loyalists" coming back for food "bursting with flavor"; smitten supporters suggest "introduce the cuisine to kids" in a place where "service is speedy speedy" – even on "packed Saturday nights."

Theater Square Grill 20 | 23 | 18 | $46
New Jersey Performing Arts Ctr., 1 Center St. (McCarter Hwy.), Newark, 973-642-1226; www.theatersquaregrill.com

An "absolute must" if you're going to NJPAC, this Newark American-Continental serves up "well-prepared, fairly high-concept" fare and a "hip, cosmopolitan" vibe in a "cavernous", "striking" space; critical cognoscenti caution, however, that you may end up paying "high prices" for the pre-show "convenience."

| F | D | S | C |

Theresa's
| 23 | 17 | 19 | $36 |

47 Elm St. (bet. E. Broad St. & North Ave.), Westfield, 908-233-9133; www.theresasrestaurant.com

Label it an "absolute gem in a hoity-toity town" and descend with the denizens to this BYO standby in Westfield that "excels" in creating "delicious" Italian dishes and "old favorites" with a "new twist", and where the "din" in the dining room can get "ridiculous"; the no-reserve policy, though, "makes it difficult" for some to return.

3 West
| 23 | 24 | 20 | $46 |

665 Martinsville Rd. (Rte. 78), Basking Ridge, 908-647-3000

Its strip-mall location doesn't deter devotees of chef Bruce Johnson's Basking Ridge "hot spot" that draws "young corporate types" with an "imaginative", "rustic" American menu, "extensive" wine list and "active bar scene"; the "small", "beautifully decorated" private rooms (with a "modern mountain lodge" feel) help make it an "excellent choice" "for business meetings" or "a special night out."

Tick Tock Diner ☻
| 16 | 12 | 16 | $18 |

281 Allwood Rd./Rte. 3 W. (Garden State Pkwy., exit 153), Clifton, 973-777-0511

Old-timers tick off the "memories" of this "classic" Jersey diner in Clifton that's "a must" for anyone traveling the Route 3 corridor and often "the final stop of many bar-hoppers after last call"; you better believe it's a tad "tacky" and totally "typical", but it "provides hearty meals 24/7", which makes the 1949 "landmark" loved by everyone in the "fries-with-gravy" crowd.

Tim Schafer's Cuisine
| 25 | 15 | 22 | $41 |

82 Speedwell Ave. (Clinton Pl.), Morristown, 973-538-3330; www.timschaferscuisine.com

Man with a can (of beer, that is) and "genius" chef-owner Tim Schafer's "ale-infused" "culinary risks" pay off at his "much-needed" and applauded "high-end" New American BYO in Morristown; the "attractive" plate presentations and "attentive" floor crew that "answers diners' questions" about the "constantly changing menu" make up for the "strip-mally" decor.

Tina Louise
| 26 | 15 | 22 | $27 |

403 Hackensack St. (bet. Broad St. & Division Ave.), Carlstadt, 201-933-7133; www.villagerestaurantgroup.com

"Utterly unique, high-quality" Chinese-inspired Asian cooking and "owners who make you feel like family" lure more than locals to this "tiny gem" of a BYO in Carlstadt; castaways from common Cantonese comestibles claim the "inexpensive" eatery has "reawakened interest" in the cuisine, so even if the "setting is claustrophobic", "the food speaks for itself time and time again."

vote at zagat.com

| F | D | S | C |

Tisha's Fine Dining ▽ 24 | 21 | 21 | $45
714 Beach Ave. (Stockton Ave.), Cape May, 609-884-9119;
www.tishasfinedining.com
A "lovely surprise" overlooking the ocean, this "small" Cape May New American BYO "earns loyalty" not just for the "gorgeous view from the outdoor porch" and the "sounds of waves", but for the "wonderful" food and "elegant Victorian" atmosphere; all of the above serve to "perfectly describe" a "magical" experience.

Tomatoes 26 | 25 | 22 | $50
9300 Amherst Ave. (Washington Ave.), Margate, 609-822-7535
This "trendy" Margate Cal-Eclectic draws an "Armani-clad" company of "beautiful people" who dine on "beautifully presented" and prepared food in a "sophisticated, serene" setting; it "can be crazy in summer", but if you cool your heels at the "busy bar" over a glass of vino from the 300-bottle list, you may just judge it "fabulous."

Tony Da Caneca 22 | 15 | 22 | $35
72 Elm Rd. (Houston St.), Newark, 973-589-6882;
www.tonydacaneca.com
"Enormous" portions of "first-rate" seafood are the highlights at this Newark Iberian "off the Ferry Street strip" that's seen as a "cut above others"; though "it could use a face-lift", "if you can find it, you'll love it", claim connoisseurs of the "quality and quantity" genre.

Top Notch 17 | 16 | 18 | $30
700 Bloomfield Ave. (bet. St. Luke's Pl. & Valley Rd.),
Montclair, 973-746-5699
An "old reliable" to some may be a "same old, same old" to others, but this American-German in Montclair is a "fixture for the BYO" brigade and "popular" with an "older" crew; though critics chide the stalwart's "dreary" digs, a more charitable lot tip their hats to the "friendly" staff.

Tortilla Press 23 | 18 | 20 | $25
703 Haddon Ave. (Collings Ave.), Collingswood, 856-869-3345;
www.thetortillapress.com
"Not your standard" Mexican affair, this Collingswood "eating mecca" "unlike anything in the area" creates "nuevo" fare that provides an "anti–Taco Bell" antidote for its fans; tequilaphiliacs should note the BYO offers "margarita mixes" if you tote your own.

Tortuga's Mexican Village 23 | 10 | 18 | $20
44 Leigh Ave. (bet. John & Witherspoon Sts.), Princeton,
609-924-5143
11½ Church St. (Union St.), Lambertville, 609-397-7272
www.tortugasmv.com
"Ignore the tattered walls" at this "kitschy" culinary crash pad in Princeton that presents "fantastic", "authentic"

| F | D | S | C |

Mexican goods and possibly "the best salsa on the planet"; "you can't get a better value in town", which may be why it's "jam-packed", but if you're willing to saddle up and head northwest to Lambertville, there's a new (and non-BYO) outpost cloistered comfortably behind an old tavern.

Trap Rock
20 | 20 | 17 | $39

279 Springfield Ave. (bet. Snyder & Union Aves.), Berkeley Heights, 908-665-1755; www.traprockrest.com

Combine "awesome" beers and "well-prepared" New American chow and you've got the makings of a rock-solid microbrewery in Berkeley Heights where those looking for more than "ordinary pub food" "hit pay dirt"; the "ski-lodge" thing adds to the allure of this "adult night out" spot that's "smoky, but very sophisticated."

Trattoria Fratelli
16 | 15 | 15 | $30

119 E. Ridgewood Ave. (bet. Oak & Walnut Sts.), Ridgewood, 201-447-9377

If you're looking for "family-oriented" Italian with "good" food and a "casual, warm" environment, take a gander at this Ridgewood BYO; on the other hand, detractors dish that "erratic service" and "ordinary" offerings make it like "hundreds" of others.

Tre Figlio
∇ 24 | 21 | 23 | $42

500 W. White Horse Pike (Mannheim Ave.), Egg Harbor, 609-965-3303; www.trefiglio.com

Take a ride out of Atlantic City and aim straight for this "out-of-the-way" Italian "jewel" in Egg Harbor City noted for food that "harmoniously" unites both "homestyle" and "modern" sensibilities; a 200-plus-label wine list and "professional, down-to-earth" floor crew keep things flowing in the right direction.

Tre Piani
19 | 20 | 19 | $43

Forrestal Village Shopping Ctr., 120 Rockingham Row (College Rd. W.), Plainsboro, 609-452-1515; www.trepiani.com

Find "thoughtfully prepared" Med-Italian provisions at this Plainsboro "underappreciated treasure", the unofficial "center of the Slow Food movement" (i.e. sustainable agriculture, a commitment to high-quality ingredients, etc.) in central Jersey that sports a "downstairs bistro" and "upstairs dining room" that's "popular for business lunches"; "disappointed" diners, though, think there are "better choices" nearby.

Tre Vigne
22 | 20 | 21 | $49

95 Morristown Rd. (bet. Maple & N. Finley Aves.), Basking Ridge, 908-221-0017; www.trevignerestaurant.com

"One of the better restaurants" in Somerset Hills, this "graceful and earnest" Med-Italian in Basking Ridge is a "peaceful place" to enjoy "wonderful" food and a staff "that doesn't come any better"; though the room and clientele

| F | D | S | C |

may remind some of "an early-bird seating on a cruise ship", many put it "on the top of their list."

Triumph Brewing Company | 16 | 19 | 16 | $28 |
138 Nassau St. (Washington Rd.), Princeton, 609-924-7855; www.triumphbrewing.com
"Have a pint, eat and strike up a conversation" at this "faux industrial", "trendy and loud" microbrewery in Princeton; an Eclectic menu that "covers the bases", from casual bar food to "nouvelle dinner entrees", satisfies the student set, while pickier palates pout about "standard" grub and "go for the beer."

Tsuki ⑤ | 22 | 13 | 17 | $29 |
23 Mine Brook Rd. (Mt. Airy Rd.), Bernardsville, 908-953-0450
"The artful chef" keeps 'em coming back for more at this Japanese in Bernardsville where the lure includes "tasty", tantalizingly tagged rolls (how about the "Viagra"?) that make giggly raw-fish fans give a "thumbs up" to; so brush aside the "brusque" service and "grab a quick bite before a movie" at the nearby theater.

Tuckers Eating & Drinking Establishment | 18 | 18 | 18 | $28 |
101 West Ave. (Engleside Ave.), Beach Haven, 609-492-2300
Establishing itself as a "Shore bet", this "busy", "reliable" Beach Haven bar/eatery supplies "original" Traditional American aliments, bartenders "full of personality" and a deck on a "sunny day" to take advantage of the "right-by-the-bay" location; acolytes advise it may be prudent to arrive with "tavern expectations and you may be very pleasantly surprised."

Tun Tavern | 16 | 16 | 16 | $24 |
Sheraton Hotel, 2 Miss America Way (Kirkman Blvd.), Atlantic City, 609-347-7800; www.tuntavern.com
Ale aficionados admire the "great" selection of housemade microbrews at this pub purveying a slate of Traditional American eats and T-shirts, caps and the like on-site; dissers hiss it's a place to go "when you don't want to hear what's being said at your table", and that the "beer's great, but after that . . . "

Tuptim | 22 | 17 | 20 | $27 |
600 Bloomfield Ave. (bet. Park St. & Valley Rd.), Montclair, 973-783-3800; www.tuptimthaicuisine.com
Take a "mini-vacation to Bangkok" at this "good option" in Montclair "for pad Thai or other favorites"; the decor is "a bit spartan", but a separate menu of non-meat items is a "vegetarian's paradise", adding interest to the BYO that's "one of the original" Thai places around before the onset of its "trendier" brethren.

| F | D | S | C |

Tuscany Trattoria | 17 | 18 | 17 | $35 |
284 Center Ave. (bet. Irvington St. & Westwood Ave.), Westwood, 201-666-1166; www.tuscanytrattoria.com
Find a "bit of old Italia" in Westwood at this "pleasant" and "popular" locale with "pretty Tuscan murals" and a "wide selection" of specialties shepherded by "friendly servers"; connoisseurs of red, white and green cuisine, however, bluntly state it's "nothing special."

Tuzzio's | 20 | 11 | 19 | $28 |
224 Westwood Ave. (Morris Ave.), Long Branch, 732-222-9614
Italian "comfort food" "just like grandma makes" reigns at this longtime eatery in Long Branch where "lots of regulars" flock for the "mixed salad for one that feeds up to six"; it "provides taste and character" in copious amounts "for the money", Shore supporters say, so even if the decor's "nothing to rave about", shuddup and slurp the "red sauce."

Two If By Sea | 22 | 14 | 19 | $45 |
141 Shrewsbury Ave. (Herbert St.), Red Bank, 732-747-1586; www.twoifbysea.com
It's "worth a trip to the other side" of Red Bank to this "nondescript" New American for its "absolutely top-notch" fare with strong seafood representation on a seasonal menu; while a few feel it "was better" at its previous locale, others see an "inspirational comeback" in a place that had "lost its way for a while"; P.S. check out the "none-too-shabby" wine list.

2Senza Ristorante | 20 | 18 | 18 | $42 |
The Galleria, 2 Bridge Ave. (W. Front St.), Red Bank, 732-758-0999; www.2senza.com
There's a "warm neighborhood vibe" at this "bustling" BYO in a "beautifully restored" "old warehouse" on the west side of Red Bank, where an open kitchen dispenses "NYC-inspired" Mediterranean fare to an "upscale" crowd; it's all "special" to some, while the less enthused find "indifferent" service from a place that's "2expensive."

Ugly Mug | 15 | 14 | 15 | $20 |
426 Washington St. (Decatur St.), Cape May, 609-884-3459; www.uglymugenterprises.com
Belly up to this bar/"institution" "with character", where chowing down the "solid pub grub" served at the American "hangout" is a "tradition" in Cape May; according to Shore lore, it's "nothing fancy", so "throw on a pair of jeans and a T-shirt" and "hunker down over a burger and fries."

Union Landing | 15 | 17 | 16 | $32 |
622 Green Ave. (Union Ln.), Brielle, 732-528-6665; www.unionlanding.com
"The fight for a table in the summer can be intense, but it's worth it" at this seafooder "overlooking a marina" along

vote at zagat.com

| F | D | S | C |

the Manasquan River in Brielle; if you're stuck on "typical" fare, try a "cocktail" and "watch the sunset", regulars reveal, since the setting "trumps any concerns you may have" of "one of the best places to relax" around.

Valentino
| 22 | 20 | 21 | $49 |

150 South St. (bet. Elm & Pine Sts.), Morristown, 973-993-8066
"Feel like Hollywood royalty" right in Morristown at this "great date place" where you can "meet at the piano bar then mosey over" to the dining room for "consistently good" bites of Italian goods; it's favored by "40-year-olds and divorcees", swear those charmed by its "formal style", and add that the "upscale" gal, though a "bit pricey", is "worth it."

Valentino's
| 19 | 17 | 18 | $42 |

103 Spring Valley Rd. (bet. Fremont & Grand Aves.), Park Ridge, 201-391-2230; www.valentinosrestaurantparkridge.com
Though there may be "no big surprises" at this "romantic" Park Ridge Italian, the "over-50 crowd" attached to the "friendly servers" calls it a "nice place to celebrate a quiet birthday or anniversary"; but surveyors split over the "classic" brand it either a "lovely suburban oasis" or an "anachronism" in need of an across the board "shake-up."

Venezia
| ▽ 19 | 15 | 19 | $31 |

Chester Springs Shopping Ctr., 237 Rte. 206 N. (bet. Old Chester Rd. & Rte. 24), Chester, 908-879-2848
"Gracious service rounds out a delightful dining experience" at this Italian "hidden pleasure" in a Chester strip mall that gets little air play, but does, however, "allow for a fancy dinner without a large bill" thanks to BYO status; reviewers reserving criticism for a reservations book that could be "better managed" still say it's worth "a go."

Ventura's Greenhouse ◐
| 18 | 17 | 17 | $31 |

106 S. Benson Ave. (Atlantic Ave.), Margate, 609-822-0140
"After a hard day at the beach", check out this Margate Italian dispensing "dependable" food but where it's all about "location, location, location" – and "bikinis, bikinis, bikinis"; with its "laid-back, totally Shore atmosphere", this paradigm of people-watching places prides itself on an outdoor deck where you can make sport of eyeing a "strange brew" of "bikers", "muscle men" and "families."

Venue
| – | – | – | E |

518 Washington St. (bet. 5th & 6th Sts.), Hoboken, 201-653-6111; www.venue-restaurant.com
Operating *way* outside the culinary box, this Hoboken arrival's bold, trippy New American menu via chef-owner James George Sarkar (ex March, NYC) features mind-benders from lamb cappuccino to pineapple carpaccio, in an

| F | D | S | C |

ultracool, ultramod and soothing bi-level space; you'll be hard-pressed to find anything like it around; N.B. BYO, and open for dinner only.

Verjus
24 | 19 | 21 | $45

1790 Springfield Ave. (Rutgers St.), Maplewood, 973-378-8990; www.verjusrestaurant.com

"Real French in the suburbs" translates as a "real find" to reviewers who rave over the "well-executed" classics at this "low-key" "surprise" in Maplewood; the "great attention to detail" is evident in a "fabulous brunch", "prompt" service and "affordable, original wine list", which, in plain English, means it's "a winner."

Verve
23 | 19 | 20 | $45

18 E. Main St. (bet. Grove & N. Bridge Sts.), Somerville, 908-707-8655; www.vervestyle.com

A "swank" setting gives this "cool" hybrid of a lounge/eatery in Somerville enough "allure" to host a huddle of hipsters who groove to its "tasty" French–New American chow and "great" live weekend jazz; P.S. "nonsmokers" need not apply.

Vic's
20 | 10 | 17 | $20

60 Main St. (Evergreen Ave.), Bradley Beach, 732-774-8225; www.vicspizza.com

"Bring a whole gang of kids" to this "family-oriented" throwback to "the '50s" in Bradley Beach where the "retro surroundings" are home to "awesome" thin-crust pizza and "waitresses who've been there forever"; yeah, the Italian looks a bit "run-down", but for locals, there's little need to explain the "old schooler's" appeal, since it's simply "a tradition."

Villa Amalfi
20 | 20 | 20 | $46

793 Palisade Ave. (Marion Ave.), Cliffside Park, 201-886-8626; www.villaamalfi.com

This "comfortable" Cliffside Park "classic" churns out Italian food that may be "uninteresting", yet "very good" in an ambiance that can only be described as one that escapes "being trendy"; modernists moan a "newer menu" may be the cure, but traditionalists like everything just fine and are "never disappointed."

Village Gourmet
21 | 18 | 18 | $27

73-75 Park Ave. (Ridge Rd.), Rutherford, 201-438-9404; www.villagerestaurantgroup.com

"You can't go wrong" with this BYO "treasure" in Rutherford where the "in-house liquor store keeps the bill for drinks way down" and the "interesting variety" of foodstuffs keeps interest in the Eclectic lineup way up; maybe there's a bit of a "green" in the staff, but since it's "steady" and "delivers a consistent meal at a reasonable price", respondents "keep going back."

| F | D | S | C |

VILLAGE GREEN ⊠   26 | 19 | 21 | $50
36 Prospect St. (Hudson St.), Ridgewood, 201-445-2914
"A quiet, cozy nook of epicurean delight", this Ridgewood New American's "exquisite preparations" come in the form of tasting menus known for "intense flavors" – "expect to spend a long time going through the many courses"; add in a staff that "knows what they're talking about", and this "prix fixe gem" gets "an A+."

Villa Vittoria   21 | 17 | 20 | $36
2700 Hooper Ave. (Cedar Bridge Rd.), Brick, 732-920-1550; www.villavittoria.com
"Good old Italian cooking with lots of oomph" and a floor crew comprised of "strolling serenaders" turn this Brick standby "near the Shore" into "a welcome option to the chains and fast-food joints that surround it"; loyalists insist new owners (members of the former proprietor's staff) are keeping things "consistent."

Walpack Inn   19 | 21 | 18 | $34
Rte. 615 (Rte. 206 N.), Wallpack Center, 973-948-3890; www.walpackinn.com
Take a "beautiful drive through scenic countryside" to this "red-meat haven" in Wallpack dressed up like a "hunting lodge" and sample "simple", "well-prepared" American food "like grandma used to make"; sit before a "crackling fire" and "watch deer grazing in the field outside" as you nibble on "brown bread to die for" and dine in the "midst of forest lands."

Wasabi Asian Plates   25 | – | 22 | $28
12 W. Main St. (N. Bridge St.), Somerville, 908-203-8881
Wasabi House
Colchester Plaza, 77 Tices Ln. (Rte. 18), East Brunswick, 732-254-9988
The "new reigning sushi champion" in Somerville is this "buzzy" "upscale" Japanese yearling (in the former Asian Plates spot) employing a "helpful" staff dishing "innovative" raw fare including a sake menu; at the "homey and friendly" Wasabi House in East Brunswick, the chefs "constantly come up with new ways to prepare the food", so even if the "location is so-so" and appearance "drab", the BYO is still "popular."

WASHINGTON INN   27 | 25 | 26 | $54
801 Washington St. (Jefferson St.), Cape May, 609-884-5697; www.washingtoninn.com
"Unlike the weather, you can always count on it to be great" say diehards of this American that's "as good as it gets in Cape May", an "always on-the-money", "up-to-date" "favorite" with "fantastic" fare and an "outstanding" 900-bottle wine list; other restaurants "should send their staff here for training", since "no detail is forgotten", so even

| | F | D | S | C |

though it may be "tough on the pocketbook", the entire package is deemed "total class all the way."

West Lake Seafood Restaurant ▽ | 25 | 13 | 19 | $24
1016 Rte. 34 (Garden State Pkwy., exit 123), Matawan, 732-290-2988
It's "as authentic as you can get" at this "superb" BYO Chinese seafood specialist in Matawan, where the "unique dishes" ("the steamed live shrimp are to die for") "not commonly" found at take-out joints lure more than locals; "knowledgeable servers" guide novices through the weekend dim sum and other items on the menu, while "kids can't take their eyes off the fish tanks."

What's Your Beef? | 21 | 14 | 17 | $37
21 W. River Rd. (Lafayette St.), Rumson, 732-842-6205
Rumsonites who want "a little control over their steak" head to this "dependable" hangout where meat eaters select slabs that are "cut to their liking" and then "grilled to perfection by expert hands"; indulge in the "horseradish cheese spread and crackers" at the bar or the "best-ever salad bar" that's "chock-full of fresh veggies" if your stomach has a cow over the "long waits."

WHISPERS | 27 | 23 | 25 | $52
Hewitt Wellington Hotel, 200 Monmouth Ave. (2nd Ave.), Spring Lake, 732-974-9755; www.whispersrestaurant.com
If the "sublime" is what you seek, by all means try this chandeliered New American "wonder" in Spring Lake offering an "awesome, intimate dining experience" that's even more "memorable in the off-season"; its "heavenly" fare, BYO status and staff "on standby" to serve may soften the screams of those who say you'll need "a high credit limit" on that platinum.

WHITE HOUSE ⌀ | 27 | 8 | 15 | $12
2301 Arctic Ave. (Mississippi Ave.), Atlantic City, 609-345-1564
"Hail to the chief"! of cheese steaks, hoagies, subs – whatever you want to call them, since this Atlantic City "landmark" (our *Survey*'s No. 1 Bang for the Buck) is known to have patrons who've "driven the 100-mile round-trip on many occasions" just to pick up the "best sandwiches on earth"; now listen, there's "no decor except the wall-to-wall pictures of famous clientele", and ya bettah unnerstan' you can't reserve a table even "if you're Jerry Vale."

Wild Ginger | 24 | 14 | 18 | $48
6 E. Palisade Ave. (bet. Dean & S. Van Brunt Sts.), Englewood, 201-567-2660
"The absolute benchmark for creative and delicious" Japanese in Englewood is this "new wave" raw-fish specialist where "imaginative" meals are the norm; "culinary genius" comes with a price, even supporters

vote at zagat.com

of the BYO sigh, so "mortgage your house before going" since ordering "a few special rolls" may cause "your check to double before you can say 'sushi.'"

Willie's Taverne 15 | 15 | 17 | $30
Lamington Rd./Rte. 202 N. (Hillside Ave.), Bedminster, 908-234-1596; www.williestaverne.com
"Don't let the crowded parking lot scare you – it's a huge place", advise insiders who frequent this Bedminster American mainstay, be it following "a local softball game or after work"; it "won't wow you", and the "mishmash of country-kitchen and manor styles" doesn't thrill, but if you "stick with the pub-style items, you'll be safe."

Windansea 18 | 19 | 18 | $36
56 Shrewsbury Ave. (Bay Ave.), Highlands, 732-872-2266; www.windanseanj.com
The "fresh" fare "doesn't disappoint" at this "waterfront" watering hole/seafooder in Highlands that appeals to "families" and a weekend "twentysomething crowd racing for the dance floor when dinner's done"; that's right, it tends to turn into a "rowdy singles scene", so "come early" if you wish to avoid it.

Wolfgang Puck Express 18 | 15 | 14 | $18
100 Sinatra Dr. (1st St.), Hoboken, 201-876-8600; www.wolfgangpuck.com
A satellite in the Puck universe, this Downtown Hoboken semi-self-serve child of a fast-food joint and a "high-class" restaurant whips up "healthy, tasty" Cal-American bites at "affordable prices" for those who wish to eat in the "upscale" "cafeteria" setting or others who opt to get the goods delivered; P.S. it's "great" for stroller mommies.

Wonder Seafood ∇ 21 | 10 | 14 | $22
1984 Rte. 27 (Langstaff Ave.), Edison, 732-287-6328
"You'd swear you were in Chinatown for dim sum" exclaim advocates of this Edison BYO with a seafood emphasis but "plenty of pork buns" and other land animal items if you need them; "go with friends to share", though be advised "a lot of locals" make for "long lines", and the "bright", "glaring room" is invariably "packed to capacity."

Word of Mouth 23 | 23 | 21 | $38
729 Haddon Ave. (bet. Collings & Washington Aves.), Collingswood, 856-858-2228
The word on the street is that Food for Thought's relative offers evidence of "Philadelphians crossing the bridge to dine in Jersey": this "simply wonderful" New American BYO in "newly hip" Collingswood has surveyors savoring "the kind of meal that leaves everyone happily full" amid a "beautifully appointed" space featuring stained-glass windows; you'll now understand why the area "is becoming known for fine dining."

| F | D | S | C |

Wu's Bistro
▽ 25 | 14 | 23 | $22

Plaza 70 E., 70 Rte. 70 E. (Maple Ave.), Marlton, 856-596-5599

Wooed by Elena Wu's "casual" BYO, voters who've vetted her Chinese spot in Marlton say it's "well worth" your time; it may be in a "nondescript strip mall", but "vegetable spring rolls that are a quick addiction", "unique takes" on standards and "attentive" service give it an edge.

Yankee Doodle Tap Room
15 | 19 | 14 | $28

Nassau Inn, 10 Palmer Sq. (Nassau St.), Princeton, 609-921-7500; www.nassauinn.com

You'll feel like you're in "Aaron Burr country" at this Princeton pub in the Nassau Inn (circa 1756) whose Norman Rockwell mural "makes the trip worthwhile" to its "wood-paneled" quarters; "make allowances" for the "dark", if not "dungeon"-like decor, and remember that despite "mundane" American chow, there's always "Guinness."

Yellow Fin
26 | 16 | 20 | $44

104 Long Beach Blvd. (24th St.), Surf City, 609-494-7001

"Imaginative" New American cuisine "favored by the seashore set" sets the pace at this Surf City spot with food that's "big on taste"; the "chef works masterfully", so even if the "snippy" servers make some sniff "they should move the place to the Hamptons", a majority "makes reservations way in advance" and spears it the "best on LBI."

Yoshi-Sono
20 | 13 | 18 | $30

643 Eagle Rock Ave. (Pleasant Valley Way), West Orange, 973-325-2005

"Smiles" from the staff and "fresh" sushi keep supporters of this Japanese flowing to its West Orange home; though some surveyors swimming in a different direction snip this one's fins, calling the food "average", most think otherwise and stream to it for fare they find "very good."

Zafra
25 | 18 | 19 | $30

301 Willow Ave. (3rd St.), Hoboken, 201-610-9801

"Close your eyes and blindly point to anything on the menu" at this "superior" Hoboken Pan-Latino with "too many delicious dishes to highlight" and too little room to make folks feel anything other than "cramped"; still, chef-scholar Maricel Presilla makes it a "pleasure to dine" at her "colorful" BYO whose "high-quality" fare turns any meal into an "affordable" experience; in simple words, go and "wait on line" if you must.

Zarolé
25 | 23 | 20 | $51

20 E. Ridgewood Ave. (Broad St.), Ridgewood, 201-670-5701; www.zarole.com

"A find in restaurant-saturated" Ridgewood is this French–New American BYO whose menu "hits the mark" with

F | **D** | **S** | **C**

"superb" fare that's a fine fit for the "beautiful" "minimalism" of the decor; if there's debate over staff services (it's "improved" but "not at the level it should be"), most maintain "many try, but few succeed as exquisitely as this one does."

Zio Michel 21 | 16 | 22 | $32
354 Lawton Ave. (Anderson Ave.), Cliffside Park, 201-945-3484
"Featuring all the dishes on the all-time Italian hit parade", this BYO in Cliffside Park proffers "interesting" seafood and "above-average" pasta, and if you want to bypass the main menu, the daily specials are "mind-boggling"; the move to a new locale a year back is either "puzzling" to a few or pleasing to those who find it "more spacious."

ZOE'S BY THE LAKE 26 | 23 | 25 | $51
112 Tomahawk Trail (2 mi. east of Rte. 15), Sparta, 973-726-7226; www.zoesbythelake.com
Called "a miracle in the boondocks of northwestern New Jersey", this bi-level "find" has gushers grateful for its "seriously thoughtful" French menu that "grabs your attention" and for the "scrumptious food that keeps it"; with owners and a staff who "charm" and "classy, understated elegance" pervading the setting overlooking Seneca Lake, this one would be "outstanding anywhere."

Indexes

**CUISINES
LOCATIONS
SPECIAL FEATURES**

CUISINES

Afghan
Pamir

American (New)
Acacia
Amanda's
American Fare
André's
Anton's/Swan
Arthur's Landing
Assembly Steak
Atrio Cafe
Bacari Grill
Bazzini
Beignet's Pub
Bell's Mansion
Bernards Inn
Black Swan
Black Trumpet
Boulevard Grille
Brandl.
Brass Rail
Cafe at Rosemont
Cafe Loren
Cafe Zbra
Captain Jack's
Chakra
Chez Z
City Bistro
Clydz
Colligan's
Daniel's on B'way
Dan's on Main
Dennis Foy's
Dining Room
Dish
Dish
Doris & Ed's
Ebbitt Room
Elements Café
Esty Street
Fat Kat
Felicity's
Ferry House
Fiddleheads
Fish Outta Water
Food for Thought
Frog & Peach
Gaebel's
Grenville
Grill 73
Harvest Moon
Heatwave Cafe
Highlawn Pavilion
Hobby's Deli
Huntley Taverne
Hurricane House
Joe & Maggie's
Karen & Rei's
Krogh's
Lana's
Lawrenceville Inn
Light Horse
Lila
Lulu's Bistro
Madison B&G
Mahogany Grille
Main St. Bistro
Main St. Cafe
Main St. Euro
Marco & Pepe
Matisse
Meritage
Metuchen Inn
Molly Pitcher
M-R Chefs Café
Napa Valley
Nauvoo Grill
Nicholas
Ninety Grand
No. 9
Olde Corner Deli
Onieal's
Orbis Bistro
Pasta Fresca
Pastels
Pelican Club

Cuisines

Perryville Inn
Peter Shields
Pine Tavern
Plantation
Raven & Peach
Raymond's
Red
Renault Winery
Restaurant
Rosemary & Sage
Ruga
Saddle River Inn
Scarborough Fair
Sergeantsville Inn
75 South
Shipwreck Grill
Shubox Café
Simply Radishing
Slowly
Smithville Inn
SoHo on George
Sonoma Grill
Southwinds
Spargo's Grille
Stage Left
Steve & Cookie's
Sweet Vidalia
Terra Christa's
Tewksbury Inn
Tim Schafer's
Tisha's
Trap Rock
Two If By Sea
Venue
Verve
Village Green
Whispers
Word of Mouth
Yellow Fin
Zarolé

American (Traditional)
Abbey
Alchemist/Barrister
Allendale B&G
An American Grill
Arthur's Tavern
Avon Pavilion
Bamboo Grille
Barnacle Bill's
Basil T's
Baumgart's Café
Beechwood Cafe
Bell's
Bell's Mansion
Black Horse
Blue Eyes
Braddock's
Broadway B&G
Cabin
Champps
Charley's
Chart House
Cheesecake Factory
Christopher's
Clark's Landing
Country Pancake
Cranbury Inn
Dock's Oyster
Doris & Ed's
Famished Frog
Full Moon
Gaslight
Grain House
Groff's
Harbor View
Harry's Lobster
Helmers' Cafe
H.I. Rib & Co.
Homestead Inn
Hunt Club
Inn at Millrace
Inn/Hawke
Irish Pub
Java Moon
Lafayette House
Laguna Grill
Lambertville Station
Latour
Liberty House
Limestone Cafe
Mad Batter

vote at zagat.com

Cuisines

Maize
Manor
Mastoris
McLoone's
Meil's
Melissa's Bistro
Merion Inn
Mile Square
Mill at Spring Lake
Moon St.
Nag's Head
Old Man Rafferty
Olive
Pacific Grille
Paramount Steak
Pilot House
Quiet Man
Ram's Head Inn
Robin's Nest
Rod's Olde Irish
Sallee Tee's
Salt Creek
Scuttlebutt's
Shadowbrook
Soho 33
South City Grill
Store
Texas Arizona
Theater Sq. Grill
3 West
Top Notch
Tuckers
Tun Tavern
Ugly Mug
Walpack Inn
Washington Inn
Willie's Taverne
Wolfgang Puck
Yankee Doodle

Armenian
Café Everest

Asian
Chez Elena Wu
Meritage
Metropolitan Cafe
Ritz Seafood
Taro
Tina Louise

Asian Fusion
Ming
Mixx
Noodle House
Rice

Bakeries
Baker's Treat

Barbecue
Big Ed's BBQ
Cubby's BBQ
H.I. Rib & Co.
Indigo Smoke
Memphis Pig Out
Red Hot & Blue

Brazilian
Brasilia
Green Grill

Cajun
Bayou Cafe
Beignet's Pub
Creole Cafe
Luchento's
Mélange Cafe
Oddfellows
Old Bay

Californian
Blue
Napa Valley
Tomatoes
Wolfgang Puck

Caribbean
Bahama Breeze
410 Bank St.

Central European
Red Hen Cafe

Chinese
(* dim sum specialist)
Baumgart's Café
Cathay 22

Cuisines

Chengdu 46
Crown Palace*
Edo Sushi
Far East Taste
Hunan Chinese
Hunan Spring
Hunan Taste
Ivangie Tea
Joe's Peking
Look See
Lotus Cafe
Meemah
Mr. Chu
P.F. Chang's
Sally Ling
Seafood Empire
Shanghai Jazz
Suilan
Sunny Garden
Taipei Noodle
Tang Dynasty
West Lake
Wonder Seafood*
Wu's Bistro

Coffee Shops/Diners
Baumgart's Café
Mastoris
Mustache Bill's
Ponzio's
Tick Tock

Colombian
El Familiar

Continental
Bareli's
Black Forest Inn
Blue Danube
Café Gallery
Champps
Court Street
Don Pepe's Steak
Farnsworth House
Ho-Ho-Kus Inn
Inn at Millrace
Ivy Inn
Lincroft Inn
Mansion on Main
Mattar's
Pheasants Landing
Spain
Stony Hill Inn
Theater Sq. Grill

Creole
Beignet's Pub
Creole Cafe
410 Bank St.
Luchento's
Oddfellows
Old Bay
Orleans

Cuban
Azúcar
Babalu Grill
Diaz
Hard Grove
La Isla
Martino's
Rebecca's

Delis/Sandwich Shops
Eppes Essen
Hobby's Deli
Jack Cooper's
Jerry & Harvey's
Kibbitz/Shore
Kibitz Room
Olde Corner Deli
Richard's

Dessert
Cheesecake Factory
Old Man Rafferty

Dominican
Diaz
Ria's Café

Eastern European
Blue Danube
Red Hen Cafe

Cuisines

Eclectic
Anthony David's
Bamboo Grille
Bistro at Red Bank
Black Duck
Black Swan
Blue
Brix 67
Bula World Cuisine
Cafe Matisse
Cafe Metro
Cafe Panache
California Grill
Clouseau's
Echo
Elements
Eurasian Eatery
Fantasea Reef
Fedora Cafe
Frenchtown Inn
Garlic Rose
Grand Colonial
Green Gables
Jonathan's
Labrador Lounge
Laguna Grill
Liberté
Lilly's on Canal
Little Café
Market Roost
Metropolitan Cafe
mojo
Park & Orchard
Reef Club
Sails
Sallee Tee's
Savaradio
Tomatoes
Triumph Brewing
Village Gourmet

English
Ship Inn

Ethiopian
Makeda

Fondue
Magic Pot
Melting Pot

French
Alexander's
Alisa Cafe
Andaman
Aozora
Beau Rivage
Café Gallery
Chez Catherine
Chez Dominique
Chez Elena Wu
Clouseau's
Colligan's
Déjà Vu
Ferry House
Frenchtown Inn
Fromagerie
Grand Cafe
Ixora
Jocelyne's
La Campagne
Lahiere's
Latour
Le Petit Chateau
Le Rendez-Vous
Liberté
Lilac
Madeleine's
Mariques
Max's Fine Dining
Misto
Saddle River Inn
Silver Spring
Siri's Thai French
Soufflé
Suilan
Verjus
Verve
Zarolé
Zoe's

French (Bistro)
Chef's Table
Dennis Foy's

Cuisines

Elysian Cafe
Harvest Bistro
Indigo Moon
La Petite France
Le Fandy
Madame Claude
Manon
Pierre's
Sophie's Bistro

French (Brasserie)
Epernay

French (New)
Brothers Moon
Le Plumet Royal
Origin
Rat's
Ryland Inn
Serenade
Stage House

German
Black Forest
Black Forest Inn
Helmers' Cafe
Top Notch

Greek
Athenian Garden
Athens Café
It's Greek To Me
Mazi
Opa B&G

Hamburgers
Allendale B&G
Barnacle Bill's
Broadway B&G
Dry Dock

Hot Dogs
Hot Dog Johnny's

Ice Cream Parlor
Dry Dock

Indian
Aamantran
Aangan
Akbar
Bombay Gardens
Chand Palace
Cloves
Ganges
India on Hudson
Karma Kafe
King of India
Masala Grill
Mela
Moghul
Namaskaar
Neelam
Passage to India
Raagini
Saffron

Indonesian
Nusantara

Irish
Quiet Man

Italian
(N=Northern; S=Southern)
Acqua
Acquaviva (N)
Alan@594 (N)
Al Dente (N)
Aldo & Gianni
Amarone (N)
Amici Milano
Andiamo
Angelo's
Anjelica's (S)
Anna's Italian
Anthony David's (N)
Aquila Cucina
Aria Ristorante (N)
Arturo's (S)
Augustino's (S)
Bareli's
Barone's
Barrel's
Basilico (N)
Basil T's
Bazzarelli

vote at zagat.com

Cuisines

Bella Sogno	Filomena (S)
Bellissimo's	Fiorino (N)
Bell's	Formia (N)
Belmont Tavern	Francesca's
Belvedere	Frankie Fed's
Benito's (N)	Frescos
Berta's Chateau (N)	Fresco Steak
Brioso	Gaetano's
Brooklyn's Pizza	Gaslight
Brunello	Girasole (S)
Bruschetta	Girasole
Buca di Beppo	Giumarello's (N)
Cafe Abbraci	Grappa
Cafe Arugula	Grissini
Cafe Coloré	Ho-Ho-Kus Inn
Cafe Cucina	Homestead Inn
Cafe Emilia	Il Capriccio
Cafe Graziella	Il Forno (S)
Cafe Italiano	Il Mondo (N)
Caffe Aldo Lamberti	Il Mulino (N)
Capriccio	Il Pomodoro (N)
Cara Mia Café	Il Porto
Carpaccio	Il Tulipano
Caruso's Tuscan (N)	Il Villaggio
Casa Dante (S)	Il Villino (N)
Casa Giuseppe (S)	Italian Bistro
Catelli	Italianissimo
Cenzino	Jimmy's (S)
Chef Vola's	Kinchley's Tavern
Christie's	La Campagna
Cinque Figlie	Laceno Italian
Columbia Inn	La Cipollina
Cucina Rosa	La Couronne
da Filippo	La Focaccia (N)
Dante's	La Fontana
Da Vinci (N)	La Mezzaluna
De Anna's	La Nonna/Piancone's
Diamond's	La Pastaria
Due Amici	La Scala (N)
E & V	La Spiaggia
Eccola	La Strada
Espo's (S)	La Tartuferia (N)
Fascino	La Vecchia
Federici's	LouCás
Ferrari's	Luchento's
Ferraro's	Luigi's

Cuisines

Luka's
Lu Nello (N)
Marcello & Dino
Margherita's
Marra's
Marsilio's
Max's Fine Dining
Mélange Cafe
Mia Sorella
Misto
Nanni Ristorante
Nunzio
Ocino
Ombra
Osteria Dante
Palazzo
Palm (N)
Panevino
Panico's
Pietro's Pizzeria
Portobello
Portofino's
Porto Leggero
Posillipo
Primavera
Pronto Cena
Puccini's
Radicchio
Raimondo's
Reservoir Tavern
Ristorante Benito
Rivoli's
Roberto's Dolce
Roberto's II
Rocca
RosaLuca's
San Remo
Savanna
Scalini Fedeli (N)
Settebello (N)
Sogno
Solari's
South St. Trattoria
Specchio
Spirito Grill
Squan Tavern
Starlite
Stony Hill Inn
Tattoni's Cafe
Teresa's
Tesauro's
Theresa's
Trattoria Fratelli
Tre Figlio
Tre Piani
Tre Vigne
Tuscany Trattoria (N)
Tuzzio's
Valentino
Valentino's
Venezia
Ventura's
Vic's
Villa Amalfi
Villa Vittoria
Zio Michel

Japanese
(* sushi specialist)
Ajihei*
Aozora
Baumgart's Café*
Brix 67*
Dai-Kichi*
East*
East Tokyo*
Edo Sushi*
Fuji*
Ginza Steak*
Ichiban*
Isohama*
Ixora*
Kiku*
K.O.B.E.*
Komegashi*
Konbu*
Mahzu*
Makoto Steak*
Midori*
Mikado*
Nikko*
Nobi*
Ota-Ya*

vote at zagat.com

Cuisines

Robongi
Sagami
Sakura-Bana*
Sapporo*
Sawa Steak*
Shogun*
Shumi*
Sono Sushi*
Sushi by Kazu*
Sushi Lounge*
Tang Dynasty*
Tsuki*
Wasabi House*
Wild Ginger*
Yoshi-Sono*

Jewish
Eppes Essen
Hobby's Deli
Kibbitz/Shore
Kibitz Room

Korean
(* Barbecue specialist)
So Moon Nan Jip*

Kosher
Jerry & Harvey's

Lebanese
Aladin's

Malaysian
Meemah
Nusantara
Penang
Taste of Asia

Mediterranean
Bella Sogno
Frescos
Hamilton's Grill
Il Pomodoro
Il Villino
La Terraza
Mazi
Mediterra
Moonstruck
Napa Valley
Northstar Café
Olive
Opa B&G
Seven Hills
Terrace Rest.
Tre Piani
Tre Vigne
2Senza

Mexican
Aby's Mexican
Baja
Blue Moon
Casa Maya
Chilangos
El Azteca
El Familiar
El Meson
El Tanampa
Jose's Mexican
Juanito's
Los Amigos
Mexicali Rose
Mexican Food
Mexico Lindo
Surf Taco
Tortilla Press
Tortuga's Mexican

Middle Eastern
Ali Baba
Norma's

Moroccan
Marakesh
Norma's

Noodle Shops
Bien Hoa
Noodle House
Penang
Taipei Noodle

Nuevo Latino
Nova Terra
Sabor

Pacific Rim
Pacific Grille

Cuisines

Pan-Asian
Soonja's
Teak

Pan-Latin
Lua
Mixx
Zafra

Peruvian
Cuzco

Pizza
Benny Tudino's
Brooklyn's Pizza
Columbia Inn
DeLorenzo's
Federici's
Ferraro's
Frankie Fed's
Grimaldi's Pizza
Kinchley's Tavern
Margherita's
Pietro's Pizzeria
Reservoir Tavern
Starlite
Tacconelli's
Vic's

Portuguese
Adega Grill
Bistro Olé
Casa Vasca
Don Pepe
Europa South
Heart of Portugal
Iberia
Mazi
Pearl of the Sea
Portuguese Manor
Segovia
Tony Da Caneca

Pub Food
Alchemist/Barrister
Champps
Light Horse
Quiet Man
Rod's Olde Irish
Scuttlebutt's
Ship Inn
Ugly Mug

Puerto Rican
Diaz

Russian
Café Everest
Lada Cafe

Salvadoran
El Salvadoreno

Sandwiches
Sallee Tee's
White House

Seafood
Athenian Garden
Axelsson's
Bahrs Landing
Barnacle Ben's
Berkeley
Big Fish
Bloomfield Steak
Blue Eyes
Blue Point
Bobby Chez
Busch's Seafood
Capt'n Ed's
Charley's
Chart House
Christie's
Clark's Landing
Crab's Claw
Crab Trap
da Filippo
Daniel's on B'way
Dock's Oyster
Don Pepe's Steak
Doris & Ed's
Emerald Fish
Fantasea Reef
Ferrari's
Fish Outta Water
Fresco Steak
Fulton Crab
Groff's

Cuisines

Harbor View
Hardshell Cafe
Harry's Lobster
Harvey Cedars
Hunt Club
John Henry's
Klein's Fish Market
Laceno Italian
Legal Sea Foods
Little Tuna
Lobster House
LouCás
McCormick/Schmick
McLoone's
Mill at Spring Lake
Mud City
Navesink Fishery
Ninety Grand
Opah Grille
Pacific Grille
Park
Pearl of the Sea
Pelican Club
Ray's Little Silver
Red's Lobster
Reef Club
Ritz Seafood
Rod's Steak
Rooney's
Seafood Empire
Sea Shack
Shipwreck Grill
Smoke Chophouse
South City Grill
Spike's
Tony Da Caneca
Two If By Sea
Union Landing
West Lake
Windansea
Wonder Seafood

Small Plates
Chakra
Coconut Bay
Copper Canyon
Cucharamama
Echo
Elements
El Familiar
Grand Colonial
K.O.B.E.
Lila
Lodos
Lua
Marco & Pepe
Mixx
Northstar Café
Nova Terra
Ombra
Sabor
Savanna
Teak

Soul Food
Delta's
Je's

South American
Cucharamama

Southeast Asian
Coconut Bay

Southern
Delta's
Je's
Niecy's

Southwestern
Copper Canyon
La Bahia
Los Amigos
Mojave Grille
Rattlesnake Ranch

Spanish
(* tapas specialist)
Adega Grill
Bistro Olé
Casa Vasca
Don Pepe
El Cid
Europa South
Fornos of Spain

Cuisines

Iberia
La Terraza
Málaga
Meson Madrid
Portuguese Manor
Savanna
Segovia
Spain
Spain 92
Spanish Tavern
Tapas de Espana*
Tony Da Caneca

Steakhouses
Arthur's Tavern
Assembly Steak
BayPoint Prime
Bloomfield Steak
Blue Eyes
Brighton Steak
Capt'n Ed's
Don Pepe's Steak
Fleming's
Frankie & Johnnie
Fresco Steak
Hunt Club
Kiku
Makoto Steak
Manhattan Steak
Mignon Steak
Mill at Spring Lake
Morton's Steak
Nero's Grille
Old Homestead
Palm
Paramount Steak
Park
Pub
River Palm
Rod's Steak
Ruth's Chris
Sammy's Cider
Shogun
Smoke Chophouse
Strip House
What's Your Beef?

Thai
Alisa Cafe
Andaman
Bamboo Leaf
Bangkok Garden
Baumgart's Café
Chao Phaya
Déjà Vu
Far East Taste
Ginger Thai
Mie Thai
New Main
Origin
Pad Thai
Penang
Rice
Siam
Siam Garden
Sirin
Siri's Thai French
Sri Thai
Thai Chef
Thai Kitchen
Thai Thai
Tuptim

Turkish
Beyti Kebab
Lodos
Samdan
Seven Hills

Vegetarian
(* vegan)
Chand Palace
Down to Earth*
East Coast Vegan*
Tuptim

Vietnamese
Bamboo Leaf
Bien Hoa
Nha Tranh
Saigon R
Taste of Vietnam

vote at zagat.com 173

LOCATIONS

METRO NYC AREA

Allendale
Allendale B&G

Alpine
Kiku

Bergenfield
Chez Dominique

Berkeley Heights
Trap Rock

Bloomfield
Belmont Tavern
Bloomfield Steak
Formia

Carlstadt
Il Villaggio
Tina Louise

Cedar Grove
Il Tulipano
Shubox Café

Clark
Lana's

Cliffside Park
Fulton Crab
It's Greek To Me
Lada Cafe
Villa Amalfi
Zio Michel

Clifton
Belvedere
Chengdu 46
Tick Tock

Closter
Harvest Bistro

Cranford
Garlic Rose

Cresskill
Samdan

East Rutherford
Park & Orchard
Sonoma Grill

Edgewater
Azúcar
Baumgart's Café
Brooklyn's Pizza
Fleming's
La Vecchia
Magic Pot
Rebecca's
River Palm
Roberto's II

Emerson
Arthur's Tavern

Englewood
Baumgart's Café
Blue Moon
It's Greek To Me
Moon St.
Ninety Grand
Saigon R
Smoke Chophouse
Tapas de Espana
Thai Chef
Wild Ginger

Englewood Cliffs
Assembly Steak
Cafe Italiano
Grissini

Fairfield
Aria Ristorante
Bruschetta

Fair Lawn
River Palm

Fort Lee
It's Greek To Me
Sally Ling

Locations

Franklin Lakes
Chef's Table

Glen Rock
Rocca

Hackensack
Bangkok Garden
Brooklyn's Pizza
Cheesecake Factory
Cubby's BBQ
Green Grill
Lotus Cafe
McCormick/Schmick
Morton's Steak
Restaurant
Sea Shack
Solari's
Stony Hill Inn
Thai Chef

Harrington Park
Marcello & Dino

Hasbrouck Heights
Ivy Inn

Haworth
Andiamo

Hoboken
Ali Baba
Amanda's
Anthony David's
Arthur's Tavern
Augustino's
Baja
Benny Tudino's
Brass Rail
City Bistro
Court Street
Cucharamama
Da Vinci
Elysian Cafe
Frankie & Johnnie
Gaslight
Grimaldi's Pizza
Helmers' Cafe
India on Hudson
It's Greek To Me
Karma Kafe
La Isla
La Tartuferia
Lua
Madison B&G
Margherita's
Mile Square
Oddfellows
Onieal's
Robongi
Sri Thai
Sushi Lounge
Texas Arizona
Venue
Wolfgang Puck
Zafra

Ho-Ho-Kus
Ho-Ho-Kus Inn

Jersey City
Baja
Beechwood Cafe
Casa Dante
Hard Grove
Komegashi
Liberty House
Light Horse
Madame Claude
Marco & Pepe
Nha Tranh
Oddfellows
Porto Leggero
Pronto Cena
Puccini's
Ria's Café
South City Grill

Kenilworth
Le Rendez-Vous

Little Falls
Bellissimo's

Little Ferry
Fat Kat

Livingston
Eppes Essen
Lulu's Bistro

vote at zagat.com 175

Locations

Nero's Grille
Panevino
Strip House

Mahwah
Boulevard Grille
Pastels
River Palm

Maplewood
American Fare
Jocelyne's
Verjus

Midland Park
Arturo's

Millburn
Basilico
Lilac

Montclair
Aozora
Déjà Vu
Epernay
Fascino
Indigo Smoke
La Couronne
Liberté
Mexicali Rose
Palazzo
Raymond's
Taro
Thai Chef
Top Notch
Tuptim

Montvale
Aldo & Gianni

Moonachie
Bazzarelli
Segovia

Mountainside
Raagini
Spanish Tavern

Newark
Adega Grill
Brasilia

Casa Vasca
Don Pepe
Fornos of Spain
Hobby's Deli
Iberia
Je's
Maize
Pronto Cena
Spain
Spanish Tavern
Theater Sq. Grill
Tony Da Caneca

New Milford
Lodos

New Providence
Aquila Cucina
Chez Z
Jose's Mexican

North Bergen
Sabor
Tapas de Espana

Northvale
Madeleine's

Nutley
Scuttlebutt's

Oakland
Cenzino
Portobello
Ruga

Old Tappan
Blue Moon

Palisades Park
Meson Madrid
So Moon Nan Jip

Paramus
Caruso's Tuscan
Chakra
El Cid
Kiku
Legal Sea Foods
Namaskaar
Napa Valley

Locations

Park Ridge
Esty Street
Park
Valentino's

Passaic
Dish

Paterson
E & V

Ramsey
Abbey
Cafe Panache
Kinchley's Tavern
Look See

Ridgefield Park
Luka's

Ridgewood
Baumgart's Café
Bazzini
Brooklyn's Pizza
Country Pancake
It's Greek To Me
Ivangie Tea
Latour
Marra's
Mela
Radicchio
Sakura-Bana
Trattoria Fratelli
Village Green
Zarolé

Rochelle Park
Nanni Ristorante
South City Grill

Rutherford
Cafe Matisse
Mignon Steak
Village Gourmet

Saddle River
Saddle River Inn

Scotch Plains
Stage House

Secaucus
Bareli's

Short Hills
Dining Room
Legal Sea Foods
Terrace Rest.

South Hackensack
Aldo & Gianni

South Orange
Cafe Arugula
Neelam
Niecy's
Taste of Asia

Springfield
Cathay 22
Hunan Spring

Summit
Brix 67
Fiorino
Hunt Club
Huntley Taverne
La Focaccia
La Pastaria
Soufflé

Teaneck
Amarone
East
Taipei Noodle

Totowa
Lu Nello

Union
Ristorante Benito

Union City
Beyti Kebab

Upper Montclair
Alan@594
Dai-Kichi
Orbis Bistro

Waldwick
Il Villino

Locations

Wanaque
Berta's Chateau

Washington
Ocino

Washington Township
Bacari Grill

Wayne
Brunello

Weehawken
Arthur's Landing
Chart House
Ruth's Chris
Spirito Grill

West Caldwell
Italianissimo

Westfield
Acquaviva
Chez Catherine
Ferraro's

Mojave Grille
Theresa's

West New York
P.F. Chang's

West Orange
Due Amici
Highlawn Pavilion
Manor
Primavera
Starlite
Yoshi-Sono

Westwood
It's Greek To Me
Melting Pot
Tuscany Trattoria

Woodcliff Lake
Blue Moon

Wyckoff
Blue Moon

ROUTE 287 CORRIDOR

Basking Ridge
Bamboo Grille
Grain House
Store
3 West
Tre Vigne

Bedminster
Willie's Taverne

Bernardsville
Bernards Inn
Grill 73
Le Petit Chateau
Tsuki

Boonton
Reservoir Tavern

Bound Brook
Girasole

Branchburg
Cafe Cucina

Bridgewater
Cafe Emilia
McCormick/Schmick
Thai Kitchen

Budd Lake
Cloves

Chatham
New Main
Scalini Fedeli
Serenade
Taste of Asia

Chester
Benito's
Venezia

Convent Station
Rod's Steak

Cranbury
Cranbury Inn

Locations

Denville
Cafe Metro
Hunan Taste
Midori
Rattlesnake Ranch
Thai Chef

Dover
Quiet Man

East Brunswick
Bombay Gardens
Shogun
Wasabi House

East Hanover
East Tokyo
Luigi's
Mr. Chu
Penang
Saffron

Edison
Akbar
Bien Hoa
Champps
Cheesecake Factory
Jack Cooper's
LouCás
Meemah
Ming
Moghul
Penang
Wonder Seafood

Flanders
Silver Spring

Gladstone
Opah Grille

Green Brook
Shogun

Highland Park
Pad Thai
Seven Hills

Hillsborough
Cafe Graziella
Old Man Rafferty

Pheasants Landing
Thai Kitchen

Iselin
Casa Giuseppe

Jamesburg
Fiddleheads

Kendall Park
Shogun

Madison
Garlic Rose
Il Mondo
Main St. Cafe
Shanghai Jazz
Soho 33

Manville
Mia Sorella

Mendham
Black Horse
Dante's
Mariques
Sammy's Cider

Metuchen
Cafe Abbraci
Clouseau's
Dan's on Main
Metuchen Inn

Meyersville
Casa Maya

Middlesex
Carpaccio

Milltown
Fresco Steak

Montville
Columbia Inn

Morris Plains
Arthur's Tavern
Hunan Chinese
Nusantara

Morristown
Andaman
Cinque Figlie

vote at zagat.com 179

Locations

Famished Frog
Grand Cafe
La Campagna
Moghul
Origin
Pamir
Pierre's
Portofino's
Settebello
Sirin
South St. Trattoria
Tim Schafer's
Valentino

Mountain Lakes
South City Grill

New Brunswick
Clydz
Delta's
Frog & Peach
Gaebel's
La Fontana
Makeda
Northstar Café
Nova Terra
Old Bay
Old Man Rafferty
Panico's
Sapporo
SoHo on George
Stage Left

North Brunswick
Arthur's Tavern
Noodle House
Seafood Empire

Old Bridge
Big Ed's BBQ
Pine Tavern

Parsippany
Chand Palace
Eccola
Marakesh
Ruth's Chris

Peapack
Limestone Cafe

Perth Amboy
Portuguese Manor

Pine Brook
Don Pepe
Don Pepe's Steak

Piscataway
Al Dente

Plainsboro
Tre Piani

Randolph
An American Grill
La Strada

Raritan
Acqua
Cafe Zbra
Espo's
Spain 92

Riverdale
Rosemary & Sage

Somerset
Sophie's Bistro

Somerville
Aladin's
Chao Phaya
da Filippo
Il Pomodoro
La Scala
Martino's
Melting Pot
Origin
Shumi
Thai Chef
Verve
Wasabi House

South Amboy
Taste of Vietnam

South River
Cuzco

Locations

Stirling
Thai Thai

Warren
Grappa
Il Forno
Jose's Mexican

Whippany
Il Capriccio
Nikko

Woodbridge
Mie Thai

DELAWARE VALLEY

Allamuchy
Mattar's

Bethlehem
RosaLuca's

Buttzville
Hot Dog Johnny's

Flemington
Baker's Treat
California Grill
Il Mulino
Market Roost

Frenchtown
Frenchtown Inn
Lila

Hackettstown
Cara Mia Café

Hamilton
Málaga
Rat's

Hope
Inn at Millrace

Hopewell
Brothers Moon

Lafayette
Lafayette House

Lambertville
Anton's/Swan
Baker's Treat
Bell's
De Anna's
Full Moon
Hamilton's Grill
Inn/Hawke
Lambertville Station
Lilly's on Canal
Manon
No. 9
Ota-Ya
Siam
Tortuga's Mexican

Lawrence
Lawrenceville Inn

Lawrenceville
Acacia
Fedora Cafe
Passage to India
Simply Radishing

Milford
Ship Inn

Newton
André's
Bula World Cuisine

Oldwick
Tewksbury Inn

Pennington
Edo Sushi
H.I. Rib & Co.

Princeton
Ajihei
Alchemist/Barrister
Big Fish
Blue Point
Ferry House
Ichiban
Lahiere's

vote at zagat.com

Locations

La Mezzaluna
La Terraza
Le Plumet Royal
Main St. Euro
Masala Grill
Mediterra
Soonja's
Teresa's
Tortuga's Mexican
Triumph Brewing
Yankee Doodle

Ringoes
Harvest Moon

Rosemont
Cafe at Rosemont

Sergeantsville
Sergeantsville Inn

Sparta
Francesca's
Il Porto
Krogh's
Zoe's

Stanhope
Bell's Mansion
Black Forest Inn

Stockton
Atrio Cafe
Colligan's
Meil's

Trenton
Amici Milano
Blue Danube
DeLorenzo's
Homestead Inn
John Henry's
Marsilio's
Tattoni's Cafe

Union Township
Grand Colonial
Perryville Inn

Wallpack Center
Walpack Inn

West Trenton
Diamond's

West Windsor
Ganges
Penang
Sunny Garden

Whitehouse
Ryland Inn

Whitehouse Station
Ixora

NORTH SHORE

Aberdeen
Mahzu

Allentown
Black Forest

Asbury Park
Bistro Olé
Jimmy's
Moonstruck
Posillipo

Atlantic Highlands
Copper Canyon
Indigo Moon
Memphis Pig Out

Avon-by-the-Sea
Avon Pavilion
Diaz
M-R Chefs Café

Barnegat
Hurricane House

Locations

Barnegat Light
Mustache Bill's

Bay Head
Grenville
Heatwave Cafe

Beach Haven
Green Gables
Harvey Cedars
Roberto's Dolce
Sweet Vidalia
Tuckers

Belmar
Brandl.
Klein's Fish Market
Matisse

Bradley Beach
Bamboo Leaf
Bella Sogno
Juanito's
La Nonna/Piancone's
Mazi
Vic's

Brick
El Tanampa
Mexico Lindo
Pilot House
Villa Vittoria

Brielle
La Nonna/Piancone's
Shipwreck Grill
Union Landing

Colts Neck
Christopher's

Dover Township
Aamantran
El Familiar
Nobi
Rivoli's
Shogun
Tang Dynasty

Eatontown
Far East Taste
King of India
Sawa Steak

Fair Haven
Le Fandy
Nauvoo Grill
Raven & Peach

Freehold
El Meson
Federici's
La Cipollina
Main St. Bistro
Metropolitan Cafe
75 South

Freehold Township
Aangan
Cafe Coloré
Ferrari's
Frankie Fed's
Ginger Thai

Harvey Cedars
Harvey Cedars
Plantation

Highlands
Bahrs Landing
Chilangos
Doris & Ed's
Orleans
Rice
Windansea

Holmdel
It's Greek To Me
K.O.B.E.

Howell
Cabin
Christie's
Heart of Portugal
Juanito's
Sushi by Kazu

vote at zagat.com 183

Locations

Island Heights
Olde Corner Deli

Jackson
Java Moon

Lacey
Southwinds

Lavallette
Crab's Claw

Little Silver
Ray's Little Silver

Long Beach Township
Fish Outta Water

Long Branch
Charley's
Joe & Maggie's
Pearl of the Sea
Reef Club
Richard's
Rooney's
Tuzzio's

Manahawkin
Mud City

Manalapan
Java Moon
Konbu
Spargo's Grille

Manasquan
Bayou Cafe
Mahogany Grille
Paramount Steak
Siam Garden
Squan Tavern
Surf Taco

Marlboro
Brioso
Crown Palace
Jerry & Harvey's

Matawan
Aby's Mexican
Terra Christa's
West Lake

Middletown
Anna's Italian
Crown Palace
Lincroft Inn
Navesink Fishery
Neelam
Nicholas
Sono Sushi

Millstone
Luchento's

Monmouth Beach
Sallee Tee's

Normandy Beach
Labrador Lounge

Ocean Grove
Captain Jack's

Ocean Township
Manhattan Steak

Ortley Beach
Diamond's

Point Pleasant
Capt'n Ed's
Clark's Landing

Point Pleasant Beach
BayPoint Prime
Broadway B&G
Dennis Foy's
Europa South
Isohama
Red's Lobster
Spike's
Surf Taco
Tesauro's

Red Bank
Basil T's
Bistro at Red Bank
Café Everest
Dish
Down to Earth
Echo
El Salvadoreno
Eurasian Eatery

Locations

Gaetano's
Juanito's
La Pastaria
La Petite France
Melting Pot
Molly Pitcher
Osteria Dante
Red
Savanna
Siam Garden
Sogno
Teak
Two If By Sea
2Senza

Rumson
Barnacle Bill's
Fromagerie
Salt Creek
What's Your Beef?

Sea Bright
Anjelica's
Elements
Harry's Lobster
McLoone's

Sea Girt
Rod's Olde Irish

Seaside Heights
Beignet's Pub

Ship Bottom
La Spiaggia
Raimondo's

Shrewsbury
Java Moon
Pasta Fresca
San Remo
Shadowbrook

South Seaside Park
Berkeley

Spring Lake
Black Trumpet
Whispers

Spring Lake Heights
Mill at Spring Lake

Stafford
La Bahia
Makoto Steak

Surf City
Blue
Yellow Fin

Toms River
East Coast Vegan
Slowly

Wall
Java Moon
Meritage
Scarborough Fair

Waretown
Big Ed's BBQ

SOUTH SHORE

Atlantic City
Angelo's
Babalu Grill
Brighton Steak
Capriccio
Chef Vola's
Dock's Oyster
Fantasea Reef
Girasole
Irish Pub
Jonathan's
Los Amigos
Mixx
Old Homestead
Ombra
Opa B&G
Palm
P.F. Chang's
Specchio
Suilan
Tun Tavern
White House

Locations

Avalon
Cafe Loren

Brigantine
Laguna Grill

Cape May
Alexander's
Axelsson's
Cucina Rosa
Dry Dock
Ebbitt Room
410 Bank St.
Frescos
Harbor View
Lobster House
Mad Batter
Merion Inn
Pelican Club
Peter Shields
Tisha's
Ugly Mug
Washington Inn

Clermont
Karen & Rei's

Egg Harbor
Ginza Steak
Renault Winery
Tre Figlio

Galloway
Ram's Head Inn

Galloway Township
Athenian Garden

Linwood
Barrel's

Longport
Little Tuna

Margate
Barrel's
Bobby Chez
Melissa's Bistro
Mikado
mojo
Steve & Cookie's
Tomatoes
Ventura's

North Wildwood
Claude's

Ocean City
Barrel's
Kibbitz/Shore
Nag's Head

Sea Isle City
Busch's Seafood

Smithville
Smithville Inn

Somers Point
Crab Trap
Felicity's
Sails

Ventnor
Savaradio

West Cape May
Black Duck
Daniel's on B'way

Wildwood
Groff's

DEEP SOUTH

Berlin
Filomena

Bordentown
Farnsworth House
Mastoris

Burlington
Big Ed's BBQ
Café Gallery

Cherry Hill
Alisa Cafe
Athens Café

Locations

Bahama Breeze
Barone's
Bobby Chez
Buca di Beppo
Caffe Aldo Lamberti
Emerald Fish
Italian Bistro
Kibitz Room
La Campagne
Mélange Cafe
Mikado
Misto
Norma's
Olive
Ponzio's
Red Hot & Blue
Siri's Thai French

Cinnaminson
Fuji
Max's Fine Dining

Clementon
Filomena

Collingswood
Bobby Chez
Nunzio
Sagami
Tortilla Press
Barone's
Word of Mouth

Deptford
Filomena

Haddonfield
Little Tuna

Haddon Heights
Elements Café

Maple Shade
Tacconelli's

Marlton
Champps
Food for Thought
Hardshell Cafe
Joe's Peking

Mexican Food
P.F. Chang's
Pietro's Pizzeria
Wu's Bistro

Medford
Beau Rivage
Braddock's
Red Hen Cafe

Moorestown
Barnacle Ben's
Barone's

Mount Holly
Robin's Nest

Mount Laurel
Black Swan
El Azteca
Pacific Grille

Pennsauken
Pub

Sewell
Blue Eyes
Italian Bistro

Voorhees
Bobby Chez
Catelli
Chez Elena Wu
Coconut Bay
Laceno Italian
Little Café
Mansion on Main
Ritz Seafood

West Berlin
Los Amigos

Westmont
Giumarello's

Williamstown
Creole Cafe

vote at zagat.com

Special Features

SPECIAL FEATURES

(Indexes list the best in each category. Multi-location restaurants' features may vary by branch.)

Breakfast
(See also Hotel Dining)
Avon Pavilion
Christopher's
Country Pancake
Eppes Essen
Full Moon
Hobby's Deli
Hurricane House
Java Moon
Je's
Market Roost
Meil's
Zafra

Brunch
Amanda's
American Fare
Anthony David's
Brothers Moon
Cafe at Rosemont
Chart House
Christopher's
Court Street
Crown Palace
Daniel's on B'way
Dan's on Main
Déjà Vu
Fiddleheads
Frenchtown Inn
Grenville
Grill 73
Harvest Bistro
Labrador Lounge
La Campagne
Madame Claude
Manon
Marco & Pepe
Molly Pitcher
Napa Valley
Rat's
Restaurant
Strip House
Terrace Rest.
Tortilla Press
Verjus
Zafra

Buffet Served
(Check availability)
Aamantran
Aangan
Akbar
Allendale B&G
Assembly Steak
Bayou Cafe
Bombay Gardens
Café Gallery
Captain Jack's
Chand Palace
Clark's Landing
Cloves
Dan's on Main
Fantasea Reef
Ganges
Grain House
Grappa
Green Grill
Hunt Club
India on Hudson
Karma Kafe
King of India
Málaga
Manor
Mansion on Main
Masala Grill
Matisse
Meritage
Mile Square
Mill at Spring Lake
Moghul
Molly Pitcher

Special Features

Namaskaar
Neelam
Noodle House
Nusantara
Pamir
Passage to India
Pierre's
Raagini
Rat's
Rod's Steak
Saffron
Salt Creek
Seafood Empire
Shanghai Jazz
Smithville Inn
South St. Trattoria
Southwinds
Terrace Rest.
Willie's Taverne

Business Dining
Assembly Steak
Chez Catherine
Dining Room
Fascino
Fiorino
Highlawn Pavilion
Ho-Ho-Kus Inn
Il Tulipano
K.O.B.E.
Lawrenceville Inn
Lu Nello
Manhattan Steak
Mill at Spring Lake
Morton's Steak
Old Homestead
Panico's
Passage to India
Pierre's
Raven & Peach
River Palm
Smoke Chophouse
Specchio
Spirito Grill
Stony Hill Inn
Terra Christa's

Tre Vigne
Wasabi House
Willie's Taverne

BYO
Aamantran
Aangan
Aby's Mexican
Acacia
Ajihei
Aladin's
Alan@594
Aldo & Gianni
Alexander's
Ali Baba
Alisa Cafe
American Fare
Andaman
Anjelica's
Anna's Italian
Anthony David's
Aozora
Aquila Cucina
Aria Ristorante
Athenian Garden
Athens Café
Atrio Cafe
Avon Pavilion
Azúcar
Bamboo Leaf
Barnacle Ben's
Barone's
Barrel's
Basilico
Baumgart's Café
Bayou Cafe
BayPoint Prime
Bazzini
Beechwood Cafe
Bella Sogno
Benito's
Bien Hoa
Bistro at Red Bank
Bistro Olé
Black Duck
Black Forest

vote at zagat.com   189

Special Features

Black Swan
Black Trumpet
Blue
Blue Moon
Blue Point
Bobby Chez
Bombay Gardens
Boulevard Grille
Brandl.
Brasilia
Brioso
Brix 67
Brooklyn's Pizza
Brothers Moon
Bula World Cuisine
Cafe Abbraci
Cafe Arugula
Cafe at Rosemont
Cafe Coloré
Café Everest
Cafe Graziella
Cafe Italiano
Cafe Loren
Cafe Matisse
Cafe Metro
Cafe Panache
Cafe Zbra
California Grill
Captain Jack's
Capt'n Ed's
Cara Mia Café
Casa Maya
Chand Palace
Chao Phaya
Chef's Table
Chef Vola's
Chez Dominique
Chez Elena Wu
Chez Z
Christie's
Christopher's
Clouseau's
Cloves
Coconut Bay
Creole Cafe
Cucina Rosa
Cuzco
da Filippo
Dai-Kichi
Daniel's on B'way
Dan's on Main
Dante's
De Anna's
Déjà Vu
DeLorenzo's
Dennis Foy's
Diaz
Dish
Down to Earth
Dry Dock
Due Amici
Edo Sushi
El Azteca
Elements Café
El Familiar
El Meson
El Salvadoreno
El Tanampa
Emerald Fish
Epernay
Eppes Essen
Eurasian Eatery
Far East Taste
Fascino
Fat Kat
Fedora Cafe
Felicity's
Ferrari's
Ferry House
Fiddleheads
Fish Outta Water
Food for Thought
Frankie Fed's
Frescos
Fresco Steak
Fuji
Full Moon
Gaetano's
Ganges
Garlic Rose
Ginger Thai
Ginza Steak

Special Features

Girasole
Green Gables
Grenville
Grill 73
Groff's
Hamilton's Grill
Hardshell Cafe
Harvey Cedars
Heart of Portugal
Heatwave Cafe
Hunan Spring
Hurricane House
Ichiban
Il Forno
Il Mondo
Il Mulino
Il Porto
Indigo Moon
Indigo Smoke
Isohama
Italianissimo
It's Greek To Me
Ivangie Tea
Ixora
Jack Cooper's
Java Moon
Jocelyne's
Joe's Peking
Jose's Mexican
Juanito's
Karen & Rei's
Kibitz Room
Klein's Fish Market
K.O.B.E.
Konbu
Labrador Lounge
La Campagna
La Campagne
Laceno Italian
La Cipollina
La Couronne
Lada Cafe
La Focaccia
La Isla
La Mezzaluna
La Pastaria
La Petite France
La Scala
La Spiaggia
La Terraza
Latour
Le Fandy
Le Rendez-Vous
Liberté
Lilac
Lilly's on Canal
Limestone Cafe
Little Café
Little Tuna
Lodos
Look See
Lotus Cafe
LouCás
Luchento's
Luka's
Lulu's Bistro
Madame Claude
Mad Batter
Magic Pot
Mahzu
Main St. Bistro
Makoto Steak
Manon
Marakesh
Margherita's
Mariques
Market Roost
Marra's
Martino's
Masala Grill
Matisse
Max's Fine Dining
Mazi
Meemah
Meil's
Mela
Mélange Cafe
Melissa's Bistro
Mexicali Rose
Mexico Lindo
Midori
Mie Thai

vote at zagat.com

Special Features

Mignon Steak
Mikado
Ming
Misto
Moghul
Mojave Grille
Mr. Chu
Mud City
Navesink Fishery
Neelam
New Main
Nobi
No. 9
Noodle House
Norma's
Nunzio
Nusantara
Orbis Bistro
Origin
Osteria Dante
Ota-Ya
Pacific Grille
Palazzo
Pamir
Paramount Steak
Pasta Fresca
Pastels
Penang
Peter Shields
Portofino's
Radicchio
Raimondo's
Raymond's
Ray's Little Silver
Rebecca's
Red Hen Cafe
Red's Lobster
Ria's Café
Ritz Seafood
Rivoli's
Roberto's Dolce
Robongi
Rocca
Saddle River Inn
Saffron
Sagami

Saigon R
Sakura-Bana
Samdan
San Remo
Savanna
Savaradio
Sawa Steak
Seafood Empire
Settebello
Seven Hills
75 South
Shumi
Siam
Siam Garden
Simply Radishing
Sirin
Siri's Thai French
Slowly
Sogno
Soho 33
Sono Sushi
Soonja's
Soufflé
South St. Trattoria
Spargo's Grille
Spike's
Sri Thai
Sunny Garden
Surf Taco
Sushi by Kazu
Sweet Vidalia
Tacconelli's
Taipei Noodle
Tang Dynasty
Taro
Taste of Asia
Taste of Vietnam
Terra Christa's
Thai Chef
Thai Kitchen
Thai Thai
Theresa's
Tim Schafer's
Tina Louise
Tisha's
Top Notch

Special Features

Tortilla Press
Tortuga's Mexican
Trattoria Fratelli
Tsuki
Tuptim
Venezia
Venue
Village Gourmet
Village Green
Wasabi House
West Lake
Whispers
Wild Ginger
Wonder Seafood
Word of Mouth
Wu's Bistro
Yellow Fin
Zafra
Zarolé
Zio Michel

Catering
Aamantran
Aangan
Amanda's
Andaman
André's
Anjelica's
Anthony David's
Athenian Garden
Augustino's
Azúcar
Baker's Treat
Bernards Inn
Bien Hoa
Black Swan
Bobby Chez
Bombay Gardens
Brioso
Brothers Moon
Cafe Loren
Cafe Matisse
Cafe Panache
Casa Dante
Casa Giuseppe
Catelli

Chez Elena Wu
Creole Cafe
Cucharamama
da Filippo
Daniel's on B'way
Dan's on Main
Dennis Foy's
Diaz
Dining Room
Dock's Oyster
Doris & Ed's
Emerald Fish
Eppes Essen
Esty Street
Far East Taste
Ferry House
Formia
Frog & Peach
Fromagerie
Girasole
Grand Cafe
Green Gables
Hamilton's Grill
Harvest Moon
Hobby's Deli
Hurricane House
Jocelyne's
Kibitz Room
La Campagne
Lawrenceville Inn
Le Petit Chateau
Lilac
Limestone Cafe
Little Café
Lu Nello
Makeda
Market Roost
Mattar's
Ming
Moghul
Moonstruck
Morton's Steak
Mud City
Nicholas
No. 9
Olde Corner Deli

vote at zagat.com

Special Features

Ombra
Origin
Ram's Head Inn
Rat's
Raven & Peach
Rebecca's
Robongi
Rosemary & Sage
Saigon R
San Remo
Shipwreck Grill
Siri's Thai French
Slowly
Squan Tavern
Stage House
Stage Left
Tim Schafer's
Tina Louise
Washington Inn
Whispers
Wu's Bistro
Zafra
Zarolé

Celebrity Chefs
BayPoint Prime, *Kevin Pomplun*
Bernards Inn, *Corey Heyer*
Cafe Panache, *Kevin Kohler*
Chef's Table, *Claude Baills*
Chez Dominique, *D. Payraudeau*
Cucharamama, *Maricel Presilla*
Daniel's on B'way, *Harry Gleason*
Dennis Foy's, *D. Foy*
Fascino, *Ryan DePersio*
Grand Colonial, *Paul Ingenito*
Ixora, *Timothy Chang*
Karen & Rei's, *Karen Nelson*
Latour, *Michael Latour*
Mélange Cafe, *Joe Brown*
Misto, *Alex Capasso*
Mixx, *E. Ferrari, A. Sanchez*
Nicholas, *Nicholas Harary*
Nunzio, *Nunzio Patruno*
Ombra, *Luke Palladino*
Orbis Bistro, *Nancy Caballes*
Perryville Inn, *Paul Ingenito*
Porto Leggero, *M. Cetrulo, A. Stella*
Ryland Inn, *Craig Shelton*
Scalini Fedeli, *Michael Cetrulo*
Serenade, *James Laird*
Specchio, *Luke Palladino*
Suilan, *Susanna Foo*
Tim Schafer's, *Tim Schafer*
Zafra, *Maricel Presilla*

Child-Friendly
(Alternatives to the usual fast-food places; * children's menu available)
Aby's Mexican*
Acacia
Alisa Cafe
Amanda's
André's
Anjelica's
Athenian Garden*
Athens Café
Axelsson's*
Bahama Breeze*
Bamboo Leaf
Bareli's
Barone's*
Baumgart's Café*
Bazzini*
Bellissimo's
Bell's
Bell's Mansion*
Beyti Kebab
Big Ed's BBQ*
Bistro Olé
Black Duck
Black Forest Inn
Blue
Blue Point*
Bobby Chez
Bombay Gardens
Braddock's*
Brioso
Cabin*
Cafe Loren
Caffe Aldo Lamberti
Capriccio

Special Features

Captain Jack's
Casa Dante
Casa Giuseppe
Casa Vasca
Catelli
Cenzino
Champps*
Chao Phaya
Cheesecake Factory
Chengdu 46
Christie's*
Clydz
Cucharamama
da Filippo
Daniel's on B'way
Diaz*
Dock's Oyster*
Doris & Ed's*
Down to Earth
E & V
El Azteca*
Elements Café
El Meson*
Emerald Fish
Espo's*
Esty Street
Far East Taste
Fat Kat
Ferry House
Filomena*
Fish Outta Water*
Food for Thought
Fornos of Spain
410 Bank St.
Frankie Fed's*
Frenchtown Inn
Fuji*
Ginza Steak
Grand Cafe
Hardshell Cafe*
Harvest Moon
Hobby's Deli
Homestead Inn
Hurricane House*
Indigo Moon

Inn/Hawke*
Italian Bistro*
It's Greek To Me*
Ixora
Java Moon*
John Henry's
Jonathan's*
Kibitz Room*
Labrador Lounge*
La Campagne
Laceno Italian
La Scala
Legal Sea Foods*
Little Café*
Little Tuna*
Lu Nello
Mahogany Grille
Manon
Manor
Mansion on Main
Margherita's
Mazi
Meil's
Mélange Cafe
Mexican Food*
Mexico Lindo*
Midori
Mie Thai
Mikado
Ming
Moghul
mojo
Mud City*
Nag's Head*
Nanni Ristorante
Navesink Fishery
New Main
Ninety Grand
No. 9
Norma's*
Nunzio
Opah Grille*
Origin
Ota-Ya
Pacific Grille*

vote at zagat.com

Special Features

Panico's
Park & Orchard*
Passage to India
P.F. Chang's
Pierre's
Pietro's Pizzeria*
Ponzio's*
Pub*
Raimondo's*
Ram's Head Inn*
Rat's
Rebecca's
Red Hen Cafe
Red Hot & Blue*
Reservoir Tavern
Ristorante Benito
Ritz Seafood
Robongi
Rosemary & Sage
Ruga
Sabor
Saffron
Sagami
Saigon R
Sawa Steak*
Serenade
Sergeantsville Inn
Shipwreck Grill
Shumi
Siri's Thai French
Slowly
Sogno*
SoHo on George
Sono Sushi*
Southwinds*
Steve & Cookie's
Sushi by Kazu
Tang Dynasty
Thai Kitchen
Thai Thai
Theresa's*
Tim Schafer's*
Tina Louise
Tomatoes
Tortilla Press*
Tre Figlio*
Tuckers*
Verjus
Wasabi House
West Lake
White House
Wild Ginger
Word of Mouth
Wu's Bistro
Zafra
Zarolé
Zoe's

Cigars Welcome
Al Dente
Allendale B&G
Arthur's Landing
Arturo's
Assembly Steak
Azúcar
Bacari Grill
Bareli's
Caruso's Tuscan
Casa Dante
Champps
Diamond's
Italian Bistro
Jonathan's
Krogh's
Maize
Manhattan Steak
Metuchen Inn
Mill at Spring Lake
Mixx
Morton's Steak
Nero's Grille
Ninety Grand
Oddfellows
Old Homestead
Park
Perryville Inn
Rod's Steak
Ruth's Chris
Sergeantsville Inn
Smoke Chophouse
Tun Tavern
Valentino

Special Features

Dancing
Acqua
Baja
Busch's Seafood
Colligan's
Filomena
Laguna Grill
Málaga
Mill at Spring Lake
Mixx
Olive
Orleans
Portuguese Manor
Rat's
Restaurant
Sabor
South City Grill
Teak
Tesauro's
Tuscany Trattoria
Villa Amalfi
Windansea

Delivery/Takeout
(D=delivery, T=takeout)
Aamantran (D,T)
Aby's Mexican (D,T)
Alisa Cafe (T)
Athenian Garden (T)
Babalu Grill (T)
Bahama Breeze (T)
Baumgart's Café (T)
Bayou Cafe (D)
Bell's (T)
Belmont Tavern (T)
Beyti Kebab (T)
Bien Hoa (T)
Big Ed's BBQ (T)
Blue Danube (T)
Blue Moon (D)
Bobby Chez (T)
Brooklyn's Pizza (T)
Cafe at Rosemont (T)
Café Everest (T)
California Grill (T)
Casa Dante (D)
Casa Maya (T)
Chao Phaya (T)
Chilangos (T)
Cloves (T)
Crown Palace (T)
DeLorenzo's (T)
Diaz (T)
Down to Earth (T)
Dry Dock (T)
East Coast Vegan (T)
El Familiar (T)
El Meson (T)
Eppes Essen (T)
Far East Taste (T)
Federici's (T)
Filomena (T)
Frankie Fed's (T)
Fuji (T)
Full Moon (T)
Ganges (T)
Grimaldi's Pizza (D)
Harvey Cedars (T)
Hobby's Deli (D,T)
Hot Dog Johnny's (T)
Hunan Chinese (T)
Hurricane House (T)
India on Hudson (D)
Indigo Smoke (T)
It's Greek To Me (T)
Java Moon (T)
Je's (D,T)
Joe's Peking (T)
Juanito's (T)
Karma Kafe (D)
Komegashi (D,T)
La Bahia (D)
Lada Cafe (T)
La Terraza (T)
Limestone Cafe (T)
Little Café (D)
Los Amigos (T)
Lotus Cafe (D)
Madison B&G (T)
Mahzu (T)
Margherita's (D)
Market Roost (T)

vote at zagat.com

Special Features

Mastoris (T)
Meemah (T)
Meil's (T)
Memphis Pig Out (T)
Mexico Lindo (T)
Mie Thai (T)
Mikado (T)
Moghul (T)
Mustache Bill's (T)
New Main (T)
Niecy's (T)
Nobi (T)
Noodle House (T)
Norma's (T)
Old Man Rafferty (T)
Ota-Ya (T)
Pad Thai (T)
Passage to India (T)
Penang (D,T)
P.F. Chang's (T)
Raagini (D,T)
Reservoir Tavern (T)
Richard's (T)
Robongi (D,T)
Saffron (D)
Sagami (T)
Saigon R (T)
Sakura-Bana (T)
Seafood Empire (T)
Seven Hills (T)
Shogun (T)
Shumi (T)
Siam (T)
Sono Sushi (T)
Spike's (T)
Sri Thai (D)
Sunny Garden (T)
Sushi Lounge (D,T)
Taipei Noodle (T)
Tang Dynasty (D,T)
Taste of Asia (T)
Thai Chef (T)
Thai Kitchen (T)
Tina Louise (T)
Tortuga's Mexican (T)
Tuzzio's (T)
Vic's (D,T)
Wasabi House (D,T)
West Lake (T)
White House (T)
Wolfgang Puck (T)
Wonder Seafood (T)

Dessert
Aquila Cucina
Baumgart's Café
Café Everest
Chakra
Cheesecake Factory
Fascino
Fedora Cafe
Karen & Rei's
Raymond's
Robin's Nest
75 South
Shubox Café

Entertainment
(Call for days and times of performances)
Bahama Breeze (live music)
Beignet's Pub (jazz)
Bernards Inn (piano)
Beyti Kebab (belly dancing)
Black Swan (piano)
Blue Eyes (vocals)
Blue Point (jazz)
Brighton Steak (piano)
Bula World Cuisine (jazz)
Cafe Matisse (jazz/guitar)
Cafe Panache (guitar)
Catelli (jazz)
da Filippo (piano)
Dining Room (jazz/guitar)
Dock's Oyster (piano)
Ebbitt Room (piano)
Elements (DJs)
Food for Thought (piano)
Gaebel's (DJs/bands)
Grand Cafe (piano)
Harvest Moon (piano)
Il Capriccio (piano)

Special Features

Indigo Smoke (jazz/R&B)
Le Petit Chateau (varies)
Lila (bands)
Makeda (jazz/funk)
Matisse (jazz)
Mattar's (piano)
McLoone's (jazz/rock)
Mixx (DJs/percussion)
Molly Pitcher (piano)
Moonstruck (jazz/piano)
Nanni Ristorante (piano)
Northstar Café (jazz)
Nova Terra (Latin bands)
Peter Shields (piano)
Quiet Man (guitar/piano)
Ram's Head Inn (piano)
Rat's (piano)
Raven & Peach (guitar/piano)
Ryland Inn (piano)
Sabor (DJs/jazz)
Shanghai Jazz (jazz)
Shipwreck Grill (jazz)
South City Grill (varies)
Steve & Cookie's (varies)
Tre Figlio (varies)
Verve (DJs/jazz)
Windansea (dancing)

Family-Style
Adega Grill
Green Grill
Italian Bistro
Marakesh
Ocino
Pad Thai
Pearl of the Sea
Saigon R
Spanish Tavern

Fireplaces
Abbey
Adega Grill
Amanda's
Aria Ristorante
Bamboo Grille
Bareli's
Beau Rivage
Bernards Inn
Berta's Chateau
Black Horse
Black Trumpet
Bloomfield Steak
Blue Moon
Braddock's
Bruschetta
Cabin
Caruso's Tuscan
Champps
Christopher's
Clark's Landing
Clydz
Colligan's
Crab's Claw
Cranbury Inn
Diamond's
Fat Kat
Filomena
Frenchtown Inn
Fromagerie
Giumarello's
Grain House
Grand Cafe
Grenville
Harry's Lobster
Harvest Moon
H.I. Rib & Co.
Huntley Taverne
Il Mulino
Il Villino
Inn at Millrace
Inn/Hawke
Ivy Inn
Jonathan's
Karen & Rei's
La Campagne
Lafayette House
Mad Batter
Mahogany Grille
Main St. Euro
Marcello & Dino
Mariques
Max's Fine Dining
McLoone's

vote at zagat.com 199

Special Features

Meritage
Metuchen Inn
Molly Pitcher
Moon St.
Nag's Head
Nauvoo Grill
Nero's Grille
Ocino
Orleans
Perryville Inn
Peter Shields
Plantation
Portobello
Pub
Ram's Head Inn
Rat's
Ryland Inn
Scarborough Fair
Serenade
Sergeantsville Inn
Settebello
Seven Hills
75 South
Shadowbrook
Shanghai Jazz
Smithville Inn
Spain 92
Spirito Grill
Stage House
Stage Left
Steve & Cookie's
Tesauro's
3 West
Trap Rock
Tuckers
Union Landing
Walpack Inn
Washington Inn
Whispers
Yankee Doodle

Historic Places
(Year opened; * building)
1676 Bloomfield Steak*
1685 Grand Colonial*
1697 Lincroft Inn*
1700 Daniel's on B'way*
1710 Colligan's*
1734 Sergeantsville Inn*
1737 Stage House*
1742 Black Horse*
1750 Cranbury Inn*
1768 Grain House*
1775 Willie's Taverne*
1787 Smithville Inn*
1790 Ho-Ho-Kus Inn*
1800 Bell's Mansion*
1800 Cafe at Rosemont*
1800 Store*
1800 Tewksbury Inn*
1805 Frenchtown Inn*
1818 Stony Hill Inn*
1823 Braddock's*
1843 Metuchen Inn*
1850 Delta's*
1850 Light Horse*
1851 Lila*
1860 Inn/Hawke*
1864 Renault Winery*
1870 Silver Spring*
1874 Saddle River Inn*
1875 75 South*
1879 Ebbitt Room*
1882 Busch's Seafood
1883 Alexander's*
1890 Grenville*
1890 Whispers*
1895 Amanda's*
1895 Elysian Cafe*
1897 Dock's Oyster
1900 Athenian Garden*
1900 Doris & Ed's*
1900 Robin's Nest*
1900 Scarborough Fair*
1903 Columbia Inn*
1903 Irish Pub
1907 Shadowbrook*
1909 Highlawn Pavilion*
1910 Stage Left*
1912 Grill 73*
1912 Hobby's Deli
1917 Bahrs Landing

subscribe to zagat.com

Special Features

1919 Lahiere's
1920 Ugly Mug*
1921 Chef Vola's
1921 Federici's
1925 Groff's
1926 Iberia
1926 Spike's
1927 Berta's Chateau*
1927 Krogh's*
1928 Molly Pitcher*
1929 Hunt Club
1929 Posillipo*
1932 Helmers' Cafe
1932 Lobster House
1932 Spanish Tavern
1933 Harry's Lobster
1933 Sammy's Cider
1935 Allendale B&G
1935 Angelo's
1936 Reservoir Tavern
1937 Kinchley's Tavern
1937 Yankee Doodle
1938 Mill at Spring Lake
1939 Bell's
1939 Homestead Inn
1939 Solari's
1944 Hot Dog Johnny's
1945 Berkeley
1947 DeLorenzo's
1947 Vic's
1951 Marsilio's
1951 Pub
1951 Rod's Steak
1915 Heatwave Cafe*
1920 Venue*
1928 Azúcar*
1930 Pheasants Landing*
1930 RosaLuca's*
1936 Steve & Cookie's*
1940 La Spiaggia*
1941 Walpack Inn*
1942 Tuzzio's*
1943 Broadway B&G*
1946 White House*
1949 Tick Tock*
1950 Fat Kat*
1950 Main St. Euro*
1950 Starlite*

Hotel Dining
Alexander's Inn
  Alexander's
Blue Bay Inn
  Copper Canyon
Borgata Hotel, Casino & Spa
  Mixx
  Old Homestead
  Ombra
  Specchio
  Suilan
Carroll Villa Hotel
  Mad Batter
Colligan's Stockton Inn
  Colligan's
Grand Summit Hotel
  Hunt Club
Green Gables Inn
  Green Gables
Grenville Hotel
  Grenville
Hewitt Wellington Hotel
  Whispers
Hilton at Short Hills
  Dining Room
  Terrace Rest.
Hilton Hotel
  Ruth's Chris
Ho-Ho-Kus Inn
  Ho-Ho-Kus Inn
Holiday Inn
  Red Hot & Blue
Madison Hotel, The
  Rod's Steak
Marquis de Lafayette Hotel
  Pelican Club
Molly Pitcher Inn
  Molly Pitcher
Nassau Inn
  Yankee Doodle
National Hotel
  Lila
  Lilac
Ocean Club Condos
  Girasole

Special Features

Olde Mill Inn
   Grain House
Peacock Inn, The
   Le Plumet Royal
Resorts Atlantic City Casino
   Capriccio
Robert Treat Hotel
   Maize
Sandpiper Inn, The
   Black Trumpet
Sands Hotel & Casino
   Brighton Steak
Sheraton Hotel
   Tun Tavern
Sheraton Suites Hotel
   Spirito Grill
Somerset Hills Hotel
   Grappa
Swan Hotel
   Anton's/Swan
Virginia Hotel
   Ebbitt Room
Westminster Hotel
   Strip House
Wilshire Grand
   Primavera

Jacket Required
Beau Rivage
Bernards Inn
Highlawn Pavilion
Le Petit Chateau
Manor
Mariques
Molly Pitcher
Saddle River Inn

Late Dining
(Weekday closing hour)
Allendale B&G (1 AM)
Basil T's (12 AM)
Benny Tudino's (12:45 AM)
Broadway B&G (1 AM)
Clydz (1:30 AM)
Elements (12 AM)
Elysian Cafe (12 AM)
Iberia (1:30 AM)
Irish Pub (24 hrs.)
Kinchley's Tavern (12 AM)
Light Horse (12 AM)
Los Amigos (varies)
Maize (12 AM)
Mastoris (1 AM)
Opa B&G (12 AM)
P.F. Chang's (varies)
Ponzio's (1 AM)
So Moon Nan Jip (3 AM)
Tick Tock (24 hrs.)
Ventura's (1 AM)

Local Favorites
Aby's Mexican
Acacia
Aldo & Gianni
Allendale B&G
Andiamo
Anna's Italian
Anthony David's
Arthur's Tavern
Athenian Garden
Atrio Cafe
Axelsson's
Bacari Grill
Bahrs Landing
Bareli's
Barnacle Bill's
BayPoint Prime
Bell's
Belmont Tavern
Benny Tudino's
Bien Hoa
Bistro Olé
Black Horse
Bobby Chez
Brooklyn's Pizza
Busch's Seafood
Cafe Abbraci
Cafe Arugula
Cafe Emilia
Cafe Graziella
Cafe Italiano
Caffe Aldo Lamberti
Captain Jack's
Cathay 22

Special Features

Charley's
Chef Vola's
Christie's
Christopher's
Country Pancake
Cucharamama
Dante's
De Anna's
Dry Dock
E & V
Edo Sushi
El Salvadoreno
Emerald Fish
Espo's
Federici's
Ferraro's
Fiddleheads
Filomena
Fish Outta Water
Formia
Fuji
Girasole
Grain House
Grimaldi's Pizza
Groff's
Hardshell Cafe
Harry's Lobster
Harvey Cedars
Hobby's Deli
Hunan Spring
Indigo Moon
Inn/Hawke
Italianissimo
It's Greek To Me
Ivangie Tea
Java Moon
Je's
Jimmy's
Juanito's
Kiku
Kinchley's Tavern
Konbu
Laceno Italian
La Focaccia
La Nonna/Piancone's
La Pastaria

La Scala
La Spiaggia
La Terraza
Lila
Limestone Cafe
Los Amigos
LouCás
Luchento's
Luka's
Madison B&G
Magic Pot
Mahzu
Makoto Steak
Marcello & Dino
Marco & Pepe
Margherita's
Mariques
Marsilio's
Mattar's
Mediterra
Meil's
Mela
Mélange Cafe
Melissa's Bistro
Melting Pot
Mexicali Rose
Mexican Food
Mia Sorella
Mie Thai
Misto
Moghul
Mr. Chu
Mud City
Mustache Bill's
Navesink Fishery
Neelam
Nero's Grille
Nha Tranh
Nikko
Nobi
Nunzio
Old Man Rafferty
Opah Grille
Ota-Ya
Pacific Grille
Panevino

vote at zagat.com

Special Features

Paramount Steak
Park
Pasta Fresca
Pilot House
Pine Tavern
Plantation
Portofino's
Posillipo
Primavera
Pub
Quiet Man
Raagini
Radicchio
Raimondo's
Raymond's
Ray's Little Silver
Red
Red's Lobster
Reservoir Tavern
Rivoli's
Robongi
Saffron
Saigon R
Sallee Tee's
Sally Ling
Salt Creek
San Remo
Shipwreck Grill
Siam
Siam Garden
Slowly
South City Grill
South St. Trattoria
Southwinds
Spain 92
Spargo's Grille
Squan Tavern
Sri Thai
Store
Sushi by Kazu
Taipei Noodle
Tattoni's Cafe
Teak
Teresa's
Tesauro's
Thai Chef
Theresa's
Tina Louise
Tony Da Caneca
Tsuki
Tuckers
Tuptim
Tuzzio's
Valentino
Venezia
Vic's
Villa Amalfi
Village Gourmet
Villa Vittoria
Wasabi House
West Lake
What's Your Beef?
White House
Windansea
Zarolé
Zoe's

Meet for a Drink
Acqua
Adega Grill
Arturo's
Babalu Grill
Barnacle Bill's
Basil T's
Bell's
Black Horse
Cenzino
Charley's
Chilangos
Clark's Landing
Copper Canyon
Crab's Claw
Cucharamama
Echo
Elements
Espo's
Famished Frog
Frankie & Johnnie
Gaebel's
Gaslight
Hunt Club
Huntley Taverne

Special Features

Inn/Hawke
Irish Pub
Krogh's
Lila
Los Amigos
Lua
Marco & Pepe
McLoone's
Mediterra
Meritage
Metropolitan Cafe
Mile Square
Mixx
Moon St.
Northstar Café
Oddfellows
Old Bay
Old Man Rafferty
Onieal's
Opah Grille
Pilot House
Pine Tavern
Plantation
Quiet Man
Restaurant
Rice
Rod's Olde Irish
Sails
Sallee Tee's
Salt Creek
Scuttlebutt's
Ship Inn
South City Grill
Stage Left
Sushi Lounge
Teak
Tewksbury Inn
Trap Rock
Tre Vigne
Triumph Brewing
Tuckers
Tun Tavern
Two If By Sea
Ugly Mug
Union Landing
Valentino

Windansea
Yankee Doodle

Microbreweries
Basil T's
Krogh's
Ship Inn
Trap Rock
Triumph Brewing

Noteworthy Newcomers
Alan@594
Aozora
BayPoint Prime
Beechwood Cafe
Bell's Mansion
Black Trumpet
Blue Eyes
Bula World Cuisine
Chakra
Cloves
Coconut Bay
Cucharamama
Elements
Fascino
Ganges
Grand Colonial
Indigo Smoke
La Bahia
Lada Cafe
Lawrenceville Inn
Lila
Lodos
Lua
Madame Claude
Marco & Pepe
Misto
Ocino
Olde Corner Deli
Palm
Porto Leggero
Ria's Café
Saffron
Sails
Savanna
Slowly
Teak

Special Features

Venue
West Lake
Wu's Bistro
Zoe's

Offbeat

Aangan
Aby's Mexican
Aladin's
Ali Baba
Azúcar
Bangkok Garden
Baumgart's Café
Bayou Cafe
Beyti Kebab
Bien Hoa
Blue
Blue Danube
Buca di Beppo
Café Everest
Chand Palace
Chao Phaya
Chef Vola's
Chilangos
Cucharamama
Cuzco
Dan's on Main
Déjà Vu
Diaz
Down to Earth
El Meson
El Salvadoreno
Far East Taste
Fedora Cafe
Garlic Rose
Hard Grove
It's Greek To Me
Ivangie Tea
Je's
Karma Kafe
King of India
K.O.B.E.
La Bahia
La Isla
Little Café
Madame Claude
Mad Batter
Makeda
Málaga
Manon
Marakesh
Martino's
Meemah
Meil's
Mela
Mexico Lindo
Mie Thai
Ming
Moghul
Namaskaar
Navesink Fishery
New Main
Nha Tranh
Niecy's
Norma's
Northstar Café
Old Bay
Opa B&G
Orleans
Ota-Ya
Pamir
Park & Orchard
Passage to India
Penang
Raagini
Rat's
Red Hen Cafe
Saffron
Saigon R
Seafood Empire
Seven Hills
Siam
Siam Garden
Siri's Thai French
Soonja's
Spain 92
Sunny Garden
Tang Dynasty
Taro
Taste of Asia
Taste of Vietnam
Teak

Special Features

Tina Louise
West Lake
Wild Ginger

Outdoor Dining
(G=garden; P=patio;
S=sidewalk; T=terrace)
Anthony David's (S)
Arthur's Landing (T)
Avon Pavilion (T)
Axelsson's (G)
Bamboo Leaf (S)
Bernards Inn (T)
Blue (P)
Blue Point (P)
Bobby Chez (P,S)
Brothers Moon (S)
Cafe Matisse (G)
Cucharamama (S)
Daniel's on B'way (G)
Dennis Foy's (P)
Diamond's (P)
Diaz (S)
Elysian Cafe (P,S)
Frenchtown Inn (P)
Frog & Peach (P)
Girasole (P)
Girasole (P)
Giumarello's (P)
Grand Cafe (P)
Green Gables (P)
Hamilton's Grill (T)
Harvest Moon (G)
India on Hudson (S)
Jonathan's (T)
Klein's Fish Market (P,T)
La Campagne (G,T)
La Petite France (G)
La Tartuferia (P)
Latour (S)
Le Rendez-Vous (S)
Lila (P)
Lilly's on Canal (P)
Matisse (T)
Mélange Cafe (P)
Mill at Spring Lake (T)

Misto (P)
Moonstruck (T)
Nag's Head (P)
Perryville Inn (P)
Peter Shields (T)
Rat's (T)
Raven & Peach (P)
Rebecca's (P)
Reef Club (T)
Rice (P)
Robongi (S)
Ruth's Chris (S)
Ship Inn (S)
Shipwreck Grill (T)
Southwinds (P)
Stage House (G)
Stage Left (P)
Tisha's (P)
Tuckers (P)
Union Landing (P)
Village Green (S)
Windansea (T)
Zafra (P)
Zarolé (S)
Zoe's (P)

People-Watching
Babalu Grill
Bernards Inn
Brix 67
Chart House
Clark's Landing
Clydz
Cucharamama
Delta's
Eccola
Echo
Elements
Huntley Taverne
Ixora
Limestone Cafe
Lua
Makeda
Misto
Mixx
Molly Pitcher

vote at zagat.com

Special Features

Reef Club
Sails
Salt Creek
Sammy's Cider
South City Grill
Tapas de Espana
Teak
3 West
Zoe's

Power Scenes
Basilico
BayPoint Prime
Bernards Inn
Cafe Panache
Casa Dante
Chakra
Chez Catherine
Fascino
410 Bank St.
Grain House
Hunt Club
Il Mondo
Lawrenceville Inn
Marsilio's
McLoone's
Morton's Steak
Old Homestead
Opah Grille
Pierre's
Ryland Inn
Saddle River Inn
Serenade
Solari's
Suilan
Washington Inn

Pre-Theater Dining
(Call for prices and times)
Arthur's Landing
Black Trumpet
Hunt Club
Laguna Grill
La Mezzaluna
Maize
Makeda
Northstar Café

2Senza
Willie's Taverne

Private Rooms
(Restaurants charge less at off times; call for capacity)
Amanda's
André's
Bernards Inn
Bistro Olé
Black Duck
Blue Point
Cafe Matisse
Chakra
Chez Catherine
Daniel's on B'way
Dining Room
Ebbitt Room
Elements
Fascino
Girasole
Giumarello's
Green Gables
Harvest Bistro
Ixora
Jocelyne's
Karen & Rei's
La Tartuferia
Mattar's
Nauvoo Grill
Nicholas
Perryville Inn
Porto Leggero
Ryland Inn
Savanna
Serenade
Siri's Thai French
Stage House
Stage Left
Suilan
Tomatoes
Washington Inn
Zoe's

Prix Fixe Menus
(Call for prices and times)
André's
Anthony David's

Special Features

Bernards Inn
Brighton Steak
Cafe at Rosemont
Cafe Matisse
Cafe Panache
Chez Catherine
Chez Dominique
Dennis Foy's
Dining Room
Ebbitt Room
Fascino
Felicity's
Frenchtown Inn
Frog & Peach
Fromagerie
Ganges
Green Gables
Ixora
Latour
Le Rendez-Vous
Matisse
Mattar's
Nicholas
Nunzio
Perryville Inn
Rat's
Rosemary & Sage
Ryland Inn
Saffron
Savaradio
Scalini Fedeli
Serenade
75 South
Sono Sushi
Stage House
Stage Left
Strip House
Verjus
Village Green
Zoe's

Quick Bites
Aby's Mexican
Alchemist/Barrister
Babalu Grill
Cubby's BBQ
East Coast Vegan
Full Moon
Hobby's Deli
Irish Pub
Jack Cooper's
Jerry & Harvey's
Main St. Cafe
Mastoris
Mustache Bill's
Nha Tranh
Noodle House
Ponzio's
Shubox Café
Simply Radishing
Tick Tock
Windansea

Quiet Conversation
Braddock's
Brass Rail
Captain Jack's
Chez Catherine
Colligan's
Cuzco
Farnsworth House
Fiorino
Food for Thought
Frenchtown Inn
Lawrenceville Inn
Le Plumet Royal
Lila
Melting Pot
Molly Pitcher
Slowly
Soufflé
Suilan
Village Green
Whispers

Raw Bars
Axelsson's
Bahrs Landing
BayPoint Prime
Berkeley
Big Fish
Blue Eyes
Blue Point

Special Features

Cafe Arugula
Chart House
Clark's Landing
Diamond's
Dock's Oyster
Elysian Cafe
Fresco Steak
Fulton Crab
Grand Colonial
Grill 73
Harvey Cedars
Ixora
Klein's Fish Market
La Focaccia
Legal Sea Foods
Liberty House
Lobster House
McCormick/Schmick
McLoone's
Mixx
Nero's Grille
Old Homestead
Olive
Plantation
Red's Lobster
Sallee Tee's
Shipwreck Grill
Soufflé
South City Grill
Spike's
Steve & Cookie's
Union Landing

Romantic Places
Acquaviva
Amanda's
Beau Rivage
Cafe Matisse
Catelli
Colligan's
Creole Cafe
Daniel's on B'way
Dining Room
Ebbitt Room
Fat Kat
Frenchtown Inn
Gaslight
Giumarello's
Grand Cafe
Green Gables
Grenville
Harvest Moon
Heatwave Cafe
Il Capriccio
Inn at Millrace
Ivy Inn
Jose's Mexican
K.O.B.E.
La Cipollina
Lawrenceville Inn
Le Rendez-Vous
Liberté
Lila
Lilac
Melting Pot
Metuchen Inn
Molly Pitcher
Pelican Club
Perryville Inn
Peter Shields
Plantation
Ram's Head Inn
Rat's
Raven & Peach
Rebecca's
Rod's Steak
Ryland Inn
Savanna
Scalini Fedeli
Scarborough Fair
Sergeantsville Inn
75 South
Slowly
Stony Hill Inn
Suilan
Tewksbury Inn
Washington Inn
Whispers

Senior Appeal
Abbey
Athenian Garden

Special Features

Bahrs Landing
Berkeley
Big Ed's BBQ
Buca di Beppo
California Grill
Capt'n Ed's
Christopher's
Clouseau's
Crab Trap
Don Pepe
Don Pepe's Steak
E & V
El Cid
Fantasea Reef
Fish Outta Water
Fornos of Spain
Green Grill
Grenville
Groff's
Harbor View
Iberia
Italian Bistro
Jack Cooper's
Java Moon
Klein's Fish Market
La Couronne
Lafayette House
Lahiere's
Legal Sea Foods
Le Plumet Royal
Little Tuna
Lobster House
LouCás
McCormick/Schmick
Mill at Spring Lake
Nanni Ristorante
La Nonna/Piancone's
Portobello
Portuguese Manor
Rivoli's
Sea Shack
Shadowbrook
Smithville Inn
Store
Tang Dynasty
Top Notch
Valentino's
Villa Amalfi
Villa Vittoria

Singles Scenes

Acqua
Babalu Grill
Big Ed's BBQ
Brooklyn's Pizza
Bruschetta
Cenzino
Champps
City Bistro
Clark's Landing
Clydz
Cucharamama
Elements
Gaebel's
Krogh's
La Nonna/Piancone's
Lua
McLoone's
Meritage
Metropolitan Cafe
Mixx
Northstar Café
Old Man Rafferty
Opa B&G
Orleans
Pilot House
Plantation
Quiet Man
Red
Reef Club
Restaurant
Rooney's
Sails
Sallee Tee's
Scuttlebutt's
Shipwreck Grill
South City Grill
Teak
Texas Arizona
Trap Rock
Verve
Windansea

Special Features

Sleepers
(Good to excellent food, but little known)

Aamantran
Aangan
Aby's Mexican
Alexander's
Andaman
Aozora
Athenian Garden
Atrio Cafe
Bamboo Leaf
Bareli's
Bayou Cafe
Beyti Kebab
Black Duck
Black Swan
Bombay Gardens
Cafe Loren
Cafe Zbra
Casa Giuseppe
Creole Cafe
Dai-Kichi
De Anna's
Diaz
Down to Earth
Edo Sushi
Fat Kat
Felicity's
Formia
Frescos
Fresco Steak
Fuji
Ginza Steak
Homestead Inn
Indigo Smoke
Isohama
Ivy Inn
Je's
John Henry's
Jonathan's
Karen & Rei's
Kibbitz/Shore
K.O.B.E.
Labrador Lounge
Lana's
La Strada
Lila
Little Café
Mattar's
Mazi
Mexico Lindo
Mie Thai
Misto
Mud City
Nag's Head
Nanni Ristorante
Nobi
Pearl of the Sea
Puccini's
Red Hen Cafe
Robin's Nest
RosaLuca's
Rosemary & Sage
Saffron
Silver Spring
Slowly
So Moon Nan Jip
Sushi by Kazu
Tang Dynasty
Tattoni's Cafe
Tina Louise
Tisha's
Tre Figlio
West Lake
Wu's Bistro

Special Occasions
Bacari Grill
Beau Rivage
Cafe Matisse
Cafe Panache
Catelli
Chakra
Chart House
Chef's Table
Chengdu 46
Chez Catherine
Cucharamama
Daniel's on B'way
Dish
Doris & Ed's

Special Features

Fat Kat
Ferry House
Food for Thought
Frenchtown Inn
Giumarello's
Grand Cafe
Harvest Moon
Heatwave Cafe
Highlawn Pavilion
Il Capriccio
Indigo Moon
Ivy Inn
Ixora
Jocelyne's
Joe & Maggie's
Karen & Rei's
K.O.B.E.
La Tartuferia
Latour
Lawrenceville Inn
Lila
Madeleine's
Maize
Málaga
Manor
Mattar's
Max's Fine Dining
Meritage
Misto
mojo
Moon St.
Napa Valley
Nicholas
Ninety Grand
No. 9
Nunzio
Peter Shields
Posillipo
Pronto Cena
Ram's Head Inn
Rat's
Raven & Peach
Rebecca's
Robin's Nest
Rod's Steak
RosaLuca's

Ryland Inn
Saddle River Inn
Serenade
Shadowbrook
Shanghai Jazz
Slowly
Specchio
Stage House
Stony Hill Inn
Suilan
Taro
3 West
Washington Inn
Wild Ginger
Zoe's

Tasting Menus
American Fare
Anthony David's
Basil T's
Bella Sogno
Bernards Inn
Black Trumpet
Cafe Matisse
Cafe Panache
Cafe Zbra
Chez Catherine
Dennis Foy's
Dining Room
Ebbitt Room
Fascino
Felicity's
Frog & Peach
Fromagerie
La Campagne
Lana's
Le Petit Chateau
Lincroft Inn
Marakesh
Nicholas
Norma's
Nunzio
Pastels
Perryville Inn
Rat's
Renault Winery

Special Features

Rosemary & Sage
Ryland Inn
Serenade
Spargo's Grille
Stage House
Stage Left
Tre Vigne
Venue
Village Green
Zoe's

Transporting Experiences
Anton's/Swan
Avon Pavilion
Blue Danube
Chakra
Chao Phaya
Cucharamama
Dining Room
Ebbitt Room
Epernay
Fascino
Hamilton's Grill
Ixora
K.O.B.E.
La Campagne
Makeda
Málaga
Manon
Marakesh
Ming
Pamir
Perryville Inn
Rat's
Ryland Inn
Saddle River Inn
Seven Hills
Shanghai Jazz
Siri's Thai French
Suilan
Taro
Walpack Inn

Trendy
Anna's Italian
Axelsson's

Babalu Grill
Basilico
Bistro Olé
Blue
Cafe Matisse
Capt'n Ed's
Chakra
Chef Vola's
Clydz
Cucharamama
DeLorenzo's
Delta's
Dish
Dock's Oyster
Doris & Ed's
Down to Earth
Dry Dock
Elements
Far East Taste
Fascino
Federici's
Frescos
Fuji
Gaetano's
Garlic Rose
Girasole
Harvest Moon
Highlawn Pavilion
Homestead Inn
Hurricane House
Il Mondo
K.O.B.E.
Labrador Lounge
La Campagna
Latour
Lila
Lobster House
Lua
Mad Batter
Mahzu
Makeda
Marco & Pepe
Martino's
Mélange Cafe
Mixx
Mojave Grille

Special Features

mojo
Mud City
Niecy's
Nikko
Ninety Grand
No. 9
Nunzio
Old Homestead
Origin
Paramount Steak
Park & Orchard
Pine Tavern
Plantation
Rat's
Rebecca's
Reservoir Tavern
Rice
River Palm
Rod's Olde Irish
Rosemary & Sage
Sagami
Saigon R
Sails
Scalini Fedeli
Shanghai Jazz
Siam
Siri's Thai French
Slowly
Steve & Cookie's
Taste of Asia
Teak
Theresa's
3 West
Tim Schafer's
Trattoria Fratelli
2Senza
Venue
Verve
Vic's
White House
Yellow Fin
Zafra

Twentysomethings
Avon Pavilion
Babalu Grill
Baja
Basil T's
Big Ed's BBQ
Champps
City Bistro
Cubby's BBQ
Cucharamama
Down to Earth
Elements
Famished Frog
Gaebel's
Los Amigos
Main St. Cafe
Mexican Food
Mile Square
Mixx
Oddfellows
Old Bay
Old Man Rafferty
Pine Tavern
Rattlesnake Ranch
Red
South City Grill
Squan Tavern
Sushi Lounge
Tacconelli's
Tapas de Espana
Teresa's
Triumph Brewing
Yankee Doodle

Views
Arthur's Landing
Athenian Garden
Avon Pavilion
Bahrs Landing
Baumgart's Café
Berkeley
Café Gallery
Cafe Matisse
Capriccio
Chart House
City Bistro
Clark's Landing
Diamond's
Doris & Ed's

Special Features

Felicity's
Hamilton's Grill
Harbor View
Highlawn Pavilion
Hot Dog Johnny's
Il Porto
Jonathan's
Komegashi
Krogh's
Labrador Lounge
Liberty House
Little Tuna
Lua
Mansion on Main
Matisse
McLoone's
Melissa's Bistro
Meson Madrid
Mill at Spring Lake
Molly Pitcher
Moonstruck
Opa B&G
Plantation
Rat's
Red
Reef Club
Robin's Nest
Rooney's
Sallee Tee's
Shadowbrook
Ship Inn
Smithville Inn
Tapas de Espana
Tisha's
Trattoria Fratelli
Tuckers
Union Landing
Ventura's
Walpack Inn
Windansea
Zoe's

Visitors on Expense Account
BayPoint Prime
Brighton Steak
Capriccio
Chez Catherine
Esty Street
Fascino
Fat Kat
Fromagerie
Girasole
Grand Cafe
Green Gables
Harry's Lobster
Il Tulipano
Il Villaggio
La Fontana
Lahiere's
La Mezzaluna
La Petite France
Lawrenceville Inn
Le Petit Chateau
Lu Nello
Mahogany Grille
Manhattan Steak
Morton's Steak
Nicholas
Old Homestead
Panico's
Ram's Head Inn
Ristorante Benito
Scalini Fedeli
Smoke Chophouse
Specchio
Stage Left
Suilan
3 West

Warm Welcome
Amanda's
Angelo's
Benito's
Berta's Chateau
Blue Point
Casa Giuseppe
Chez Catherine
Chez Dominique
Cucharamama
da Filippo
Far East Taste

Special Features

Jocelyne's
La Bahia
Labrador Lounge
Le Rendez-Vous
Madeleine's
Mustache Bill's
Nunzio
Opah Grille
Plantation
Pronto Cena
Quiet Man
Ristorante Benito
Rod's Olde Irish
RosaLuca's
Seafood Empire
Venezia

Waterside
Avon Pavilion
Axelsson's
Bahrs Landing
Barnacle Bill's
Baumgart's Café
Café Gallery
Capriccio
Chart House
Colligan's
Crab Trap
Diamond's
Felicity's
Hamilton's Grill
Hot Dog Johnny's
Il Porto
Klein's Fish Market
Komegashi
Liberty House
Lilly's on Canal
Lua
Matisse
McLoone's
Mill at Spring Lake
Molly Pitcher
Peter Shields
Pilot House
Pronto Cena
Red's Lobster

Reef Club
Robin's Nest
Rooney's
Sallee Tee's
Silver Spring
Tisha's
Tuckers
Union Landing
Ventura's
Windansea
Zoe's

Winning Wine Lists
Beau Rivage
Bernards Inn
Berta's Chateau
Black Forest Inn
Brass Rail
Chakra
Court Street
Crab's Claw
Cucharamama
Doris & Ed's
Esty Street
Fromagerie
Harvest Moon
Il Villino
Le Petit Chateau
Manor
Mediterra
Napa Valley
Nicholas
Northstar Café
Ombra
Park & Orchard
Rat's
Ryland Inn
Scalini Fedeli
Serenade
Specchio
Stage House
Stage Left
Suilan
3 West
Tre Figlio
Tre Piani

Special Features

Two If By Sea
Washington Inn

Worth a Trip

Atlantic City
  Dock's Oyster
  White House
Basking Ridge
  3 West
Bernardsville
  Bernards Inn
Bethlehem
  RosaLuca's
Cape May
  Ebbitt Room
  410 Bank St.
  Frescos
  Pelican Club
  Peter Shields
Chatham
  Scalini Fedeli
  Serenade
Cherry Hill
  La Campagne
  Misto
Cinnaminson
  Max's Fine Dining
Clermont
  Karen & Rei's
Clifton
  Chengdu 46
Collingswood
  Nunzio
  Sagami
Edison
  Bien Hoa
Englewood
  Wild Ginger
Frenchtown
  Frenchtown Inn
Hamilton
  Rat's
Highlands
  Doris & Ed's
Hoboken
  Cucharamama
  La Tartuferia
  Zafra

Holmdel
  K.O.B.E.
Hope
  Inn at Millrace
Hopewell
  Brothers Moon
Lambertville
  Hamilton's Grill
Long Branch
  Joe & Maggie's
Madison
  Shanghai Jazz
Marlton
  Food for Thought
  Joe's Peking
Matawan
  West Lake
Montclair
  Fascino
Morristown
  Grand Cafe
Mount Holly
  Robin's Nest
Newark
  Casa Vasca
Newton
  André's
North Brunswick
  Seafood Empire
Paramus
  Chakra
Princeton
  Blue Point
Ramsey
  Cafe Panache
Ringoes
  Harvest Moon
Saddle River
  Saddle River Inn
Short Hills
  Dining Room
Somerville
  Chao Phaya
  Origin
Stanhope
  Black Forest Inn
Stockton
  Colligan's

Special Features

Toms River
  Slowly
Trenton
  DeLorenzo's
Union Township
  Perryville Inn
Voorhees
  Little Café
Wallpack Center
  Walpack Inn

Weehawken
  Arthur's Landing
West Cape May
  Daniel's on B'way
West Orange
  Highlawn Pavilion
Whitehouse
  Ryland Inn
Whitehouse Station
  Ixora

Wine Vintage Chart

This chart is designed to help you select wine to go with your meal. It is based on the same 0 to 30 scale used throughout this *Survey*. The ratings (prepared by our friend **Howard Stravitz**, a law professor at the University of South Carolina) reflect both the quality of the vintage and the wine's readiness for present consumption. Thus, if a wine is not fully mature or is over the hill, its rating has been reduced. We do not include 1987, 1991–1993 vintages because they are not especially recommended for most areas. A dash indicates that a wine is either past its peak or too young to rate.

	'85	'86	'88	'89	'90	'94	'95	'96	'97	'98	'99	'00	'01	'02	'03
WHITES															
French:															
Alsace	24	–	22	28	28	27	26	25	25	26	25	26	27	25	–
Burgundy	26	25	–	24	22	–	28	29	24	23	26	25	23	27	24
Loire Valley	–	–	–	–	24	–	20	23	22	–	24	25	23	27	26
Champagne	28	25	24	26	29	–	26	27	24	24	25	25	26	–	–
Sauternes	21	28	29	25	27	–	21	23	26	24	24	24	28	25	26
Germany	25	–	25	26	27	25	24	27	24	23	25	24	29	27	–
California (Napa, Sonoma, Mendocino):															
Chardonnay	–	–	–	–	–	–	–	24	26	25	25	24	27	29	–
Sauvignon Blanc/Semillon	–	–	–	–	–	–	–	–	–	25	25	23	27	28	26
REDS															
French:															
Bordeaux	24	25	24	26	29	22	26	25	23	25	24	28	26	23	24
Burgundy	23	–	21	24	26	–	26	28	25	22	28	22	24	27	–
Rhône	25	19	27	29	29	24	25	23	24	28	27	27	26	–	25
Beaujolais	–	–	–	–	–	–	–	–	–	–	23	24	–	25	28
California (Napa, Sonoma, Mendocino):															
Cab./Merlot	27	26	–	21	28	29	27	25	28	23	26	23	27	25	–
Pinot Noir	–	–	–	–	–	–	–	24	24	25	24	26	29	–
Zinfandel	–	–	–	–	–	–	–	–	–	–	–	–	26	26	–
Italian:															
Tuscany	–	–	–	–	25	22	25	20	29	24	28	26	25	–	–
Piedmont	–	–	–	27	28	–	23	27	27	25	25	28	23	–	–